A QUICK OVERVIEW OF THE SIGNIFICANT RULE CHANGES IN THE 2001-2004 RACING RULES OF SAILING

The following is a list of the significan*on of The Racing Rules of Sailing (RRS). T. 00 edition of the RRS as originally publish* *ide between 1998 and 2000. NOTE: These t be actual representations of the rules.*

- **Rule 16.2** (Changing Course): This new rule is an "anti-hunting" rule. When P and S are in a crossing (converging) situation, upwind or downwind, S cannot change course so close to P that P has to immediately change course to continue *keeping clear* of S.

- **Rule 17.1** (On the Same Tack; Proper Course): An addition to this rule will now make it much more difficult for S to "slam dunk" P; and much easier for judges and umpires to rule on "slam dunk" protests.

- **Rule 18.2 (d)** (Rounding and Passing Marks and Obstructions, Changing Course to Round or Pass): Now, when a right-of-way boat is changing course to round a mark, rule 16 (Changing Course) is "turned off" such that she can turn quickly and without regard to other boats required to keep clear of her (other than not colliding with them and causing damage).

- **Rule 26** (Starting Races): The RRS now include a shorter timing sequence (5-4-GO) that can be used instead of the traditional 10-5-GO sequence.

- **Rule 31** (Touching a Mark): A boat that has been forced to touch a mark is now no longer automatically exonerated when the other boat takes a penalty or retires. She must protest the other boat (hail at the time of the incident, fly her flag if required, lodge the protest on time, etc.) in order to get exonerated by the protest committee, which can do so under rule 64.1(b) (Penalties and Exoneration).

- **Rule 49** (Crew Position): It is legal to wear "hiking pants," i.e. pants with built-in stiffeners under the thighs.

- **Rule 60.4** (Right to Protest and Request Redress): The protest committee can now protest any boat involved in an incident that may have resulted in serious damage or injury, based on a report from anyone, including a competitor who did not protest.

- **Rule 61.1 (a)** (Protest Requirements, Informing the Protestee): Boats under 20 feet long (6 meters) no longer need to fly a "protest flag" when protesting. They simply must hail the word "Protest."

- **Definition "Finish"**: If a boat crosses the finishing line in the wrong direction, she is now permitted to correct her mistake and finish correctly.

AN OVERVIEW OF THE RULES...

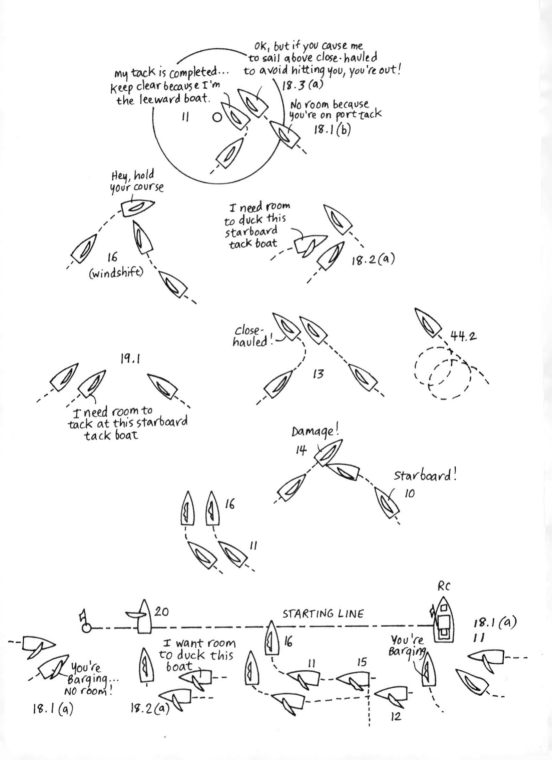

...FROM START TO FINISH

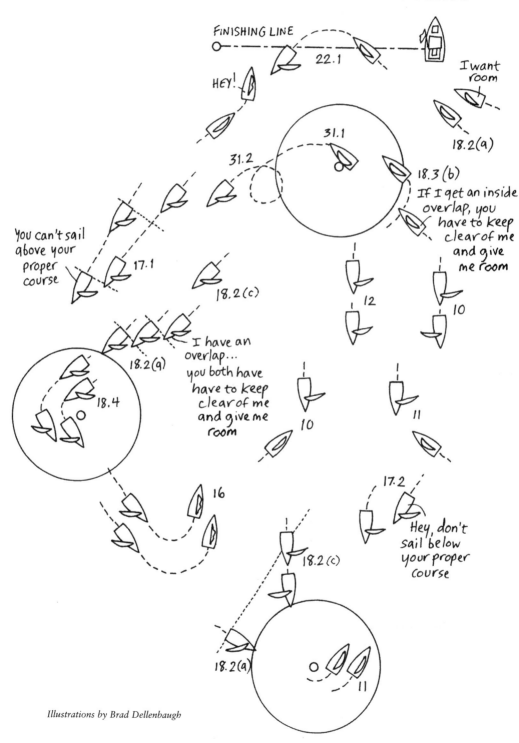

Illustrations by Brad Dellenbaugh

OTHER BOOKS BY DAVE PERRY

Dave Perry's 100 Best Racing Rules Quizzes

Winning in One-Designs

To order rulebooks, *US SAILING Appeals and ISAF Cases*, other books by Dave Perry, or US SAILING publications, please call 800 US SAIL-1 or visit www.ussailing.org

TO CONTACT US SAILING

Write: PO Box 1260, 15 Maritime Drive
Portsmouth, RI 02871 USA

Phone: 401 683-0800
Fax: 401 683-0840
Infofax: 888 US SAIL-6

Email: info@ussailing.org
www.ussailing.org

ISBN 1-882502-89-2

Published by the United States Sailing Association

© 2001 by the United States Sailing Association and Dave Perry

Illustrations © 2001 by Brad Dellenbaugh

The Racing Rules of Sailing, 2001-2004 © 2001
by the International Sailing Federation (ISAF)

Permission to reprint the *Racing Rules of Sailing, 2001-2004*
has been granted to the United States Sailing Association (US SAILING)
by the International Sailing Federation (ISAF)

Previous editions published in 1985, 1989, 1993 and 1997

Cover photograph: Onne van der Wal

UNDERSTANDING THE
RACING RULES
OF SAILING
THROUGH 2004

DAVE PERRY

Illustrations by Brad Dellenbaugh

FIFTH EDITION

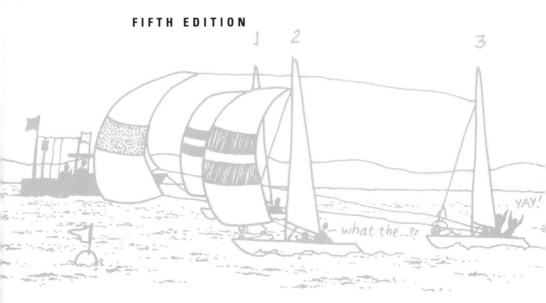

Foreword

IN 1997, the International Sailing Federation (ISAF) presented the sport with the most major rewrite of *The Racing Rules of Sailing* since the modern rules were introduced in 1961. The goal of ISAF was to provide a shorter and less complex set of rules, using more common language, that conformed to ideas of fairness accepted by most sailors and that strove to minimize contact to the greatest extent possible.

The rationale for the new code was threefold:

1) that the sport will be more attractive to newcomers if the rules are easier to understand, resulting in more boats on the starting line;

2) that less complex rules will contribute to fewer protests and more consistency in protest committee decisions; and

3) that, given the increase in the average speed of racing boats, simplifying the rules and toughening their requirements regarding contact will lead to fewer expensive collisions and unpleasant confrontations.

By all accounts it appears that the "new" rules have been successful. Worldwide it has been reported that the number of protests and collisions are down and the number of "720's" (voluntary penalty for breaking a rule) is up. And though I have not seen statistics regarding the numbers of boats on starting lines, it is clear that the game is still just as fun and challenging to play as it was under the "old" rules.

Based on this success, ISAF has worked hard to make as few changes as possible to the 2001-04 rules. The changes that were made in 1998, 1999 and 2000 (changes that were inevitable due to the extensive rewrite that had just occurred) have been incorporated into the 2001-04 rules. Otherwise, there are very few changes and only some very minor game changes this time around. That is good news.

MY HOPE is that sailors who read this book will feel confident that they do fully know and understand the rules. I realize that a rules book doesn't often make for the best bedtime reading, but I've made a conscious effort to write in an easy-to-follow, conversational style. In addition, I've taken the time to go into each rule in enough depth so that you can feel confident that you actually do understand what the rule means and how it applies to your racing. Finally, Brad Dellenbaugh has provided his usual clear and humorous diagrams that make understanding the rules even easier. In learning these new rules and their tactical implications I strongly recommend an attitude that is positive about accepting that challenge, realistic about letting go of some of what was previously known about the rules, and willing to make the effort to fully study and understand them.

IF YOU'RE NEW to sailboat racing, Chapter 2 covers the basic terms you'll hear throughout the book and around the race course; and it lists the basic rules which you will need to know so you can get out there and start having fun without feeling that you're lost and in everyone's way. But, after reading Chapter 2, I encourage you to take the extra time to read through the rest of the book. Obviously you won't be able to visualize all the situations discussed, but at least you will have been exposed to the big picture right off the bat; and I can promise that your understanding of the rules will happen much faster because you will know how to answer most of your own rule questions as they arise, which they will!

IF YOU ARE already an experienced racer, I'm confident that you will find this book an informative and useful reference. Wherever possible, I have quoted from the US SAILING Appeals and International Sailing Federation (ISAF) Cases so that you will know their authoritative interpretation of the rules. I have also gone into depth in areas that commonly cause the most problems or raise the most questions. As a result, this reference will also be extremely useful to sailors serving as judges on a protest committee. The most useful appeals are quoted or referenced with the discussion of each rule; and each discussion goes into sufficient depth to provide the answers or at least the guidelines to resolve most protests or questions as they come up. Both competitors and judges will find the extensive use and reference to the appeals very useful and timesaving when they are either lodging a protest or trying to resolve one in the hearing.

NOTE: *At the time this book was published, US SAILING and ISAF had not yet completed their revisions of their Appeals and Cases; therefore the quotes from the appeals may not be 100% accurate. I expect that the substance of the interpretations are accurate, but encourage you to double-check the actual appeals and cases.*

It is nearly impossible to race sailboats without getting involved in some rules-related situations, whether it's in a crowded mark rounding, a protest hearing, a measurement problem or an appeal. It is my hope that this book, which blends the rules and the appeals together, will answer most of your rules questions and expand your knowledge and awareness of what is in the US SAILING and ISAF appeals so that you can continue to satisfy your own rules curiosity into the future, and feel confident that you in fact do understand the rules yourself.

This book will be published every four years with the revisions of *The Racing Rules of Sailing.* As it is my goal to provide a useful and accurate reference for all sailors, I welcome your comments and suggestions concerning improvements and inaccuracies. Please send them to my attention by May 1, 2004, or sooner at: 239 Barberry Road, Southport, CT 06490.

And now, enjoy your understanding of the rules!

Good Sailing,
Dave Perry

Dedication

Sam Merrick

ALL OF US are inspired by someone, and all of us have benefited from some-one else's hard work and passion. I have both been inspired by and have benefited from Sam Merrick's devotion to the sport of sailing and his remarkable hard work to make the sport bet-ter, particularly in the areas of the racing rules and of Olympic-level racing in the U.S.

Sam began sailing at the age of 11 at the Bay Head Yacht Club on the waters of Barnegat Bay in New Jersey in Sneakboxes. He remained an active com-petitor into his 70's, successfully racing E-Scows, Thistles and the Olympic Sol-ing. Both Brad Dellenbaugh and I had the pleasure of competing against him in the Soling on many occasions, always finding him to be an ardent com-petitor and a true gentleman both on and off the race course.

After earning a bachelor's degree in engineering and a law degree, both from the University of Pennsylvania, Sam's professional life took him to Wash-ington, D.C. He was the special assistant to the general counsel of the Nation-al Labor Relations Board (1950-55), staff member of the Senate Committee on Labor and Public Welfare (1958-61), assistant to the special counsel of the mayor of Boston (1962-67) and director of Congressional relations for the United States Conference of Mayors and the National League of Cities (1971-72).

By 1977 Sam was ably prepared for his most challenging role: becoming the director of the United States Olympic Yachting Committee. His primary job was to select and prepare the U.S. Olympic Sailing Team. His efforts for the 1980 Olympics in Moscow ended when President Jimmy Carter pressured the U.S. Olympic Committee to boycott those Olympics because of the invasion of Afghanistan by Soviet troops.

Sam became the Chairman of the U.S. Olympic Yachting Committee in 1980, and he helped develop a U.S. Team that he optimistically thought could win medals in six of the seven classes. The 1984 Olympics in Los Angeles attracted 300 sailors from 62 nations; and the U.S. Sailing Team far exceeded any performance by any national sailing team, prior to or since those 1984 Games, earning a medal in every class, and three Gold and four Silver Medals at that.

For this accomplishment, in 1984 US SAILING bestowed on Sam its highest honor, the Nathanael G. Herreshoff Trophy, awarded to an individual who has made an outstanding contribution to the sport of sailing.

I WAS FORTUNATE enough to be a member of the U.S. Olympic Yachting Committee from 1981-84 and witnessed first-hand Sam's ability to harness the energies and talents of many disparate, and often competing, sources and forge them into one centralized effort to be successful. As Bob Conner, then Secretary/Treasurer of US SAILING, said upon Sam's winning the Herreshoff Trophy, "Sam is equally adept with a tiller, a telephone or a pen. All of us who have known or worked with Sam have learned to keep a clear path between him and his objective."

Sam was also a long-time member of the U.S. Racing Rules Committee, remaining on board right up through the creation of the new racing rules under which we race today. His contribution to the rules-writing process was always from his perspective as a racing sailor, and he always had what was best for the game at the foremost in his thinking. For that we can all be grateful. And what I appreciated most was that no sooner had I published another edition of this book (now in its fifth edition), then I would receive a long missive from Sam politely challenging many of my assertions and offering numerous suggestions for improvements.

I will also always remember two other character traits of Sam. One is his laugh as he went about doing his work. He truly enjoyed the process as much as the outcome in whatever he was involved in, and he made even the most difficult aspects of the work seem enjoyable. And the second is his humility.

For Sam it was all about the task at hand, and never about himself. In fact, upon accepting the Herreshoff Trophy Sam said, "In honoring me, you honor the team, and also those fine sailors who 'missed by inches'."

Sam departed from us on April 17, 2000, at the age of 86. One of Sam's last contributions was an insightful and well-researched book, entitled *The Life of His Choice*, about a sailor from Bay Head, New Jersey, named F. Slade Dale, who had been an inspiration to him. On the title page sits a 1928 photo of a 23-foot cutter, designed and built by Dale, sailing comfortably through the waters of Barnegat Bay. Beneath the photo, which in my mind is now a picture of Sam rounding a windward mark in his Soling just ahead of a tightly-packed fleet, is this quote – which Sam intended as a reflection on F. Slade Dale's life, but which I feel is just as fitting a reflection on Sam's:

> *"But unlike most of us, he had succeeded in doing the things he desired – had succeeded in living 'the life of his choice'."*

FOR LIVING THE LIFE of his choice, and for inspiring and benefiting so many with his passion and hard work along the way, I dedicate this book to Sam, whose laughter and deft touch live on every page.

Acknowledgements

I'D LIKE TO THANK the following people, and for the reasons given:
My father, Hop Perry, who began my rules interest and taught me the first rules
I knew; my mother, Jan Perry, who, along with her father Northrop Dawson,
stimulated and encouraged my desire to write; and my wife Betsy, who has
enhanced this book (and my life) with her contributions and her support.

Bill Bentsen and Dick Rose, members of both the US SAILING and ISAF
Racing Rules Committees, who have generously given me tremendous amounts
of their time and insight as I have learned more about the rules; and who have
inspired me to become a strict analyst of the exact word in each rule so as to
learn and interpret only what the rule writers wrote.

Harry Anderson, who patiently tolerated my endless rule questions during
his every visit to Yale from '73 to '77, and who answered each with the same
high care and interest to explain exactly why he gave the answer he did.
Gregg Bemis, whose countless hours of conversation on the rules I will always
cherish. David and Brad Dellenbaugh, who have helped me gain tremendous
insights into the rules by their high-minded approach to analyzing and interpreting the rules. Tom Ehman, who shares my insatiable curiosity to understand the rules. Andy Kostanecki with whom (along with Dick Rose) I shared
my first experience at writing a rule and who were wonderful to work with.
Goran Petersson, whose sincere dedication to listening to sailors and welcom-
ing their input on the racing rules I admire and appreciate so much. And my
fellow members on the US SAILING Appeals Committee for their high level
of rules interpretation and interest in the rules.

I would also like to thank the many friends with whom I've enjoyed much
open-minded and friendly, thoughtful debate on the rules, completely devoid
of any self-righteousness or the ill effects of taking debate personally; and all
the sailors I've met while sitting on protest committees, who have given clear
and honest testimonies so that the facts of what happened were clear, enabl-

ing everyone involved to learn from and enjoy the more intellectual challenge of applying the rules to the seemingly endless variety of situations we find ourselves in while racing.

I can't say enough about the talent and energy of my friend Brad Dellenbaugh, whose illustrations are an equal half of making this book fun and effective. I also thank Joy Shipman and Terry Harper of US SAILING for all their efforts towards the publication of this book. Finally, I want to acknowledge all those sailors who took the time to write to me with their critical comments and suggestions for the improvement of this book.

As individual words form together to create a rule, so have all these people formed together to become my teacher in a subject that never ceases to give me pleasure each time I feel I know and understand a rule a little more clearly.

To all of you: Thank you!

Table of Contents

The Racing Rules of Sailing
Contents

This table indicates where discussion of each rule is located. The text of *The Racing Rules of Sailing* (RRS) is printed at the end of this book. "RRS" by a rule indicates that there is no specific discussion of that rule in this book; you will find the text of the rule in *The Racing Rules of Sailing*.

Introduction

How to Learn the Most from This Book

Give me a fish and I'll eat for a day;
teach me to fish and I'll eat for the rest of my life.

It is one goal of this book to help you learn and understand the rules and the appeals better. It is an equal goal to help you see how you can continue to answer your own rules questions as they arise, whether in the position of a competitor, a race committee member or a judge. Here are some suggestions that will make it much easier for you to accomplish both.

DON'T TRY TO MEMORIZE THE RULES

It is the wrong approach to try to memorize the eight situations where a *port-tack* boat has right of way over a *starboard-tack* boat, just as it's confusing to try to simply memorize the entire text of rule 18 (Rounding and Passing Marks and Obstructions). Each rule has a clear purpose, which I have tried to explain thoroughly. You'll learn and remember the rules faster and more clearly if you take a step back and try to see exactly what actions each rule is trying to produce or eliminate. For example, when you are over the starting line at the gun you have taken an unfair head start on your competitors. You can remedy your mistake simply by returning behind the line and starting properly; and it makes complete sense that while you are returning you have no rights over boats that have started correctly. This is the purpose of rule 20 (Starting Errors; Penalty Turns; Moving Astern) and rule 29.1 (On the Course Side at the Start), which you can easily understand and apply in your racing without knowing the exact wording of each rule.

LET GO OF PREVIOUS INTERPRETATIONS OF THE RULES

My advice is: read this book with an open mind. Be careful not to hurry through sections that you feel you already know. Read each word and discussion carefully. It's very common and easy to superimpose what you "think" a rule says or should say; and in many cases this causes you to miss a subtle difference in what the rule is actually saying. Sailors seriously interested in understanding the rules will find real pleasure and benefit in learning a rule correctly.

WHEN ALL ELSE FAILS, READ THE DIRECTIONS

It is usually not difficult to answer your own rules questions if you follow this route. When you have a question, first look in the Index of Subjects in the ISAF *Racing Rules of Sailing* (RRS) to see which rule(s) may apply. Also look through the Contents of the RRS at the titles of the Parts, then the Sections and finally the rules themselves to find the one(s) that might pertain to your situation. For example, if it involves two or more boats, the appropriate rule(s) are probably in Part 2. To find the rule(s), first determine what the relationships of the boats are just before, during and just after the incident. For instance, have they been converging for some time or does one of the boats suddenly change course and cause the convergence; are they on the same or opposite *tacks*; are they *overlapped* or not, and so forth. Also determine where they are on the course; i.e. are they behind the starting line, near a *mark* or halfway down a reaching leg? Then look through the titles of the rules in Part 2 for the description most similar to the situation.

When you have found the rule you feel applies, read it out loud. As Bill Bentsen, member of the US SAILING and ISAF Racing Rules Committees for many years, says, "Before answering a rules question I always reread the rule first." Then read the discussion of the rule in this book, along with each appeal referenced in the discussion. It is also good advice to reread the definition of each italicized word in the rule. If you have access to the US SAILING Appeals and ISAF Cases (available from US SAILING), check the helpful index and read any appeals that may pertain to your situation. If you are still not confident in the answer, write down your question in the back of your rule book and discuss it with the local rules expert or one of the US SAILING Certified Judges in your area.

USEFUL FEATURES OF THIS BOOK

Brad and I have included the following features in the book with the hope that they will be useful to you:

1)   A **"blimp's eye" chart** in the front of the book which shows an entire race course with the rule numbers for the situations that commonly arise in each location. This feature should be very useful when you're involved in a *protest* but you're not sure what rule number applies.

2)   A **"question and answer" format,** indicated by the sailor's head in the margin, in which I ask and answer the most commonly asked rules questions. Perhaps you'll recognize some as questions you may have.

3)   When a term defined in the Definitions is used in its defined sense, I have printed it in *italic* type. To emphasize words or phrases throughout my explanations and discussions of the rules, I have used **bold** type.

4)   **A Glossary of Terms** explaining the meaning of terms commonly used in discussing the rules but not defined in *The Racing Rules of Sailing*. (Located after this Introduction.)

5)   **A table for calculating** boat speed, distance and time that will be useful when preparing for a protest or hearing one. (Located after this Introduction.)

6)   **The complete text** of *The Racing Rules of Sailing*, including its appendices. (In the back of this book.)

7)   **A detailed index** of rule subjects and the rule(s) in which they are located, prepared by ISAF and included in *The Racing Rules of Sailing*. (In the back of this book.)

8)   **An index** listing each 2001-2004 rule number and where the primary discussion of that rule is located in this book. (Located after the Table of Contents in this book.)

9)   **A summary** of the significant changes in the rules. (First page of this book.)

Glossary of Terms

To keep the rules short and simple, the rule writers use common terms when possible. When a term is not defined in *The Racing Rules of Sailing* (RRS), it is intended to be interpreted in its common, everyday dictionary meaning (see RRS Introduction, Terminology).

The following is a glossary of some of the terms you will find in *The Racing Rules of Sailing* and their discussion that are not defined in the RRS themselves:

Bearing Away	turning away from the direction of the wind
Luffing	turning toward the direction of the wind
Heading Up	another term for "luffing"
Can or May	means permissive; have option of doing it
Beating to Windward	a boat is "beating to windward" whenever her fastest course to the next *mark* is close-hauled or above
Close-hauled Course	the course a boat will sail when racing upwind and sailing as close to the wind as she can
Fetching a Mark	a boat is "fetching a *mark*" when it can pass the *mark* without sailing past head to wind
Gybing	the maneuver involving changing *tacks* with the boat's bow away from the wind; when sailing downwind, a boat changes tacks the moment her mainsail crosses her centerline
Shall	means mandatory; must do it
Tacking	the maneuver involving changing *tacks* with the boat's bow toward the wind; when sailing upwind, a boat changes *tacks* the moment her bow passes head to wind

Code

Throughout this book, in order to consolidate space and to conform to the appeals, I have used the following code:

> **S** *starboard-tack* boat
>
> **P** *port-tack* boat
>
> **L** *leeward* boat
>
> **W** *windward* boat
>
> **A** boat *clear ahead*
>
> **B** boat *clear astern* (behind)
>
> **M** middle or intervening boat
>
> **I** inside boat (at a *mark* or *obstruction*)
>
> **O** outside boat (at a *mark* or *obstruction*)

When combined, the codes work like this:

> **SL** the boat is on *starboard-tack* and *overlapped* to *leeward* of the other boat.
>
> **PI** the boat is on *port-tack* and *overlapped* on the inside of the other boat.

Speed, Distance & Time Table

(1 knot = 6076 feet per hour)

Boat speed	Feet per second	Meters per second
1 knot	1.69	0.51
2 knots	3.38	1.01
3 knots	5.06	1.52
4 knots	6.75	2.03
5 knots	8.44	2.53
6 knots	10.13	3.04
7 knots	11.81	3.54
8 knots	13.50	4.05
9 knots	15.19	4.56
10 knots	16.88	5.06

In other words, if your boat is going 4 knots, you will travel 6.75 feet per second. One way to determine your boat's speed is to sail by a buoy or other fixed object and count how many seconds it takes for the buoy to go from your bow to your stern. If in a Melges 24 it takes 3 seconds to go by the buoy, you are going 8 feet per second, or just under 5 knots.

It's very useful to know your boat's approximate speed on all points of sail in all wind and wave conditions, particularly in a protest hearing. For instance, in the above example you know that the *two-length zone* is about 6 seconds' worth of sailing before the *mark*. You also know that if you tack in front of another boat and she claims to have hit you only 3 seconds after you became close-hauled, you can point out that, by her own testimony, she held her course for a full boat-length after you were close-hauled.

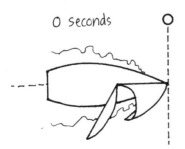

O seconds

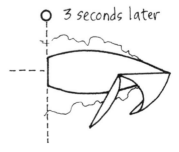

3 seconds later

19.1

I need room to
tack at this starboard
tack boat

16

11

An Overview of the Rules System

Here is an overview of how the rules system works, and where the rules and their interpretations are located.

BRIEF HISTORY

Up through the early 1920s, different parts of the world had their own versions of racing rules. Then, as more sailors started traveling to other countries for international regattas, the European and United States yacht racing associations agreed on a common set of right-of-way rules in 1929. However, as racing grew in popularity and the boats were getting smaller, the existing rules were not clear and precise enough to make them easily enforceable.

In the mid-1930s Mike Vanderbilt, defender of the America's Cup in the J-boats *Enterprise* (1930), *Rainbow* (1934) and *Ranger* (1937) began work on a new draft of the rules based on the three basic relative positions boats can be in: on the same tack, on different tacks, and in the act of changing tacks. In 1948 the North American Yacht Racing Union (NAYRU), predecessor to the United States Sailing Association (US SAILING) and the Canadian Yachting Association (CYA), adopted Vanderbilt's draft as their official rules.

In 1949 the International Yacht Racing Union (IYRU) created a Racing Rules Committee to study the various racing rules that were being used throughout the world. From 1950 to 1959, Mike Vanderbilt and Gregg Bemis of the United States, Gerald Sambrooke-Sturgess of Great Britain and others worked hard to draft one set of rules under which the entire world would race. In 1960 the IYRU adopted a draft, largely based on the "Vanderbilt draft," and these rules came into effect in 1961. Since then, racing through-out the world has been done under the same code of rules.

Beginning in 1961, the IYRU'S policy became that these rules would be locked in place for four-year periods lasting through the Olympic Games. During these four-year periods, sailors would communicate their ideas for improvements to their Racing Rules Committees, which would also study the rules for areas of improvement. After each Olympics, the IYRU would adopt a revised set of rules for the next four-year period.

Over the years since 1961, in the process of being revised to clarify their meaning and to meet changes in the sport, the rules became longer and long-er. As newcomers joined the sport, they (and those who taught them) found learning the rules to be a formidable task. In 1991 the IYRU took formal action to simplify the rules. A draft of "experimental rules" was offered to sailors each year from 1993-1996 for their review, trial and input. This "world-wide" re-search project resulted in a highly refined and simpler set of rules that went into effect in 1997.

For a more detailed history of the racing rules, read Rob MacArthur's *Room at the Mark*.

THE RULES AND HOW THEY ARE UPDATED

The rules are *The Racing Rules of Sailing*. They are published by the Inter-national Sailing Federation (ISAF). Each national authority (US SAILING in the United States) adopts these rules for racing in its own country. Some rules permit each national authority to make some additions or modifications, called "prescriptions." So when racing in a different country, a sailor need only learn what prescriptions, if any, that national authority has made. But notice that there are no modifications permitted to the Definitions and "right of way" rules in Part 2, thus ensuring that these remain identical throughout the world.

Notice that the ISAF and the national authorities are very interested in hav-ing sailors study the rules for improvements and give their input. In the U.S., suggestions or comments should be sent to the Racing Rules Committee, c/o US SAILING. Notice also that rule 86 (Rule Changes) restricts which rules the sailing instructions can change; but rule 86.2 says, "*If a national author-*

ity so prescribes, these restrictions do not apply if rules are changed to devel-op or test proposed rules in local races." US SAILING prescribes *"that proposed rules may be tested in local races."* US SAILING Appeal 58 says, "Local races are those in which normally the same group of people from a limited geographic area regularly race together."

WHERE THE RULES ARE LOCATED

*The **rules** are located in the following places.*
*(See the definition **Rule**.)*

1. **The ISAF rule book (*The Racing Rules of Sailing*) and any prescriptions of the national authority.** US SAILING sells one "rule book" that includes the ISAF rules, appendices and US SAILING prescriptions. See its Contents for an overview of where each ISAF *rule* is located and what each Appendix covers. Notice that rule titles are not part of the *rules*.

2. **Class rules.** Each class publishes rules specific for that class, which are available from the class secretary. (Contact US SAILING for class office addresses.)

3. **Club or "local" rules.**

4. **The Notice of Race.** Appendix J (Notice of Race and Sailing Instructions) lists the information contained in the Notice of Race.

5. **The Sailing Instructions.** The sailing instructions are required to tell you when class and "local" rules apply, as well as when parts or the whole of an Appendix shall apply. They may even change some of *The Racing Rules of Sailing* (see rule 86, Rule Changes). Appendix J (Notice of Race and Sailing Instructions) lists all the information the sailing instructions must contain. Notice that rule 88.2(c) (Sailing Instructions) prohibits any oral instructions unless there is a procedure specifically set out in the sailing instructions; and even then, they can be given only on the water. This is obviously to avoid confusion and potential prejudice to sailors not hearing about a change.

6. **Any other conditions or documents that might apply to a particular race or series.**

   In particular, **every sailor should take a few minutes to read the sailing in-**

structions for a race or event. Normally, a race committee will not answer oral questions concerning any rule or sailing instruction for the above stated reason. You should give them your question(s) in writing in ample time for them to consider their answer, seek the judges' opinions (when necessary) and post each question with its answer in writing on the official notice board.

PROTEST SYSTEM

A *"protest"* is merely the means of bringing an incident in which a boat may have broken a *rule* to a hearing after the race where the sailors involved and the members of the protest committee can review the incident and decide how the *rules* apply.

The rules for how to lodge a *protest* are clearly stated in rule 60 (Right to Protest and Request Redress). Rules concerning how the protest hearing must be run, including a listing of all the sailor's rights, are in Part 5, Section B (Protests, Redress, Hearings, Misconduct and Appeals; Hearings and Decisions).

Appendix L (Recommendations for Protest Committees) contains detailed recommendations for how protest committees should conduct the hearing. The preamble to the Appendix clearly states the fundamental principle of "innocent until proven guilty:"

In a protest or redress hearing, the protest committee should weigh all testimony with equal care; should recognize that honest testimony can vary, and even be in conflict, as a result of different observations and recollections; should resolve such differences as best it can; should recognize that no boat or competitor is guilty until a breach of a *rule* has been established to the satisfaction of the protest committee; and should keep an open mind until all the evidence has been heard as to whether a boat or competitor has broken a *rule*.

APPEALS SYSTEM

If you are penalized in a protest hearing and you feel that the protest committee applied the *rules* incorrectly to the facts they found or failed to follow the correct procedures in hearing the *protest*, you can "appeal" their decision to a "higher court." All the rules and procedures for submitting an appeal are located in rule 70 (Right of Appeal and Requests for Interpretation) and Appendix F (Appeals Procedures), except that regional sailing associations may have additional procedures as well.

Note that you cannot appeal the facts that were found by the protest committee; only their interpretation and application of the *rules* to those facts (rule 63.6, Taking Evidence and Finding Facts; rule 70.1, Right of Appeal and Requests for Interpretation; rule 71.3, Appeal Decisions). If after a hearing you, as a *party* to the hearing, feel the protest committee found the wrong facts, you can ask them to reopen the hearing under rule 66 (Reopening a Hearing) or request redress under rule 62.1 (Redress).

In the United States the "highest court" is the US SAILING Appeals Committee. When they decide a case that to them sets a precedent or is a clear and useful interpretation of a *rule*, they publish it; they can also submit the appeal and their decision to the ISAF Racing Rules Committee, which in turn can publish the appeal in their book. Notice that ISAF does not, in most cases, decide appeals; they simply publish ones submitted by national authorities that they feel are important and useful interpretations.

US SAILING's Appeals and ISAF's Cases are available from the US SAILING office. US SAILING members receive new decisions of the US SAILING Appeals Committee in their magazine, *American Sailor*, as well as in annual supplements. (See copywrite page for information on contacting US SAILING.)

"What is the status of US SAILING's Appeals and ISAF's Cases?"

The Appeals of the national authorities (US SAILING in the United States) and the ISAF Cases are not *rules*. They are "authoritative interpretations and explanations of the rules." Sailors and protest committees can and should refer to the appeals for guidance. ISAF's Cases carry supreme weight worldwide. When a situation is identical to a published ISAF interpretation, the ISAF Case serves as a precedent. (See US SAILING Appeal 50.)

Similarly, US SAILING Appeals carry supreme weight within the United States; and in fact their appeals are highly regarded throughout the world. They do not, however, have the same weight as the ISAF Cases outside the United States, and they may sometimes be disregarded in favor of the host country's national Appeals Committee's decisions.

"What's the best way to use the appeals books?"

Both US SAILING's Appeals and ISAF's Cases are easily designed for quick reference. One index lists each appeal referring to a particular rule, and another gives a short description of each appeal. Instead of reading the appeals book from front to back, you should read each appeal pertaining to a particular rule. The appeals themselves are each very short. You are given the facts, a diagram when relevant, and then the decision. I like to read the facts, close the book, think out what my decision would be, then compare it with the actual decision.

 "Can the decision on an appeal change the results of a race or series?"

You bet. Rule 71.4 (Appeal Decisions) states, *"The decision of the national authority shall be final... all parties to the hearing and the protest committee... shall be bound by the decision."* In ISAF Case 61 it was asked, "May an authority organizing a race state in the notice of race or sailing instructions that, while appeal is not denied, final regatta standings and awards will not be affected by any appeal decision? ANSWER: No... An appeal involves not only the adjudication of a dispute on the meaning of a rule but also, in the event of a reversal of the decision of the protest committee, an adjustment of the results of the race and the final standings of the regatta on which the awards are based."

 "Can anyone appeal the decision of a protest committee?"

No. Only a *party* to the hearing can appeal the decision in that hearing (rule 70.1, Right of Appeal and Requests for Interpretations). (For more explanation on who qualifies as a *party*, see the discussion of the definition *Party*.) In particular, if you weren't a *party* to a hearing, but the decision in that hearing affected you and you believe that the protest committee acted improperly, your recourse is to request redress under rule 62.1(a) (Redress). (See US SAILING Appeal 64 and ISAF Case 55.)

 "If I'm in a situation where I feel the protest committee is prejudicing, or has prejudiced, the outcome of the hearing by denying me any of my procedural rights under Part 5, Section B (Hearings and Decisions), do I have to 'object' at the time if I want to retain my right to appeal?"

You are not required to, but I strongly encourage you to do so. Remember that an appeals committee can only base its decision on the facts as presented to them by the protest committee. When a competitor appeals on the grounds that the protest committee made a prejudicial procedural error, generally there is little or no record of it in the protest committee's "facts found." Therefore, it becomes very difficult for the appeals committee to ever learn enough facts to uphold the appeal.

Therefore, if you are in a situation where the protest committee is denying you your procedural rights, you should state your "objection" right then, so that the hearing can continue properly; or if, after the hearing, you feel the protest committee has prejudiced the outcome of the hearing by denying you any of your procedural rights, you should request redress under rule 62.1(a) (Redress).

The reason for this is that a protest committee must give you a hearing and, more importantly, must find facts and give you a decision (rule 63.1, Hearings; rule 64.2, Decisions on Redress). Otherwise, you may never get any facts regarding the alleged improprieties on which to base an appeal. Note that in the U.S., the time limit for requesting redress for a protest committee action is 6:00 pm the day following the protest committee action, or later if there is a good reason to extend this time limit.

Note that, when seeking redress, you must be prepared to point out the "improper" action or omission of the protest committee. It is not enough to claim that the protest committee should have taken alternative action that would have given you better standing.

"Are there ever times when I am not allowed to appeal?"

Yes. Rule 70.4 (Right of Appeal and Requests for Interpretations) is very clear on this:

There shall be no appeal from the decisions of an international jury constituted in compliance with Appendix M. Furthermore, if the notice of race and the sailing instructions so state, the right of appeal may be denied provided that

(a) it is essential to determine promptly the result of a race that will qualify a boat to compete in a later stage of an event or a subsequent event (a

national authority may prescribe that its approval is required for such a procedure),

(b) a national authority so approves for a particular event open only to entrants under its own jurisdiction; or

(c) a national authority after consultation with the ISAF so approves for a particular event, provided the jury is constituted as required by Appendix M, except that only two members of the jury need be International Judges.

WIND

Windward

STARBOARD

PORT

Leeward

A Simplified Version of *The Racing Rules of Sailing*

THERE'S NO disagreeing that there are a lot of rules to know when racing sailboats. But just as in every other sport, you don't need to know and completely understand them all before you go racing. I love to play soccer, and I've got the basic rules down: keep my hands off the ball, try to kick the ball into the goal to score, try not to kick the other guys in the shins, and stop when the referee blows the whistle. I'm still a bit hazy on what 'offsides' means, what the difference between an "indirect" and a "direct" kick is, and just how many elbows in the ribs I'm supposed to peacefully accept as part of the game. But I still have a great time playing, and I learn a bit more about the rules each time I go out.

Here then are a few basic rules you should know so that you can get into racing without feeling like you're just in everyone's way. At first, take the racing easy just to get the feel of how it works; and never be worried about asking too many questions; that's exactly how we all learned what was up. Of course, the one danger in learning just the basic rules is that there will be places on the course where there are exceptions or where the actual rule has more detail. So you should really take the time to read through this book. It's written in language that is easy to understand. The more you race, the more situations you'll run into that are exactly as covered and described here, and the sooner you'll be comfortable enough to get in there and mix it up out on the course.

Now, if you are just getting into sailing and racing, you've probably noticed that there are a few different words and phrases used around the track.

Clearly the rules wouldn't be using them if they didn't make things easier; so we've included some illustrations to help you understand what some of these terms mean. See also the "Glossary of Terms" on page 30.

BASIC RULES

These are simplified summaries of the basic rules that apply when you and another boat are about to hit. When one boat has the "right of way," that means that the other boat is required to "keep clear;" in other words to stay out of the way of the right-of-way boat.

1) If you are on **opposite** *tacks* (booms on different sides), the boat on *starboard tack* has the right of way over the boat on *port tack* (just as at a four-way stop, the car on the right gets to go first). (Rule 10.)

2) If you are on the **same** *tack* (booms on the same sides), the *leeward* boat has the right of way over the *windward* boat; and a boat coming up from behind can't hit the boat ahead (just as on the road). (Rules 11 and 12.)

3) If you are **tacking**, you have to stay out of the way of a boat sailing in a straight line (just as you cannot pull out onto a road immediately in front of a car driving down the road). (Rule 13.)

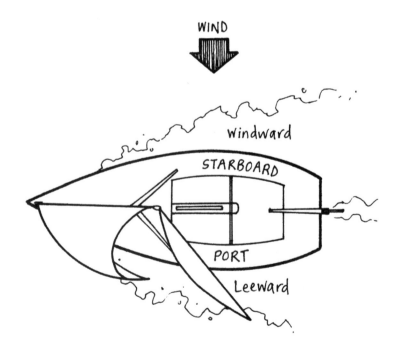

WIND

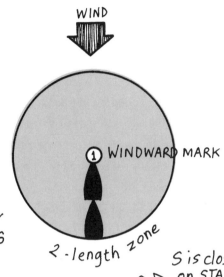

① WINDWARD MARK

S is on a reach

S

2-length zone

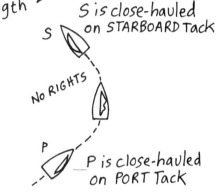

S is close-hauled
on STARBOARD Tack

S

No RIGHTS

P

P is close-hauled
on PORT Tack

gybing ② GYBE MARK

W

L

Mark ③ to ① = WINDWARD Leg or BEAT
Mark ① to ② and ② to ③ = REACHING Legs
Mark ① to ③ = LEEWARD Leg or RUN

L is the LEEWARD Boat
W is the WINDWARD Boat

I is the INSIDE Boat
O is the OUTSIDE Boat

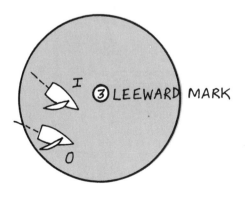

I

③ LEEWARD MARK

O

4) Before most races, the race committee will give each competitor a copy of the sailing instructions (SI's), that contain the specific information on how the races will be run. There will be an imaginary line between two *marks* called the "starting line," and a timing system to tell you when you can start the race (explained in rule 26 or the SI's). You must be completely behind this line at your start. If you are not, simply turn back and get behind the line. However, while you are returning, you must stay clear of all boats that started correctly. (Rule 20.)

5) Anytime you have the right of way and want to turn toward another boat, you must be sure that the other boat has enough time and space to get out of your way. (Rule 16.)

6) When you are two boat-lengths from a *mark* or *obstruction*, you have to give any boat between you and the *mark* or *obstruction* room to round or pass it. (Rule 18.)

7) One large exception to number 6 (above) is at the starting *marks*, where you do not have to give *windward*/inside boats room to pass between you and the starting *mark*. If the *windward*/inside boat tries to squeeze in between you and a starting *mark* (like a race committee boat), they are "barging," which is definitely illegal but unfortunately very common. (Rules 18 and 11.)

8) You must avoid all collisions if possible. (Rule 14.)

9) If you make a right-of-way boat have to **change their course** to avoid hitting you, you must take a penalty. Normally the penalty is to simply get away from the other boats immediately and sail two full circles (called a "720"). When you're done, get back in the race. (Rule 44.)

10) If you **touch any *mark***, the penalty is just one full circle. (Rule 31.)

If you have the right-of-way and another boat makes you change course to avoid hitting her, she has broken a *rule*. You can tell her this by "protesting" her. To do this, immediately hail the word "Protest." If you are racing on a boat 20 feet or longer you must **also** put up a red flag as quickly as possible (usually immediately) after the incident. Then at the finish tell the race committee which boat you are protesting, and onshore fill out the protest form the race committee will give you. Soon afterward, the protest committee (usually three knowledgeable sailors) will hold a hearing at which both boats have the opportunity to tell their story; the committee will then make its decision. (Rules 60 to 68.)

Hike hard, sail fast and enjoy!

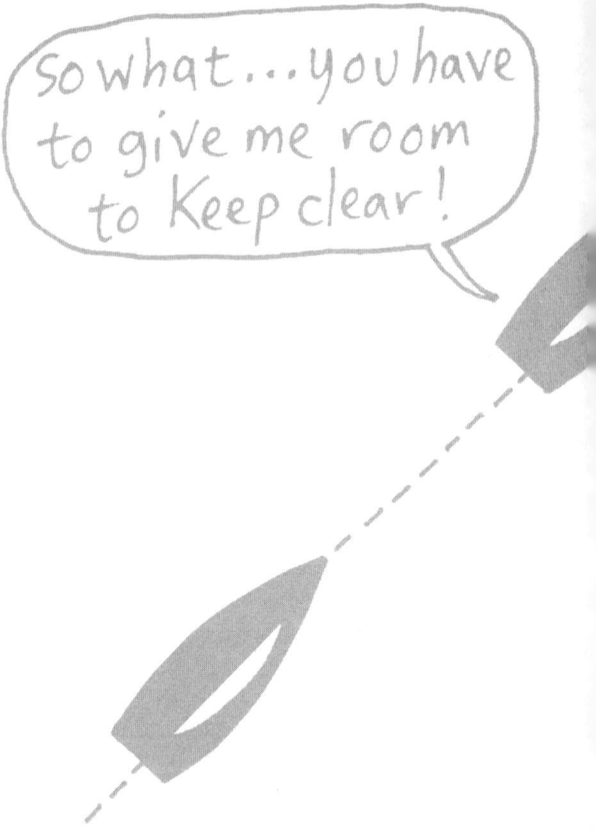
so what... you have to give me room to Keep clear!

3

Sportsmanship and the Rules

"You haven't won the race if in winning the race you have lost the respect of your competitors."

Four-time Olympic Gold Medalist,
Paul Elvström

SPORTSMANSHIP AND THE RULES

Competitors in the sport of sailing are governed by a body of *rules* that they are expected to follow and enforce. A fundamental principle of sportsmanship is that when competitors break a *rule* they will promptly take a penalty or retire.

THIS STATEMENT of principle is located in the rule book just before Part 1 (Fundamental Rules). It is no coincidence that the subject of "sportsmanship" is given a status above all the rules in our sport. The history of sailboat racing is filled with the tradition of exciting competition played out with honor and respect among the competitors and officials. In keeping with that tradition, when we race we agree to be fair and honest, to be good sports and to attempt to win using our own superior boat speed and racing skills.

At the heart of what makes our sport so fulfilling is the principle that we have a competitor-enforced, "no-referee" rules system; that is we have the responsibility to follow the *rules* on our own, to self-penalize ourselves when we break a *rule*, and to protest when we believe another boat has broken a *rule*. In this regard, our sport is unique compared with a lot of other sports. I was watching a pro tennis singles match (two players) and became amused as I counted at least ten referees: one calling each of the four lines on each side, one calling the net, and an umpire to settle disputes. Even at the highest levels of racing we "call our own lines."

The *rules* are intended to provide for safe, fair and equitable racing worldwide; and to make competitor enforcement as easy as possible by clearly defining which boat has the right of way and which boat the requirement to *keep clear* when boats meet. When competitors know they have broken a *rule*, they are expected to promptly take a penalty or retire. Competitors who "never drop out," even when they know they are in the wrong, because they think they have a chance to "win" the *protest* in the hearing just waste the time of all the people involved in the *protest* and diminish the quality of the racing for all.

Rule 44 (Penalties for Breaking a Rule of Part 2) provides that the 720-degree Turns Penalty or other voluntary penalty will always be available to a boat; and rule 31 (Touching a Mark) provides the 360-degree penalty turn for touching a *mark*.

When a competitor believes that another boat may have broken a *rule*, she can protest. A *protest* is merely the means of bringing an incident in which a boat may have broken a *rule* to a hearing after the race where the sailors involved and the members of the protest committee can review the incident and decide how the *rules* apply. *Protests* that are the result of honest differences of opinions on the *rules* or observations of the incident should never have a negative taint to them. Quite the contrary, *protests* are an essential part of our competitor-enforced rule system and are expected, particularly in situations where a boat has gained an advantage in the race or series by breaking a *rule*.

When a boat is forced to break a *rule* through no fault of her own, she is known as the "innocent victim," and can be excused from blame under rule 64.1(b) (Penalties and Exoneration). If a boat feels her finishing place has been made significantly worse by the race committee, protest committee or another competitor, she can request redress under rule 62.1 (Redress); in this case, rule 64.2 (Decisions on Redress) reminds the protest committee to make as fair an arrangement as possible for all boats affected.

The rule writers have taken some excellent measures to amplify the message that sailboat racing should be synonymous with good sportsmanship and integrity with regard to fair play. However, in the end of the day it is up to us, the sailors, to use the *rules* as they are written and intended. One problem is that some feel that the rewards from winning justify cheating, such as the "good feeling" of winning, the attention and hype, the benefit to business and sponsors and so on. Obviously, this is a personal decision that all sailors must make for themselves. The hope is that the temptations to cheat can't possibly overpower the realization that once people start bending or ignoring the *rules*, or develop their own "common law," the whole exercise of playing the game becomes meaningless for everyone involved.

Rule 2 (Fair Sailing) and rule 69 (Allegations of Gross Misconduct) provide the external "weight" to encourage strict and voluntary rule observance. However, people who race should want to know that everyone whom they've spent the time, money, and energy to race against is sailing within the *rules*; and when they know or suspect that someone isn't, then rather than joining in, they should take action under the *rules* to encourage the others to stop.

4

Part 1
Fundamental Rules

The first rules in the rule book are appropriately called the "Fundamental Rules;" and they address five very important issues in our sport: safety and helping others when in a position to do so, fairness while racing, acceptance of the rules under which we race, responsibility for one's own safety, and drug use (primarily an issue of caution for Olympic-bound racers).

RULE 1 – SAFETY

Rule 1.1 – Helping Those in Danger

A boat or competitor shall give all possible help to any person or vessel in danger.

This rule is the first fundamental rule, reaffirming that this principle must be the one to which all sailors hold above all others. Remember that the word "shall" is mandatory. If it were proved that a sailor was in a position to help another, but did not do so, he or she would be liable for disqualification. Note that the rule requires the giving of all "possible" help; this is to leave no question about the extent to which sailors should help each other when in danger.

The rule book is very supportive of this principle.

- Rule 21 (Capsized, Anchored or Aground; Rescuing) reads in part, "… *a boat shall avoid a boat that is… trying to help a person or vessel in danger.*"

- Rule 41 (Outside Help) reads, "*A boat may receive outside help as provided for in rule 1. Otherwise, she shall not receive help except for an ill or injured crew member or, after a collision, from the crew of the other boat.*"

- Rule 42.3(c) (Propulsion, Exceptions) reads, "*Any means of propulsion may be used to help a person or another vessel in danger.*"

- Rule 47 (Limitations on Equipment and Crew) reads in part, "*No person on board shall leave, unless... to help a person or vessel in danger.*"

 "If I do stop and help a boat or person in danger, can I get some compensation for the places and/or time I may have lost?"

You bet! When you have lost places and/or time as a result of a rescue, you are permitted to request redress under rule 62.1(c) (Redress), and the protest committee, acting under rule 64.2 (Decisions on Redress), can give you appropriate compensation for the places and/or time lost. In the event you go to a rescue, try, if possible, to accurately note the time and your position when you began sailing to the rescue and when you got back in the race. On boats in offshore races it is common to keep a log of times and positions to help the protest committee provide the fairest compensation.

A now famous instance of these rules at work is the rescue made by Canadian Finn sailor Larry Lemieux in the 1988 Summer Olympic Games held in the rough seas off Pusan, South Korea. While in second place midway through a race, Larry noticed a 470 sailor in the water separated from his boat and having great difficulty. Larry went to the sailor's rescue, succeeded in getting him safely back to his boat, and after the race requested redress. The Olympic Jury awarded Larry points equal to finishing second in that race!

ISAF Case 20 reads: "SUMMARY OF THE FACTS: Dinghy A capsized during a race and seeing this, dinghy B sailed over to her and offered help. A accepted help and B came alongside taking the crew of two aboard. Then all hands worked for several minutes to right A whose mast was stuck in mud. Upon reaching shore, B requested redress under rule 62.1(c). The protest committee considered several factors in its decision. First, A's helmsman was a highly experienced sailor. Secondly, the wind was light, and the tide was rising and would shortly have lifted the mast free. Thirdly, she did not ask for help; it was offered. Therefore, since neither boat nor crew was in danger, redress was refused. B appealed, stating that rule 1.1 does not place any onus on a boat giving help to decide, or to defend, a decision that danger was involved.

"DECISION: Appeal upheld. A boat in a position to help another that may be in danger is bound to do so. That a protest committee, later assessing the many factors that may cause a vessel or person to be in danger, concludes that help was offered but not requested or that no danger existed is irrelevant."

Rule 1.2 – Life-Saving Equipment and Personal Buoyancy

A boat shall carry adequate life-saving equipment for all persons on board, including one item ready for immediate use, unless her class rules make some other provision. Each competitor is individually responsible for wearing personal buoyancy adequate for the conditions.

Rule 1.2 gives the highest prominence to these safety issues. Note that it is **each sailor's** responsibility to decide when to wear his or her life-jacket (often referred to as a "personal flotation device" or "PFD"). Often class rules and/ or sailing instructions will require you to wear your life-jacket any time you go afloat. Be sure to check those rules.

Also, the race committee can require you to wear your life-jacket by displaying flag Y (rule 40, Personal Buoyancy). Note, however, that though the race committee has the option to use this signal, it does not shift away from you any of your responsibility for your own safety. Rule 40 also clarifies that wet suits and dry suits are not adequate personal buoyancy.

Finally, the US SAILING prescription to rule 40 reads, "*US SAILING prescribes that every boat shall carry life-saving equipment conforming to government regulations.*"

RULE 2 - FAIR SAILING

A boat and her owner shall compete in compliance with recognized principles of sportsmanship and fair play. A boat may be penalized under this rule only if it is clearly established that these principles have been violated. A disqualification under this rule shall not be excluded from the boat's series score.

As was discussed in Chapter 3, Sportsmanship and the Rules, when we race we should all agree to hold ourselves to the highest principles of fairness and sportsmanship. Rule 2 is a clear statement of that premise. When a boat or competitor clearly violates these principles, he or she breaks this rule and is liable to penalty.

Note that a penalty for breaking this rule is more severe than for most other rules. Rule 2 clearly states that if you are in a series which allows you to discard your worst race, a disqualification for breaking rule 2 cannot be discarded. Notice also that a boat can be penalized under rule 2, even when another *rule* applies to the situation. Therefore, in any incident or situation where the principles in rule 2 have been clearly violated, regardless of what other *rules* may also have been broken, a boat is liable to disqualification under rule 2. This becomes very significant given that a boat has to count that disqualification in her final score.

 "Could you give some examples of when you would consider the principles in rule 2 have been violated?"

Sure, recognizing that each protest committee is given the discretion to judge what they deem to be "recognized principles of sportsmanship and fair play." In deciding whether a competitor has competed in compliance with the principles in rule 2, I feel it is important to consider the motive for their actions; i.e. was it an intentional violation of one of the principles?

In ISAF Case 47, "An experienced helmsman of a port-tack boat hails 'Starboard!' to a beginner who, although on starboard tack, not being sure of himself and probably being scared of having his boat holed, tacks to port to avoid a collision. No protest was lodged. One school of thought argues that it is fair game, because if a helmsman does not know the rules, that is his own hard luck. The other school rejects this argument, on the grounds that it is quite contrary to the spirit of the rules to deceive a competitor in that way. It is known that such a trick is often played, particularly where novices were involved, and therefore guidance is sought on whether a protest committee should or should not take action under rule 2.

"ANSWER: A boat that deliberately hails 'Starboard' when she knows she is on port tack has not acted fairly and has broken rule 2. The protest committee might also consider taking action under rule 69."

Other examples:

- A *port-tack* boat is reaching by to *leeward* of a *starboard-tack* boat before the start. The *starboard-tack* boat does not change her course, but just as the boats are passing her boom suddenly flies out and hits the *port-tacker's* shroud. Clearly there is no way for *port* to keep clear at that moment. If it is determined that S's skipper let the boom out **intentionally to hit the boat on port**, I would penalize S under rule 2. If it is determined that S was simply sailing her boat, perhaps responding to a gust of wind, etc., I would penalize P for not *keeping clear*.

- Two boats come off the starting line side-by-side in very light air. Suddenly, the *leeward* boat rocks hard to windward, the tip of her mast hitting the tip of the *windward* boat's mast. The *leeward* boat does not change course. Again, if it is determined that the action was done solely to try to touch the *windward* boat, I would penalize her under rule 2. I would apply the same reasoning to a *leeward* boat whose crew goes out on the trapeze in light air or otherwise reaches out and touches the *windward* boat for the sole purpose of "fouling the other boat out."

- A boat is on a heavy-air overnight race. Each time the boat tacks, the crew down-below move the sails back and forth to the *windward* side to increase the boat's stability. Not only would I penalize this boat for breaking rule 51 (Moving Ballast), I would penalize her under rule 2 as well.

One common practice that is not a violation of rule 2 is the tactic whereby one boat tries to make it harder for another boat to do well in a race or series, including by trying to put boats between herself and the other boat at the finish, provided the boat tries to sail within the *rules* and provided her motive is to benefit her own series score.

ISAF Case 78 reads, "On a windward leg near the finish of the final race of a one-design class series, boat A is some distance ahead of boat B. Suddenly, A changes course, so that she sails back down the course towards B, and positions herself in a tactically controlling position over B. A then slows B's progress, resulting in three boats passing them. A had calculated her own and B's score, and had determined that if B were to be passed by three boats A would defeat B in the series.

"QUESTION: Was the tactic used by boat A, turning back and slowing another boat's progress, a sportsmanlike action? Is this tactic acceptable in any race and in any part of a race?

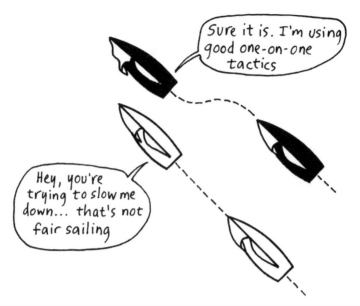

"ANSWER: A's tactic broke no rule, including rule 2, which refers to sportsmanship. It is acceptable for a boat to slow another boat's progress in a race and to use this tactic in any race of a series, at any time or place during the race, provided the tactic is intended to benefit her own series result. However, if a boat intentionally breaks a rule while using this tactic she also breaks rule 2."

Though some may shiver at the notion that it is okay for one boat to actively try to hinder another boat's race, the racing rules themselves are in no way constructed to discourage, inhibit or prevent this. In fact, it is quite common for one boat to try to start close to *leeward* of another for the purpose of hindering the other's start, to intentionally tack on someone's wind on a beat, or to luff a boat downwind. In addition, it is quite common for sailors to be aware of "who their competition is" from the outset of a race or series and to actively seek opportunities to hinder them early on. As long as it's done within the racing rules, there is no problem.

"What happens if a boat hinders my race and causes me to finish worse than I would have otherwise finished, and is found to have broken rule 2 in the process?"

You are entitled to redress under rule 62.1(d) (Redress)! You can request this yourself, or the race or protest committee can do it on your behalf (rule 60, Right to Protest and Request Redress).

When a protest committee feels that an individual competitor has acted in a way that is contrary to our sport, they can conduct a hearing under rule 69 (Allegations of Gross Misconduct).

Rule 69 - Allegations of Gross Misconduct

Rule 69.1 - Action by a Protest Committee

(a) When a protest committee, from its own observation or a report received, believes that a competitor may have committed a gross breach of a rule or of good manners or sportsmanship, or may have brought the sport into disrepute, it may call a hearing. The protest committee shall promptly inform the competitor in writing of the alleged misconduct and of the time and place of the hearing.

(b) A protest committee of at least three members shall conduct the hearing, following rules 63.2, 63.3, 63.4 and 63.6. If it decides that the competitor committed the alleged misconduct it shall either

   (1) warn the competitor or

   (2) impose a penalty by excluding the competitor, and a boat when appropriate, from a race, or the remaining races of a series or the entire series, or by taking other action within its jurisdiction.

(c) The protest committee shall promptly report a penalty, but not a warning, to the national authorities of the venue, of the competitor and of the boat owner.

d) If the competitor has left the venue and cannot be notified or fails to attend the hearing, the protest committee shall collect all available evidence and, when the allegation seems justified, make a report to the relevant national authorities.

(e) When the protest committee has left the event and a report alleging misconduct is received, the race committee or organizing authority may appoint a new protest committee to proceed under this rule.

Rule 69.1(a) permits a protest committee to call a hearing when it believes that a competitor may have committed a gross breach of a *rule* or of good manners or sportsmanship, or may have brought the sport into disrepute. The protest committee may have first-hand knowledge of the situation, or it may have received a report from someone else. Notice that a boat does not protest under rule 69; however, she can suggest in a *protest* that a hearing under rule 69 be considered.

If the protest committee decides that the competitor has acted improperly, it can warn him, exclude him (and his boat if appropriate) from one or more races in a series or the entire series, or take other action available to it. Notice that it must also report it's action, other than a warning, to the national authorities involved.

Rule 69 is to be used when the competitor's conduct is "gross." "Gross" can be generally interpreted as follows: conspicuously obvious, flagrant, deliberate, referring to offenses or errors so bad they cannot escape notice or be condoned or actions exceeding reasonable or excusable limits.

In my opinion, any **deliberate infringement** of the *rules* is a gross infringement. For example: S deliberately rams P causing damage (perhaps because the skipper of P had disqualified the skipper of S in a protest hearing the night before). Another example is when a competitor deliberately cuts a *mark* or *starts* ahead of the starting line for the purpose of hindering another competitor's race. (See ISAF Case 34.)

Further examples of a gross breach of good manners or sportsmanship include: **proved lying** in a protest hearing (as opposed to honest differences in recollection of the incident); **intentional cheating** (for instance, racing with an unmeasured sail or removing mandatory ballast, as opposed to class or racing rule violations caused by ignorance); **intentional damage** to another boat afloat or on shore, (for instance, cutting someone's shrouds in the night); **fighting**, particularly where there is injury or damage; **stealing** from another boat or from private property at a club or elsewhere; and **foul or threatening language**, particularly if it is continued after receiving a clear warning.

Obviously rule 69 is an important rule, but its effectiveness relies on the integrity of the protest committee that chooses to invoke it. Each case must be carefully examined to determine, as accurately as possible, exactly what happened, what events led up to the incident, and what the probable motives of the individuals involved were. The hearing and deliberations should be conducted as objectively as possible with an effort to keep emotions out. A competitor's previous actions should not be weighed in the case unless germane and accurately represented. Appeals that are cited as precedent must be closely examined to be sure that they are truly nearly identical in all ways. And before imposing a penalty under rule 69.1(b)(2), the protest committee must thoroughly consider if the weight of the punishment is justified by the competitor's action.

Disqualification from a series for a gross infringement of the *rules* or a gross breach of good manners or sportsmanship is a strong penalty by itself, due to the effect it generally has on the individual(s) and from the adverse publicity it can create. But in addition, this penalty must also be reported to US SAILING or the appropriate national authority. In turn they can conduct an investigation and exclude the competitor(s) or boat(s) from the sport for a period of time. This is extremely strong as it will have an impact on the sailor's life beyond just their sailing, in ways that may extend beyond just the time period of their penalty.

Note that a sailor penalized under rule 69 is a *party* to a hearing (see the definition *Party*), and as such she has the right to appeal the decision of the protest committee under rule 70.1(a) (Right of Appeal and Requests for Interpretation). A U.S. sailor also may file a grievance under Article XIV of the US SAILING Bylaws when they feel actions have been taken against them that are not in accordance with the *rules*.

RULE 3 – ACCEPTANCE OF THE RULES

By participating in a race conducted under these racing rules, each competitor and boat owner agrees

(a) to be governed by the *rules*;

(b) to accept the penalties imposed and other action taken under the *rules*, subject to the appeal and review procedures provided in them, as the final determination of any matter arising under the *rules*; and

(c) with respect to such determination, not to resort to any court or other tribunal not provided by the *rules*.

Rule 3 states that when you decide to race under the ISAF *Racing Rules of*

Sailing, you agree to be governed by those *rules*, and to keep actions made in accordance with the *rules* within the rules system of the sport; i.e. not to take them to any outside court. Note that rule J1.2(4) (Notice of Race and Sailing Instructions) requires that the Notice of Race include, when appropriate, an entry form to be signed by the boat's owner or owner's representative, containing words such as: "*'I agree to be bound by* **The Racing Rules of Sailing** *and by all other **rules** that govern this event'.*"

This agreement becomes especially important when an incident results in a high cost of repair or replacement. Rule 68 (Damages) states, "*The question of damages arising from a breach of any **rule** shall be governed by the prescriptions, if any, of the national authority.*"

In the United States, US SAILING prescribes, "*that responsibility for damages arising from any breach of the **rules** shall be based on fault as determined by application of the **rules**, and that she shall not be governed by the legal doctrine of 'assumption of risk' for monetary damages resulting from contact with other boats.*" Furthermore, the prescription states, "*A protest committee shall find facts and make decisions only in compliance with the **rules**. No protest committee or US SAILING appeal authority shall adjudicate any claim for damages. Such a claim is subject to the jurisdiction of the courts.*"

In other words, a protest committee can find only the facts; and a protest committee, or appeals committee acting on an appeal, can decide only which boat was at fault under the *rules*. They cannot decide issues of claims for damages.

When you disagree with a protest committee's application or interpretation of the *rules*, you may appeal under rule 70.1 (Right of Appeal and Requests for Interpretation), unless the right of appeal has been denied under rule 70.4. If you feel that any of your rights as a competitor have been denied by the race or protest committee and it hurt your finishing place in a race or series, you can request redress under rule 62.1 (Redress) and you can appeal that decision as well.

If ever you feel you've been aggrieved by an action not under the jurisdiction of the *rules*, you can take your grievance to the organizing authority for the race or series, or to US SAILING through Article XIV of the US SAILING By-Laws.

RULE 4 – DECISION TO RACE

The responsibility for a boat's decision to participate in a race or to continue *racing* is hers alone.

There have been attempted lawsuits brought unsuccessfully against race committees by sailors who have had accidents during races in strong winds. Their contentions have been, in part, that the race committee has jeopardized their safety by holding races in severe conditions. US SAILING Appeal 39 is crystal clear: "The decision to start, postpone, or abandon a race is a matter solely within the jurisdiction of the race committee (see rule 88.1, Race Committee). Rule 62.1 (Redress) should not be interpreted to restrict or interfere with its authority and responsibilities in matters of race management. Under rule 4, each boat has the sole responsibility to decide whether or not to race. If a boat decides not to race, she cannot claim her finishing place was made worse."

Notice that it is the **boat**'s responsibility to decide. Every sailor on a boat has the responsibility to voice their opinion as to whether or not to *start* or to continue to *race*. Nothing in this rule protects an owner, skipper or helmsman from a liability suit by their crew.

RULE 5 – DRUGS

A competitor shall neither take a substance nor use a method banned by the Olympic Movement Anti-Doping Code or the World Anti-Doping Agency and shall comply with Appendix 3 (ISAF Regulation 19, ISAF Anti-Doping Code). An alleged or actual breach of this rule shall be dealt with under regulation 19. It shall not be grounds for a *protest* and rule 63.1 does not apply.

Clearly, this is primarily of concern for Olympic-bound competitors. However, all competitors are wise to recognize that there is a strict rule forbidding the use of banned drugs in our sport. Refer to Appendix 3 in *The Racing Rules of Sailing* for more information.

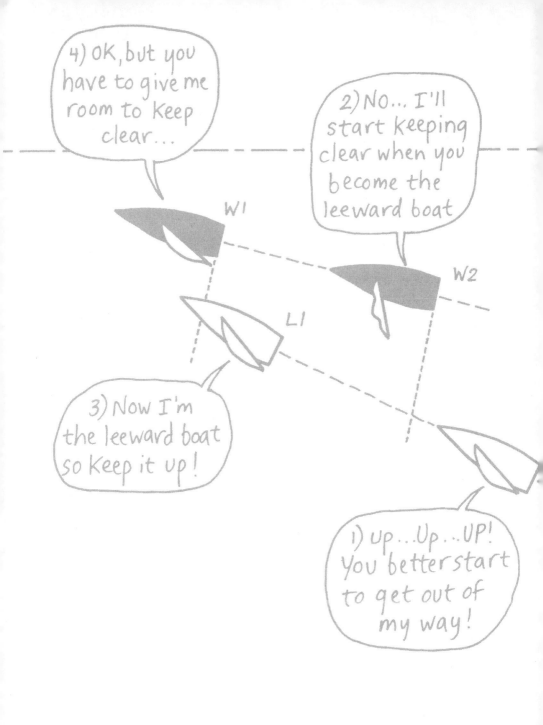

5

The Definitions

The Definitions are the "dictionary" of the rule book. Words and terms like "racing," "obstruction" and "proper course" are specifically defined so that there is no question or debate as to their meaning. When a defined word or term is used in a *rule*, it is printed in *italic* type. Before studying the *rules*, be sure to study the Definitions and then actively check back to them as you go through each *rule*; you'll find that in a short time you will be confident of each *rule*'s full meaning.

ABANDON

A race that a race committee or protest committee *abandons* is void but may be resailed.

N

A race committee can *abandon* a race before it starts (rule 27.3, Other Race Committee Actions Before the Starting Signal), while it is under way (rule 32, Shortening or Abandoning After the Start) or even after one or more boats have finished (rule 32). To signal an *abandonment*, the race committee will make three consecutive sound signals and display flag N (meaning return to the starting area for a new start), flag N over H (meaning return to the harbor and await further instructions) or flag N over A (meaning no more races that day). (See Race Signals.) A protest committee, acting on a request for redress, can *abandon* a race (rule 64.2, Decisions on Redress). A race that has been properly *abandoned* may be resailed.

N over H

Notice that once the race has started, the race committee is governed by rule 32 when deciding whether to *abandon* a race.

N over A

Rule 32.1 lists the five scenarios in which the race committee may *abandon* a race:

a) because of an error in the starting procedure,

b) because of foul weather,

c) because of insufficient wind making it unlikely that any boat will *finish* within the time limit,

d) because a *mark* is missing or out of position, or

e) for any other reason directly affecting the safety or fairness of the competition.

 "Does rule 32.1(e) mean that the race committee can abandon a race in progress when a large wind shift occurs?"

Yes, when in its judgment the wind shift has made the race an unsatisfactory test of skill and therefore "unfair." However, in my opinion it is desirable to reduce the number of subjective decisions a race committee can make once the race has started and it can see who is or isn't doing well. Therefore, once a race has been started, race committees should make every attempt to anticipate and react to wind shifts and to reposition *marks* in order to keep the race "fair" before deciding to *abandon*, particularly after the first boat has rounded the first *mark*.

After at least one boat has finished a race, the race committee and protest committee are required, before *abandoning* the race, to consider the probable consequences for all boats affected and to take appropriate evidence when doubt exists (rules 32.1 and 64.2).

CLEAR ASTERN AND CLEAR AHEAD; OVERLAP

One boat is *clear astern* of another when her hull and equipment in normal position are behind a line abeam from the aftermost point of the other boat's hull and equipment in normal position. The other boat is *clear ahead*. They *overlap* when neither is *clear astern* or when a boat between them *overlaps* both. These terms do not apply to boats on opposite *tacks* unless rule 18 applies.

Putting aside for a moment what *tack* the boats are on, let's look at two boats sailing near each other. To figure out if they are *overlapped*, take one of the

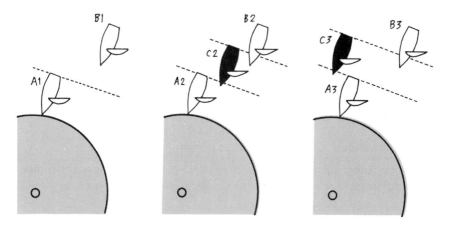

In position 1, A and B are not overlapped; A is clear ahead and B is clear astern.

In position 2, C is in between A and B and overlapped with both of them; therefore B is overlapped with A.

In position 3, C is not in between A and B; therefore B is overlapped with C, C is overlapped with A, and A and B are not overlapped.

boats and draw a line down her centerline. Then find the aftermost point of her hull or equipment in **normal position**. Draw another line perpendicular to the centerline and through the aftermost point. If the other boat's hull and equipment in **normal position** are completely behind that line, she is *clear astern* and the other boat is *clear ahead*. If she is across that line at all, then neither boat is *clear astern* of the other; therefore they are *overlapped*.

Now let's say one of the boats was *clear ahead* of the other boat by five feet. Put a third boat in between the two. If the boat that was *clear astern* now *overlaps* this middle boat and the middle boat *overlaps* the boat that was *clear ahead*, the definition says that now each boat is *overlapped* with each other.

One point worth discussing is determining the aftermost point of the hull and equipment in normal position. It literally means the point on the boat that is the farthest aft, i.e. the point that would hit a wall first if the boat were backed into one.

Notice also the term "normal position" (see the definition *Finish* for more discussion). If your auxiliary engine is tilted up, then in all likelihood the propeller is the aftermost point; and if you've been sailing the race with it up, you can't come into a mark and quickly swing the engine down just to break an *overlap* by making your boat shorter.

Finally, notice that the terms "clear astern," "clear ahead" and "overlap" do not apply to boats on opposite *tacks*, unless they are about to round or pass a *mark* or *obstruction* (rule 18, Rounding and Passing Marks and Obstructions). So two boats side by side on opposite *tacks* halfway down the run are not *overlapped*, but when they get down near the "*two-length zone*" at the *mark*, they are considered to be *overlapped*.

FINISH

A boat finishes when any part of her hull, or crew or equipment in normal position, crosses the finishing line in the direction of the course from the last *mark* either for the first time or after taking a penalty under rule 31.2 or 44.2 or, under rule 28, after correcting an error made at the finishing line.

You *finish* when any part of your hull, or of your crew or equipment in **normal position,** crosses the finish line. Therefore, in a strong adverse current for example, all you need to do is get your bow across the line to get your finishing position or time. Rule 28.1 (Sailing the Course) states, "*After finishing she need not cross the finishing line completely.*"

Notice that your crew and equipment must be in "normal position." "Normal position" is generally defined as the position where your crew or equipment is normally located in the existing wind and sea conditions. Therefore boats can't come into a close downwind finish and suddenly let their spinnaker halyards and sheets out two feet, or come into a close upwind finish in light air and suddenly have their crews jump out on the trapeze to put their heads across the line.

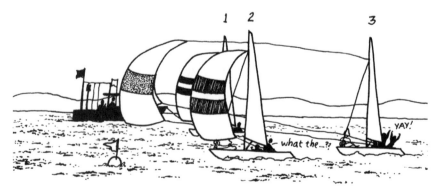

Boat 3's spinnaker is not in normal position.

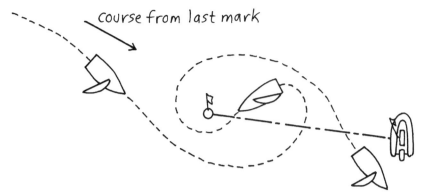

course from last mark

Boat X finishes when she crosses the finishing line the third time.

If you foul a boat at the finishing line or touch a finishing *mark*, it's possible that you will cross the finishing line before doing your "720" or "360." That is not a problem. Simply get clear of other boats, do your penalty turn(s) and then cross the finishing line again. You *finish* when you cross the line after taking your penalty; i.e. the first time you crossed the line will be disregarded.

If you do not *finish* correctly, the race committee is allowed to score you DNF (Did Not Finish) without protesting you (rule A5, Scores Determined by the Race Committee). If you feel they have incorrectly scored you DNF, you can request redress under rule 62.1(a) (Redress). However, if you *finish* but the race committee thinks it saw you touch a finishing *mark* and you do not take a penalty, or it thinks you skipped a mark or otherwise failed to sail the course correctly, it must score you as having *finished* and then protest you under rule 31.1 (Touching a Mark) or rule 28.1 (Sailing the Course) in accordance with rule 61.1(b) (Protest Requirements). (See ISAF Case 80.)

Sometimes, when coming up to a finishing line, it is not always clear which way to go across it. The definition says that a boat *finishes* when she crosses the finishing line in the direction of the course from the last *mark*. The last *mark* means the last *mark* of the course prior to the finishing line. Therefore, simply cross the line in the natural direction from the last *mark* you passed, regardless of any required sides either of the finishing *marks* may have had at other times during the race. (See ISAF Case 45.)

And if you realize you have crossed the finishing line in the wrong direction, you can correct your error so that your course complies with rule 28.1 (Sailing the Course). Remember that this may require that you "unwind your string" first before crossing the line in the correct direction (see discussion of rule 28).

INTERESTED PARTY

A person who may gain or lose as a result of a protest committee's decision, or who has a close personal interest in the decision.

Rule 63.4 (Interested Party) reads, "*A member of a protest committee who is an interested party shall not take any further part in the hearing but may appear as a witness.*" The purpose of this rule is clearly to provide competitors with the fairest possible hearing without any taint of prejudice or self-interest among the protest committee members.

There are times when race or protest committee members will initiate a *protest* against a boat; for example, under the propulsion rule (rule 42, Propulsion). In this context they are not *interested parties*, and they are allowed to be **both** a member of the protest committee as well as the protestor. However, they must give all their evidence and testimony as a witness in front of the *parties* to the hearing (see rules 63.3(a), Right to be Present, and 63.6, Taking Evidence and Finding Facts, and US SAILING Appeal 39.)

Persons who, in my opinion, **could** be considered *interested parties* are parents (or offspring), instructors or coaches, employers or employees, sponsors or financial contributors, members of the same yacht club or association, or even a fellow sailor with the same nationality. In the right set of circumstances, any of these persons could be judged to be an *interested party*.

 "What can I do if I honestly feel a member of the protest committee might be an 'interested party'?"

If you feel any member of a protest committee is an *interested party*, you may object. Rule 63.4 reads, "*A party to the hearing who believes a member of the protest committee is an **interested party** shall object as soon as possible.*" The protest committee should then consider your objection before proceeding (Appendix L2, Recommendations for Protest Committees, Before the Hearing).

In evaluating members of a protest committee as potentially *interested parties*, the important criterion is: will their hearing of the facts, their finding of the facts and their application and interpretation of the *rules* be hindered by any prejudice or favoritism toward or against any of the parties to the hearing?

If members of the protest committee honestly feel that any predisposition on their part will affect their decision in the hearing, they should respectfully decline to serve; and when you honestly feel or suspect that a protest committee member's decision-making ability might be affected for some reason, you have a right to say so and to state your reasons (rule 63.4).

KEEP CLEAR

One boat *keeps clear* of another if the other can sail her course with no need to take avoiding action and, when the boats are *overlapped* on the same *tack*, if the *leeward* boat can change course in both directions without immediately making contact with the *windward* boat.

The rules are structured so that when two boats converge on the race course, one has the right-of-way and the other must stay out of her way, i.e. *keep clear*. The preamble to Part 2, Section A reads, "*A boat has right of way when another boat is required to keep clear of her.*" I call the boat that is required to *keep clear* the "**give-way**" boat.

The principle in the definition is clear: right-of-way boats should be able to sail their race without give-way boats getting in their way. That means that not only must a give-way boat not hit a right-of-way boat, she must also not get so close that the right-of-way boat can no longer sail her straight-ahead

course because she has to take action to avoid contact with the give-way boat. Though this avoiding "action" will normally be a change of course, it could also be a change of speed or some other action.

On the issue of "need," I believe that when the right-of-way boat has a reasonable apprehension that contact will occur without action on her part, she is justified in saying she "needed" to take action, even if subsequent analysis of the situation shows that the give-way boat would have actually cleared by inches.

The last phrase in the definition closes a possible loophole caused by rule 16 (Changing Course). Rule 16 requires that when right-of-way boats change course, they give other boats *room* to *keep clear*. The loophole is that a *windward* boat (W) could position herself right next to a *leeward* boat (L) such that the moment L changed course she would hit W. W could then claim that L had broken rule 16 by not giving her *room* to *keep clear*. The definition closes that loophole by addressing **overlapped** boats on the same *tack* and telling W that she is not *keeping clear* if she allows herself to get so close to L that L couldn't change course in **both** directions at that moment without **immediately** making contact with her.

Note that the second "if" in the definition suggests that L does not need to actually hit W to prove she couldn't change course without hitting her. If the protest committee decides that L couldn't have changed course without immediately hitting W, then W has broken rule 11 (On the Same Tack, Overlapped) simply by her extreme close proximity to L.

"Do I have to keep clear of the right-of-way boat's crew, sails, equipment, spars, etc. even when they are clearly out of their 'normal position'?"

Yes. The definition makes no distinction regarding whether or not a boat is carrying her crew, sails, equipment, spars, etc. in "normal position." (See ISAF Case 91.) The only exception is in the rare instance where a boat is *keeping clear* and suddenly something from the right-of-way boat flies out unexpectedly and immediately makes contact with the give-way boat. ISAF Case 77 describes such a case where just after rounding a leeward *mark*, the head of the spinnaker of the boat *clear ahead* (A) came loose and flew back and touched the headstay of the boat *clear astern* (B). The decision concludes, "Concerning the definition *Keep Clear*, nothing B did or failed to do required

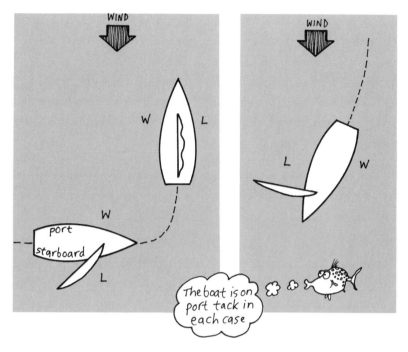

The boat on the left is reaching with her port side toward the wind; therefore her port side is her windward side and she is on port tack. When she luffs up to head to wind she remains on port tack. The boat on the right is sailing by the lee with her mainsail lying naturally on her starboard side. Therefore her port side is her windward side and she is also on port tack.

A 'to take avoiding action.' This is shown by the fact that the contact between them results exclusively from A's equipment moving out of normal position."

LEEWARD AND WINDWARD

A boat's *leeward* side is the side that is or, when she is head to wind, was away from the wind. However, when sailing by the lee or directly downwind, her *leeward* side is the side on which her mainsail lies. The other side is her *windward* side. When two boats on the same *tack overlap*, the one on the leeward side of the other is the *leeward* boat. The other is the *windward* boat.

The definition called *Tack, Starboard* or *Port* tells us that whether we are on *port* or *starboard tack* is determined by our *windward* side, i.e. if our *windward* side is our port side, we are on *port tack*.

This definition tells us that our *windward* side is the side closest to the wind, and that our *leeward* side is the opposite side. If the boat is heading directly into the wind, then whichever side **was** the *windward* side before the boat was head to wind is still considered the *windward* side.

The only exception is when the boat is heading directly downwind or "by the lee" (which means the boat has continued to turn past directly downwind without the boom changing sides). In that case, the *windward* side is the side opposite the side the boom is on.

"If I'm sailing close-hauled on port-tack in light air and heel the boat sharply to windward such that the boom falls to the port side of the boat, am I now on starboard tack; or if I'm sailing by the lee and forcibly holding the mainsail over the port side with my arm, am I still on starboard tack?"

No. Remember that when you are not sailing directly downwind or by the lee, your *tack* is determined by the side of the boat the wind is blowing over. In your first case, when you are sailing close-hauled, the wind is blowing over your port side regardless of where your boom is located; therefore you are on *port tack*. The same would be true if you are sailing along on *port tack*, and then go head to wind and push your boom out on the port side to back down. You are still on *port tack* as long as your bow doesn't **pass** head to wind. The moment it **passes** head to wind, you are now on *starboard tack*.

When you are sailing directly downwind or by the lee, your *leeward* side is the side on which your mainsail "lies." "Lies" is used intentionally to indicate that it is the side where your mainsail would **naturally** lie, i.e. be pushed by the wind, as opposed to by the control of some other force such as your arm, the mainsheet or gravity. Therefore, in your second case, you are now on *port tack* because if you released the mainsail, it would lie on your starboard side. The same would be true if, while sailing directly downwind, you trimmed the mainsail in amidships. Your *tack* will be determined by where the mainsail would lie naturally; in this case, most likely it will want to go back out to the side it was on before you trimmed it in.

Finally, there is the definition of *windward* and *leeward* boat. If the boats are **on the same** *tack* and they are *overlapped,* the one on the *leeward* side of the other is the *leeward* boat. The other is the *windward* boat. Notice that if they are not *overlapped,* they are not *windward* and *leeward* boats; they are *clear ahead* and *clear astern.*

MARK

An object the sailing instructions require a boat to leave on a specified side, and a race committee vessel surrounded by navigable water from which the starting or finishing line extends. An anchor line and objects attached temporarily or accidentally to a *mark* are not part of it.

A *mark* can be an inflatable ball, a bell buoy, a large power boat, an island or any object the sailing instructions so indicate. Notice that often the sailing instructions require that government *mark*s be passed on their required side as you sail from one turning *mark* to the next. These government *marks* are *marks* of the course as well. On a starting line between a race committee boat and a buoy, the **entire** race committee boat is a *mark* even though the actual end of the line is marked by a flag or some other specific point on the boat. Anything that is normally attached to the object is also part of the *mark*, for instance, a flag, a long antenna or a swimming platform; but something temporarily attached, such as a Whaler tied up to the race committee boat, is not part of the *mark* **unless** the sailing instructions indicate otherwise. Note that a race committee will often hang a "stand-off buoy" off the transom of their race committee boat to keep boats farther away, and that they will commonly indicate in the sailing instructions that these "stand-off" buoys are to be considered part of the *mark*.

Also note that the entire object is the *mark*, not just the above-water part.

OBSTRUCTION

An object that a boat could not pass without changing course substantially, if she were sailing directly towards it and one of her hull lengths from it. An object that can be safely passed on only one side and an area so designated by the sailing instructions are also *obstructions*. However, a boat *racing* is not an *obstruction* to other boats unless they are required to *keep clear* of her, give her room or, if rule 21 applies, avoid her.

An *obstruction* is **anything** on the race course, including another boat in your race or other vessel in the racing area, large enough to require you to change course substantially to avoid it if you are about to hit it. In determining whether the object can be considered an *obstruction*, the definition offers three criteria:

1) the object must be large enough to require you to change course substantially **if** you were aiming right at it, regardless of whether you actually are or not. In other words, it's a hypothetical test. An object does not become an *obstruction* or cease to be an *obstruction* based on where on it you are actually aiming at the time.

2) the amount of course change required is determined from a point one of your boat's overall hull lengths away from the object. This strongly suggests that you keep a lookout for anything ahead of you, as opposed to suddenly finding yourself about to hit something right in front of you and needing to slam your tiller over to miss it.

3) the size of the course change must be "substantial," i.e. a large course change. In a 20-foot boat, a course change of 10 degrees moves the bow about three-and-a-half feet. Done when one boat-length away, a 10-degree alteration will clear a seven-foot object on either side. **As my general rule** I would say that a course change less than 10 degrees is not "substantial;" i.e. a stationary object clearly less than one-third your boat's length would not be an *obstruction*, though a moving object will require a larger alteration to get around it. Obviously, a lobster pot or an average-size channel marker is not going to require you to change your course substantially, but a race committee boat, a breakwater or another sailboat in a race will.

A powerboat can be an **obstruction** if it's large enough. When a race committee decides to use a powerboat as one end of the starting line, the powerboat becomes a *mark* also. Notice that it doesn't cease to be an *obstruction*. It is always an *obstruction*, but now it also happens to be a *mark*.

 "Can you clarify the times when a boat in a race can be considered an 'obstruction'?"

Sure. A boat in a race, either your race or another race, is an "obstruction" when either:

1) it has the right of way over the other boats in the situation; or

2) it is entitled to *room* from the other boats in the situation; or

3) it is capsized or has not regained control after capsizing; or

4) it is anchored or aground; or

5) it is trying to help a person or vessel in danger.

Otherwise, boats in a race are not considered *obstructions*.

PARTY

A *party* to a hearing: a protestor; a protestee; a boat requesting redress; a boat or a competitor that may be penalized under rule 69.1; a race committee in a hearing under rule 62.1(a).

It is important to understand exactly who is, and is not, a *party* to a protest hearing. The primary reason is that the rules in Part 5, Protests, Redress, Hearings, Misconduct and Appeals, provide many specific rights and obligations for *parties* to a hearing and many requirements of a protest committee regarding *parties* to a hearing. Furthermore, only a *party* to a hearing may appeal a decision of a protest committee under rule 70.1 (Right of Appeal and Requests for Interpretation).

When boats lodge a *protest* they automatically become a *party* to the hearing (protestor), as do the boats they are protesting (protestee). The same is true when they request redress under rule 62 (Redress). When boats request redress under rule 62.1(a), claiming that an improper action or omission of the race committee made their finishing place significantly worse, the race committee also becomes a *party* to the hearing.

Often, in the course of a hearing, a third yacht will become a "suspect." Rule 61.1(c) (Protest Requirements, Informing the Protestee) says, *"During the hearing of a valid **protest** or request for redress, if the protest committee decides to protest a boat that was involved in the incident but is not a **party** to that hearing, it shall inform the boat as soon as reasonably possible of its intention, then protest her as required by rule 61.2 and proceed with a hearing as required by rule 63."* Once the protest committee protests the third boat, that boat (now a 'protestee') becomes a *party* to the hearing.

"If, after acting on another boat's request for redress, the protest committee abandons the race in which I was first, can I consider myself a 'party to the hearing' because I was 'penalized,' and as such appeal the decision?"

Absolutely not. Rule 64.1 (Protest Decisions, Penalties and Exoneration) discusses "penalties," using disqualification as the usual penalty. You were not given a specific "penalty" when the race was *abandoned*. Obviously *abandoning* the race changes series results, moving some competitors up and some down. You may have been disappointed by the *abandonment*, but you were not "penalized" by it. A "penalty" results from a rule breach either accepted voluntarily or imposed by a protest committee decision. Because you were not liable to be penalized in the incident, you are not a *party* to the hearing and are not entitled to appeal.

On the other hand, you certainly can request redress under rule 62.1(a) (Redress), making you a *party* to your redress hearing. You must be prepared to demonstrate what "**improper** action or omission" the protest committee made in reaching its decision to *abandon* the race, and how the action/omission made your finishing place significantly worse through no fault of your own. Then, once the protest committee has made a decision on your redress request, you may appeal **that** decision. Note, however, that a boat is not entitled to redress for proper action by a race or protest committee simply because alternative action would give her a better standing.

AP

Finally, boats or competitors who are liable to be penalized under rule 69.1 (Allegations of Gross Misconduct, Action by a Protest Committee) **are** a *party* to a hearing, thereby giving them standing to appeal the protest committee's decision should they want to do so.

POSTPONE

AP over H

A postponed race is delayed before its scheduled start but may be started or *abandoned* later.

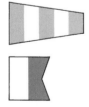

AP over A

A race can be *postponed* only if it has not been started. Once a race has been started, it can only be stopped by *abandoning* it. To signal a *postponement*, the race committee will make two consecutive sound signals and display flag AP, flag AP over H (meaning return to the harbor and await further instructions) or flag AP over A (meaning no more races that day). (See Race Signals.)

PROPER COURSE

A course a boat would sail to *finish* as soon as possible in the absence of the other boats referred to in the *rule* using the term. A boat has no *proper course* before her starting signal.

This is the most subjective definition in the book. It is also very important, particularly in applying rule 17 (On the Same Tack; Proper Course). The concept is very straightforward: your *proper course* is the course you think will get you from the starting line to the finishing line as quickly as possible, taking into account all the factors that will affect your speed. Typically, different sailors will have different ideas on what their fastest course is; thus different boats will have justifiably different *proper courses*.

One way to visualize this concept is to imagine a Time Trial. You and nine other sailors show up to race around a fixed-length triangle course, one at a time; the one with the fastest time wins. Around the windward-reach-reach course there are wind shifts, grandstands and a small man-made island on the second reach for the press and photographers. You start. You've already calculated the fastest path up the first beat, accounting for wind shifts, waves, current, time lost while tacking and so on. Down the first reach, as you approach the grandstand area you notice it's creating a huge wind shadow so you bear

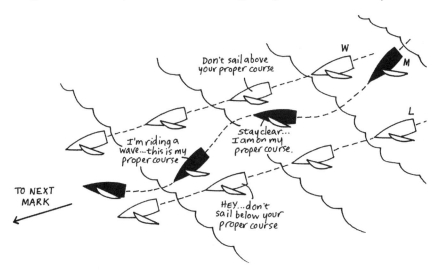

M is surfing waves in order to increase her speed in an attempt to arrive at the next mark and ultimately the finishing line as soon as possible. Therefore, her luffing and bearing away are justifiable changes in her proper course; M has not broken any rule.

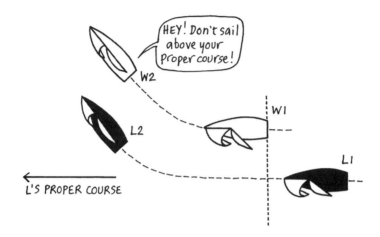

L has become overlapped from clear astern and then luffed above her proper course solely to make it more difficult for W to stay ahead of her. In W's absence L would not have luffed at all. Therefore, L has broken rule 17.1 by sailing above her proper course.

away to avoid the light air and break through to leeward as quickly as possible. On the second reach, you've calculated that passing to leeward of the press island is the shortest, fastest route to the leeward mark. You finish.

The next boat starts. But this boat goes a different way up the beat. And it doesn't think the grandstand's wind shadow is that bad, so it doesn't bear off as much. And finally it passes the press island to windward and finishes. Both boats were trying to race and finish as quickly as possible and so they were both sailing *proper courses*. In fact, all the boats may have had different opinions as to the fastest course that day. The course each boat sailed was a *proper course*.

Clearly it is possible that there may be several *proper courses* at any given moment, depending upon the particular circumstances involved. However, because it is often difficult to prove when someone is actually on a *proper course* as opposed to sailing extra high or low for tactical purposes, ISAF Case 14 suggests, "Which of two different courses is the faster one to the next mark cannot be determined in advance and is not necessarily proven by one boat or the other reaching the next mark ahead." For protest committees, two reasonable criteria for judging a *proper course* are whether the boat sailing it has a logical reason for its being a *proper course* and whether she applies it with some consistency.

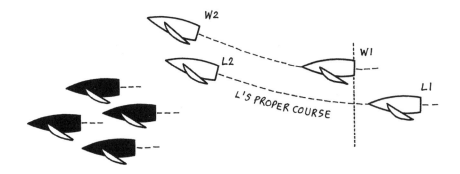

L is "limited" to sailing no higher than her proper course because she became over-
lapped from clear astern. However, L decides that she will arrive at the gybe mark
sooner by luffing and sailing to windward of the pack in front of her. Because she
would do this even in the absence of W, it is a legitimate new proper course for L and
W must keep clear under rule 11.

The phrase "*in the absence of the other boats referred to in the rule using*
the term" clarifies which boats to "remove" when determining whether a
course is a *proper course* or not. Note that it certainly does not mean 'in the
absence of all the boats in the race.' Let's say you and another boat are sailing
down a reach. You catch up and become *overlapped* to *leeward* of the other
boat (W). Rule 17.1 (On the Same Tack; Proper Course) tells you that you cannot sail above your *proper course* while *overlapped* with W. Because W is the
"other boat" referred to in rule 17.1, your *proper course* is your fastest course
in the absence of W.

As you and W continue down the reach, you begin catching up to a group
of boats in front of you going slowly. Now you have to decide whether to
head up and try to pass the group to *windward*, or bear away and try to pass
them to *leeward*. You decide that you will arrive at the gybe mark faster by
heading up and passing the group to *windward*, but by heading up, you will
collide with the *windward* boat. In this case, heading up can be considered
your *proper course* because you would do so even in the absence of W.

The point is: your *proper course* should be based on what will get **you** to
the next *mark* and ultimately to the finishing line as quickly as possible, not
on a tactical consideration such as heading up to cut off a nearby *windward*
boat. Note that the rules referring to *proper courses* are rules 17.1, 17.2, 18.1(b)
and 18.4.

Notice also that there is no *proper course* **before** the starting signal. That is because a *proper course* is the course sailed to *finish* as soon as possible. Obviously, you can't start racing toward the finishing line until you are allowed to *start*; therefore, there is no *proper course* until after the starting signal is made.

PROTEST

An allegation made under rule 61.2 by a boat, a race committee or a protest committee that a boat has broken a *rule*.

For the most part, allegations and decisions on whether boats have broken any *rules* are handled after the race in a hearing called by a protest committee. The procedure to ask for such a hearing is called a *protest*. Rules 60 (Right to Protest and Request Redress) and 61 (Protest Requirements) clearly outline the rights and requirements for boats, race committees and protest committees who wish to protest.

Note that a "request for redress" under rule 62.1 (Redress) is not a *protest*. For you to "request redress," you must make your request in writing and comply with the time limit of rule 61.3 (Protest Time Limit) or within two hours of the relevant incident, whichever is later. You don't need to fly a protest flag (rule 62.2, Redress).

RACING

A boat is *racing* from her preparatory signal until she *finishes* and clears the finishing line and *marks* or retires, or until the race committee signals a general recall, *postponement*, or *abandonment*.

It is important to know when you are *racing* because you can be penalized for breaking a rule of Part 2 (When Boats Meet) only when you are *racing*, with the exception of rule 22.1, Interfering With Another Boat (see the preamble to Part 2).

You begin *racing* at your preparatory signal. In a "5-4-GO" sequence, the four-minute signal is the preparatory signal (Rule 26, Starting Races). In a "10-5-GO" sequence, the five-minute signal is the preparatory signal. In a "3-2-1-GO" sequence, it's usually the two-minute signal. Check the sailing instructions for the race to find out when your actual preparatory signal is.

You are no longer *racing* when you have *finished* and cleared the finishing line and *marks*. US SAILING Appeal 16 reads, "When no part of a boat's hull, equipment or crew is still on the finishing line, she has cleared it."

"When am I considered to be clear of the finishing marks?"

You have "cleared the finishing *marks*" when you have left them astern without hitting them during an incident that occurred while you were *finishing*. US SAILING Appeal 26 says, "The official diagram shows that the boat in this case finished six hull lengths away from the mark that she subsequently touched. When she cleared the line, she was well clear of the mark. Thus, her contact with the mark occurred after she had finished and cleared the finishing line and finishing marks. It was a separate incident, occurring when she was no longer racing."

ROOM

The space a boat needs in the existing conditions while manoeuvring promptly in a seamanlike way.

This definition is central to applying rule 15 (Acquiring Right of Way); rule 16 (Changing Course); rule 18 (Rounding and Passing Marks and Obstructions) and rule 19 (Room to Tack at an Obstruction).

Note the word "promptly" which means "performed readily, quickly, immediately." This builds in a time element to the definition. Therefore when a *leeward* boat (L) luffs or bears away near a *windward* boat (W), rule 16 requires L to give W room to *keep clear*, but W must respond "promptly" or risk losing the protection of *room*.

To expand on "seamanlike," I would say "seamanlike" means "responsible, prudent, safety conscious." In other words, it is "seamanlike" never to put your or another boat's crew, boat or equipment at risk of injury or damage.

"Does the definition Room take into account the experience or the number of the crew on board the boat?"

No. US SAILING Appeal 77 addresses this head on by saying, "Neither the experience of IW's crew nor their number is relevant in determining 'room'... the interpretation of 'seamanlike way' must be based on the boat-handling that can reasonably be expected from a crew with average experience and of appropriate number for the boat."

US SAILING Appeal 20 talks about tactical *mark* roundings and says in essence that *room* does not include all the room an inside boat might like to take to make a tactically desirable rounding.

ISAF Case 21 gives further interpretation of *room*:

"QUESTION: What is the maximum amount of room an inside boat without right of way is entitled to take in rounding or passing a mark or obstruction? What is the minimum amount that the outside boat is required to give?

"ANSWER: The possible answers vary widely. To suggest the extremes, they might be:

1. as a minimum, enough room with sails and spars sheeted inboard, for the hull to clear by centimetres both the mark and the outside boat;
2. as a maximum, all the room the inside boat takes, setting her course as far abeam of the mark as she wishes.

"Between these extremes, neither of which is correct, are two more moderate possibilities: next to the minimum, enough extra clearance to allow for some error of judgment or execution; or, next to the maximum, enough room to make a tactically desirable rounding. The correct answer falls roughly between these two.

"As the definition states, the word 'room' in rule 18.2(a) means the space needed by an inside boat, which, in the existing conditions, is handled in a seamanlike way, to pass promptly between the outside boat and the mark or obstruction.

"The term 'existing conditions' deserves some consideration. For example, the inside one of two dinghies approaching a mark on a placid lake in light air will need and can be satisfied with relatively little space beyond her own beam. At the other extreme, when two keel boats, on open water with steep seas, are approaching a mark that is being tossed about widely and unpredictably, the inside boat may need a full hull length of room or even more to ensure safety.

"The phrase 'in a seamanlike way' applies to both boats. First, it addresses the outside boat, saying that she must provide enough room so that the inside boat need not make extraordinary or abnormal manoeuvres to keep clear of her and the mark. It also addresses the inside boat. She is not entitled to complain of insufficient room when she fails to execute with reasonable efficiency the handling of her helm, sheets and sails during a rounding."

RULE

(a) The rules in this book, including the Definitions, Race Signals, Introduction, preambles and the rules of relevant appendices, but not titles;

(b) the prescriptions of the national authority, unless the sailing instructions state that they do not apply;

(c) the class rules, or the rules of the handicapping or rating system, except any that conflict with the rules in this book;

(d) the notice of race;

(e) the sailing instructions; and

(f) any other documents that govern the event.

This is the complete list of the *rules* that govern a race. Note that sailing instructions are *rules* so it is important to read them carefully before entering a race. Sailing instructions can change certain racing rules, **but they must refer specifically to the rule being changed** and state the change (see rule 86.1(b), Rule Changes).

Also note that if a class rule conflicts with any of the ISAF *Racing Rules of Sailing*, **the class rule does not apply.** Furthermore, in accordance with rule 86.1(c), class rules are only permitted to change certain rules of *The Racing Rules of Sailing*, specifically: rule 42 (Propulsion); rule 49 (Crew Position); rule 50 (Setting and Sheeting Sails); rule 51, (Moving Ballast); rule 52 (Manual Power); rule 53 (Skin Friction) and rule 54 (Forestays and Headsail Tacks).

START

A boat *starts* when after her starting signal any part of her hull, crew or equipment first crosses the starting line and she has complied with rule 29.1 and rule 30.1 if it applies.

You cannot *start* until after the starting signal for your class. If any part of your hull, crew or equipment is on the course side of the starting line at the starting signal, you must return completely behind the line to *start* correctly

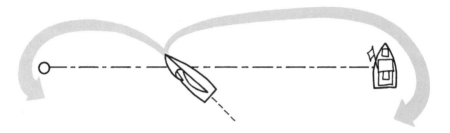

When rule 30.1 (the "Round-an-End Rule") is in effect, a boat that goes across the starting line at any time during the final minute before the starting signal must go around one of the ends before starting. She may do this immediately if she chooses; i.e. she does not need to wait for the starting signal before going around an end.

(rule 29.1, Starting; Recalls). If you don't, the race committee can score you OCS (On the Course Side) or DNS (Did Not Start) without needing to protest you (rule A5, Scores Determined by the Race Committee). If you feel they have incorrectly scored you OCS or DNS, you can request redress under rule 62.1(a) (Redress).

Notice that you *start* when, **after** the starting signal is made, **any** part of your hull, crew or equipment first crosses the starting line. There is no mention of **normal position** here. If your bow person is calling the line from the pulpit and inadvertently sticks his or her hand over the line just before the gun, or if your crew, by going out on the trapeze, mistakenly puts his or her head over the line one second before the gun, you are "on the course side." The same is true if anchored and your anchor and anchor line are over the starting line.

The definition refers to rule 30.1 (Round-an-End Rule). Notice that the race committee can signal the "Round-an-End Rule" on any start it wants simply

by displaying flag I **before, with or as** the preparatory signal. When it is lowered one minute before the starting signal, accompanied by one long sound signal, it means that the one-minute period of rule 30.1 has begun. The purpose of the rule is to keep people from charging over the line early and making it difficult for the race committee to have a fair start. The way it works is, if you are on the course side of the starting line or its extensions during the minute before your starting signal, you must return behind the line by going **around one end or the other before** *starting* correctly. Notice you can get back around an end immediately; you don't have to wait for the starting signal to be made.

Notice that anytime you are returning to the pre-start side of the starting line or its extensions **after** your starting signal, you have to *keep clear* of any boats not doing so until you are completely on the pre-start side (rule 20, Starting Errors; Penalty Turns; Moving Astern)

Notice also the more stringent starting penalties available to race committees in rules 30.2 (20% Penalty Rule) and 30.3 (Black Flag Rule).

TACK, STARBOARD OR PORT

A boat is on the *tack*, *starboard* or *port*, corresponding to her *windward* side.

When racing, you are **always** on either *starboard* or *port tack*, even when you are in the act of tacking or gybing. Your *tack* (*starboard* or *port*) is determined by your *windward* side, i.e. if your port side is your *windward* side, you are on *port tack*. For discussion on how to determine your *windward* side, see the definitions *Leeward* and *Windward*.

Let's look at a boat (P) tacking from *port tack* to *starboard tack*. At some point during her *tack*, P will pass head to wind. At the moment she passes head to wind her starboard side becomes her *windward* side; therefore she is instantly on *starboard tack*. However, rule 13 (While Tacking) requires her to *keep clear* of other boats until she is on a close-hauled course; and rule 15 (Acquiring Right of Way) requires her to initially give other boats *room* to *keep clear* once she gets the right of way.

TWO-LENGTH ZONE

The area around a *mark* or *obstruction* within a distance of two hull lengths of the boat nearer to it.

As boats are about to round or pass a *mark* or *obstruction*, rule 18 (Rounding and Passing Marks and Obstructions) provides specific instructions regarding which boats are entitled to *room*, which must give *room* to others, etc. Most of these instructions are based on the relationship of the boats when they are two lengths away from the *mark*. To make the *rules* themselves cleaner to read, the rule writers have created a defined area around a *mark/obstruction* called the "*two-length zone*."

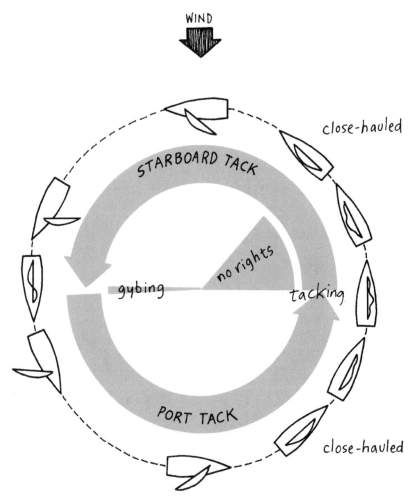

The *two-length zone* is essentially a circle with the *mark/obstruction* at its center whose radius is two hull lengths of the boat that is nearest to it. Therefore, if a 24-foot boat and a 30-foot boat are approaching a *mark* and the 24-foot boat is nearer the *mark*, the *two-length zone* is 48 feet (2 x 24) from the *mark*.

The use of the term "hull length" is intended to clarify that the *two-length zone* is based solely on the length of the hull, and not the additional length of bowsprits, overhanging mizzen booms, etc. Webster's dictionary defines the "hull" of a boat as its "frame or body, exclusive of masts, yards, sails and rigging." Note, however, that two boats *overlap* when any part of their hull or

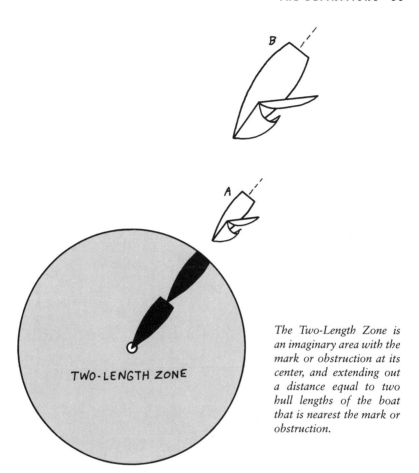

The Two-Length Zone is an imaginary area with the mark or obstruction at its center, and extending out a distance equal to two hull lengths of the boat that is nearest the mark or obstruction.

equipment in normal position are alongside each other. Therefore, a boat with a three-foot bowsprit can have a two-foot *overlap* on a boat nearby, although her bow is still a foot from the other boat's stern.

WINDWARD

See *Leeward* and *Windward*.

6

Part 2, Section A
When Boats Meet – Right of Way

When boats that are **both** *racing* meet, the rules that govern are in Part 2 of the rule book.

PREAMBLE TO PART 2

The rules of Part 2 apply between boats that are sailing in or near the racing area and intend to *race*, are *racing*, or have been *racing*. However, a boat not *racing* shall not be penalized for breaking one of these rules, except rule 22.1. The International Regulations for Preventing Collisions at Sea or government right-of-way rules apply between a boat sailing under these rules and a vessel that is not, and they replace these rules if the sailing instructions so state.

The preamble clarifies **which** *rules* apply when and to whom. Note that the "preambles" rank as *rules* (see definition *Rule*). When the Inland Navigational Rules (in U.S. waters) or the International Regulations for Preventing Collisions at Sea (outside of a country's waters) are to replace the *The Racing Rules of Sailing*, e.g. when the race will continue after sunset, the sailing instructions must specifically contain the numbers of the applicable INR or IRPCAS and state the time(s) or places(s) they will apply, as well as any night signals to be used by the race committee (Appendix J, Notice of Race and Sailing Instructions). Sailors wishing a complete copy of the INR or IRPCAS should contact the US SAILING office for information on how to get one.

Notice that the racing rules apply to boats even when they are racing in different races. Rule 63.7 (Protests Between Boats in Different Races) reads, "*A* **protest** *between boats sailing in different races conducted by different organizing authorities shall be heard by a protest committee acceptable to those authorities.*"

Also, notice that when you intend to *race*, the rules of Part 2 only apply from when you begin to sail in or near the racing area until you have left the racing area; and they only apply between boats intending to *race*. This distinction may be important in resolving a financial claim after a serious collision when the boats were not actually *racing*.

 "I realize I am technically 'racing' after my preparatory signal, but what happens if I accidentally foul a boat before or after I am racing?"

The preamble to Part 2 says, "*a boat not* **racing** *shall not be penalized for breaking one of these rules, except rule 22.1.*" (Rule 22.1, Interfering With Another Boat, says that even if you aren't *racing*, you can't interfere with a boat that is; see discussion of rule 22.1.) Rule 44.1, Taking a Penalty, says, "*A boat that may have broken a rule of Part 2* **while racing** (emphasis added) *may take a penalty at the time of the incident.*" Therefore, if you break a *rule* before your preparatory signal, apologize and continue on.

Of course, if there is damage, you and/or the other boat may choose to protest so that the protest committee can find the facts and make a decision as to who was at fault. Though neither one of you can be "penalized" under rule 64.1(a) (Penalties and Exoneration), the facts and decision of the protest committee may be necessary in determining who pays for the damage (rule 68, Damages).

Remember, under the definition of *racing*, you are *racing* from your preparatory signal until you have *finished* and cleared the finishing line and finishing *marks* or retired. So if your preparatory signal is five minutes before your starting signal and you foul someone with four and a half minutes to go, you can be disqualified if you don't take a penalty. Remember also that you are no longer *racing* the moment your transom clears the finishing line and finishing *marks* (US SAILING Appeals 16 and 26 and rule 28.1, Sailing the Course).

Note, however, that if you are not *racing* and break any other rules, other than those in Parts 2 (When Boats Meet) and 4 (Other Requirements When Racing) and rule 31 (Touching a Mark), you will receive a penalty under rule

64.1(a) (Penalties and Exoneration). For instance, you will be penalized before or after you are *racing* for breaking the sailing instructions, or for violating the principles in rule 2 (Fair Sailing), or for committing a "gross breach of a *rule* or of good manners or sportsmanship" under rule 69 (Allegations of Gross Misconduct), or for not complying with the rules of Part 6 (Entry and Qualification) which include rules 75, 78 and 79 which concern eligibility, measurement compliance and advertising. Also note that rule 64.1(c) (Protest Decisions) reads, "*If a boat has broken a rule when not **racing**, her penalty shall apply to the race sailed nearest in time to that of the incident.*"

"*If five minutes before my preparatory signal I'm near the starting line on starboard tack and despite my best effort to avoid the collision my boat gets holed by a port tacker who is also intending to race, and as a result I can't sail in the race, do I have any recourse under the rules?*"

You sure do. You should protest them under rule 10 (On Opposite Tacks) and request redress under rule 62.1(b) (Redress). Both of you were intending to *race* and were sailing in the racing area; therefore you were both governed by *The Racing Rules of Sailing*. The *port-tack* boat (P) was required to *keep clear* of you while you were on *starboard tack* under rule 10. Though P cannot be penalized for breaking this rule as she was not *racing* at the time, the protest committee is required to hold a hearing, find facts and determine which boat, if either, was at fault (rules 63.1, Hearings; 64.1, Penalties and Exoneration; and 65.1, Informing the Parties and Others). Once P is found to have broken rule 10, the protest committee must turn to your request for redress (rule 63.1); and you should be granted redress as your finishing place was made significantly worse (you were unable to race!) through no fault of your own due to the physical damage caused by P, a boat that was breaking a rule of Part 2 at the time. Furthermore, the question of financial responsibility for damages may hinge on a finding of facts and fault by the protest committee (see rule 68, Damages).

"*If I'm racing and a boat definitely fouls me, and later in the race I am converging with them and I don't have the right of way, do I have to keep clear of them even though they were wrong in the first incident?*"

You bet! When competitors know they have broken a *rule*, they are expected to promptly take a penalty or retire (see Basic Principle, Sportsmanship and the Rules in the "Introduction of the RRS"). But while a boat continues to *race*, she maintains all her rights just as any other boat. US SAILING Appeal 1 reads, "*Pilgrim* (X) and Y were involved in an incident early in a race, and each protested the other. Later in the same race, *Maori* (Z), which had observed the incident believed X to have been in the wrong, refused to yield right of way to her. X protested Z. The protest committee disqualified X for breaking a rule in the first incident. It then disqualified Z, despite her contention that X, having been disqualified for a breach of a rule in the first incident, was no longer entitled to rights under the rules. Z appealed. DECISION: The decision of the protest committee is upheld."

ISAF Case 1 reads, "Boats A, B, and C are racing with others. After an incident, boat A hails and displays her protest flag, but boat B neither retires nor takes a penalty. Later, B protests a third boat, C, after a second incident. The protest committee hears A's protest against B and disqualifies B; does this disqualification invalidate B's protest against C?

ANSWER: No. When a boat continues to race after an alleged rule breach, other boats shall continue to accord her such rights as she has under the rules of Part 2. Consequently, even though A's protest against B is upheld, B's protest against C is still valid and, when the protest committee is satisfied from the evidence that C broke a rule, she must be disqualified."

 "So do I understand it correctly that the rules of Part 2 apply even between boats that are racing in different races?"

Yes. The rules of part 2 apply between boats in different races as long as they both fit the description in the preamble of Part 2. Rule 63.7 (Protests Between Boats in Different Races) reinforces this point by saying, "*A **protest** between boats sailing in different races conducted by differing organizing authorities shall be heard by a protest committee acceptable to those authorities.*"

PREAMBLE TO SECTION A

A boat has right of way when another boat is required to *keep clear* of her. However, some rules in Sections B, C and D limit the actions of a right-of-way boat.

The rules of Part 2 are written to clearly say which boat must *keep clear* of the other. (See definition *Keep Clear* for a full discussion of the meaning of this phrase.) For example, rule 10 (On Opposite Tacks) says, "*When boats are on opposite **tacks**, a **port-tack** boat shall **keep clear** of a starboard-tack boat.*" Therefore, in learning the rules, it is helpful to learn which boats do **not** have the right of way in meeting situations, as these are the boats with the requirement to stay out of the other's way.

There are just four basic right-of-way rules (rules 10-13), and they are found in Section A. They cover the three basic relationships boats can be in (on the same tack, on the opposite tack or changing tacks), and they are:

- on opposite *tacks*................... *port tack* keeps clear of *starboard tack*
  – rule 10

- on same *tack*, overlapped ...... *windward* keeps clear of *leeward*
  – rule 11

- on same *tack*, not overlapped.. *clear astern* keeps clear of *clear ahead*
  – rule 12

- changing *tacks* by tacking ...... boat tacking *keeps clear* of other boats
  – rule 13

RULE 10, ON OPPOSITE TACKS

When boats are on opposite *tacks*, a *port-tack* boat shall *keep clear* of a starboard-tack boat.

This basic rule applies to boats that are on **opposite** *tacks*. When boats are on the **same** *tack*, rules 11 (*windward/leeward*) and 12 (*clear astern/clear ahead*) apply. Thus, if on a downwind leg a *starboard-tack* boat comes up from *clear astern* and runs into a *port-tack* boat (assuming no damage), who will be penalized under the *rules*? The *port-tack* boat under rule 10, because the two boats are on **opposite** *tacks*.

"If I'm on a beat converging with a port-tack boat and she hails "Hold your course," is that hail binding on me?

US SAILING Appeal 27 reads, "In response to the questions regarding a boat that has been hailed to hold course, it is permissible to hail, but the rules do

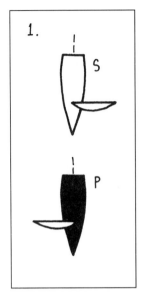

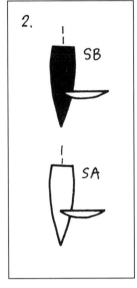

In position 1, the boats are on opposite tacks; therefore S has right of way over P under rule 10.

In position 2, both boats are on the same tack; therefore SB must keep clear of SA under rule 12.

not recognize such a hail as binding on the other boat. S can tack or bear away at any time she is satisfied that a change of course will be necessary to avoid a collision."

My opinion is that in order for the *port-tack* boat to be liable for failure to *keep clear*, it is important that as they approach each other, the *starboard-tack* boat hold her course as long as she can do so with safety. I recommend that when *port-tack* boats are about to cross close in front of *starboard-tack* boats, P should always hail "Hold your course" to S to alert her that P is there, that P realizes it will be close, and that P wants S to hold her course for as long as possible.

 "Okay, but do I have to hit the port-tacker to prove there was a foul; and if there is no contact, whom is the 'onus of proof' on?"

S does NOT have to hit P to prove that P failed to *keep clear*. S should avoid the collision and protest. Though the rule itself contains no specific "onus" (i.e. an assignment of responsibility to one boat or the other to prove the other boat's guilt), ISAF Case 50 discusses the whole issue, including the question of "onus of proof": "Rule 10 protests involving no contact are very common, and protest committees tend to handle them in very different ways. Some place an onus on the port-tack boat to prove conclusively that she would have cleared the starboard-tack boat, even when the latter's evidence

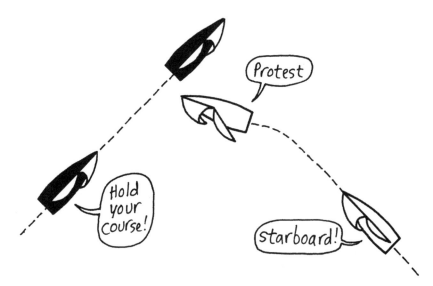

Though it is common for P to hail "Hold your course" to assure S that P is aware that she's there and to encourage S to give her every opportunity to try and cross, S is in no way bound by that hail to actually do so. S may bear away or tack at any time she has a reasonable concern that her change of course is necessary to avoid a collision.

is barely worthy of credence. No such onus appears in rule 10. Other protest committees have been reluctant to allow any rule 10 protest in the absence of contact, unless the starboard-tack boat proves conclusively that contact would have occurred had she not changed course. Both approaches are incorrect.

"A starboard-tack boat in such circumstances need not hold her course so as to prove, by hitting the port-tack boat, that a collision was inevitable. Moreover, if she does so she will break rule 14. At a protest hearing, S must establish either that contact would have occurred if she had held her course, or that there was enough doubt that P could safely cross ahead to create a reasonable apprehension of contact on S's part and that it was unlikely that S would have 'no need to take avoiding action' (see the definition 'Keep Clear').

"In her own defence, P must present adequate evidence to establish either that S did not change course or that P would have safely crossed ahead of S and that S had no need to take avoiding action. When, on all the evidence, a protest committee finds that S did not change course or that there was not a genuine and reasonable apprehension of collision on her part, it should dismiss her protest. When, however, it is satisfied that S did change course, that there was reasonable doubt that P could have crossed ahead, and that S was justified in taking avoiding action by bearing away, then P should be disqualified."

In ISAF Case 88, P and S were converging on an upwind leg. When three and then two lengths away, S hailed "Starboard" but P held her collision course. When just under two lengths away, and fearing a collision, S luffed to try to minimize the contact at the same moment P bore away sharply. S then bore away sharply to pull her transom out of P's way. P passed astern of S within two feet; there was no contact. The protest committee dismissed S's rule 10 *protest* against P and S appealed.

In its decision, the appeals committee says, "Rule 10 required P to 'keep clear' of S. 'Keep clear' means something more than 'avoid contact'; otherwise the rule would contain those or similar words. Therefore, the fact that the boats did not collide does not necessarily establish that P kept clear. The definition 'Keep Clear' in combination with the facts determines whether or not P complied with the rule. In this case, the key question raised by the definition is whether S was able to sail her course 'with no need to take avoiding action'." After listing all the considerations it took into account, the appeals committee concludes that S did have a need to take avoiding action, and disqualified P for breaking rule 10.

RULES 11 and 12 – ON THE SAME TACK

Rules 11 and 12 are the basic rules for boats on the **same** *tack*. When boats are on the same *tack* they can either be *overlapped* or not *overlapped*. If they are *overlapped*, they are either a *windward* boat or a *leeward* boat. If they are not *overlapped*, they are either *clear ahead* or *clear astern*.

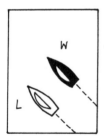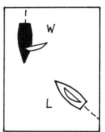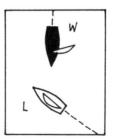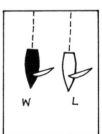

In each situation, both boats are on the same tack. The white boat is the leeward boat and the black boat must keep clear under rule 11.

RULE 11 – ON THE SAME TACK, OVERLAPPED

When boats are on the same *tack* and *overlapped*, a *windward* boat shall *keep clear* of a *leeward* boat.

When boats on the same *tack* are *overlapped*, rule 11 applies. When boats are on much different angles of sail, it is often difficult to know which is the *leeward* boat. The boat that will hit the other's *leeward* side or be hit on her own *windward* side is the *leeward* boat. As a good rule of thumb, the boat that is on the point of sail closer to the wind is the *leeward* boat; i.e. between a boat sailing downwind and a boat sailing close-hauled, the close-hauled boat is the *leeward* boat.

"I realize that when I'm the windward boat I have to keep clear of the leeward boat, but how far away do I need to stay?"

Far enough away so that while the *leeward* boat (L) is sailing on a straight line, you do not hit L or force L to take any avoiding action to miss you, e.g. have to change her course, ease her spinnaker pole forward or require any of her crew to duck or move to avoid being hit.

Furthermore, you need to be far enough away so that the *leeward* boat can change course in **both** directions without **immediately** making contact with you. If you allow yourself to get so close to L that she is physically unable to change her course without immediately hitting you, you are not *keeping clear* under the definition *Keep Clear* and are breaking rule 11. Note that the second "if" in the definition suggests that L does not need to actually hit you to prove she couldn't change course without hitting you. If the protest committee decides that L couldn't change course without immediate contact, then you have broken rule 11 simply by your extreme close proximity to L.

More importantly, **anytime** L cannot sail her course without a need to take action to avoid you, you have not *kept clear* and break rule 11. Therefore, you will be smart not to allow yourself to get so close that you will possibly interfere with L in the least. Notice also that when L is head to wind, it is quite possible that you will be required to go **beyond** head to wind (i.e. change *tacks*) in order to keep clear. If this is the case, you must do so. Also, if you are converging with L and both of you are sailing on what you each believe to be your *proper courses*, rule 11 requires you to *keep clear* of L.

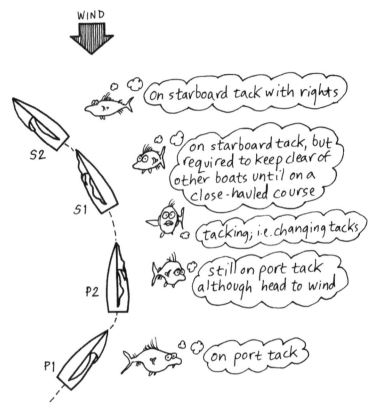

RULE 12 – ON THE SAME TACK, NOT OVERLAPPED

When boats are on the same *tack* and not *overlapped*, a boat *clear astern* shall *keep clear* of a boat *clear ahead*.

In 1949 the rule read, "A yacht Overtaking another shall keep clear while she is Clear Astern." Now the rules only talk about boats that are *clear ahead* or *clear astern*; however, the concept is still the same. A boat, as in cars on the the road, coming up from behind another boat on the same *tack*, must not hit her.

Rule 12 clearly identifies a boat or boats *clear ahead* as right-of-way boats, therefore making them *obstructions* to boats coming up from behind (definition *Obstruction*). ISAF Case 41 reads, "With respect to A [clear ahead], both boats astern must keep clear of her under rule 12. However, A also is an obstruction to both, as the last sentence of the definition Obstruction makes clear. When they are 'about to pass' A, still overlapped, rule 18 will come into effect."

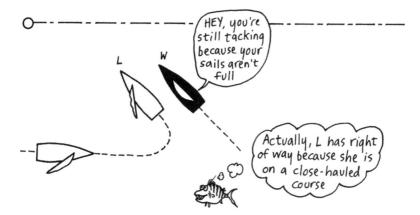

RULE 13 – WHILE TACKING

After a boat passes head to wind, she shall *keep clear* of other boats until she is on a close-hauled course. During that time, rules 10, 11 and 12 do not apply. If two boats are subject to this rule at the same time, the one on the other's port side shall *keep clear.*

Remember that under the definition *Tack, Starboard* or *Port,* you are always on one *tack* or the other. So if you are on *port tack* and turn your boat towards the wind, the moment your boat passes head to wind you are **instantly** on *starboard tack.*

Rule 13 provides a transitional rule that applies when a boat is changing *tacks* by tacking. "Tacking" is the maneuver by which a boat changes *tacks* with the bow passing head to wind. Generally that involves an approximately 90 degree turn from close-hauled to close-hauled.

Rule 13 simply says that while you are tacking, you must *keep clear* of other boats from the moment you pass head to wind until you are on a close-hauled course (on **either** *tack*). A "close-hauled course" is the course a boat will sail when racing upwind and sailing as close to the wind as she can. Notice that to be on a close-hauled course, the sails don't need to be full nor does the boat need any headway (see ISAF Case 17). Note that once you pass head to wind, rule 13 turns off rules 10, 11 and 12. Therefore, after you pass head to wind and before you're on a close-hauled course, if another boat hits you or has to change her course to avoid you, you have not *kept clear* and have broken rule 13.

In the rare instance where two boats are tacking near each other and both are past head to wind but neither is close-hauled yet, the one on the other's port side must *keep clear*; or put another way, the boat on the right has the right of way.

"Gybing" is the maneuver by which a boat changes *tacks* with the bow turning away from the wind. For instance, when sailing downwind on *port tack*, the moment the foot of your mainsail crosses the centerline you are on *starboard tack* (see the definition *Leeward* and *Windward* for a complete discussion on determining a boat's *tack* when sailing downwind or by the lee). Because the act of "gybing" is generally so momentary, there is no special transitional rule for "gybing."

"When I tack or gybe into a right-of-way position, do I have to give other boats room to keep clear of me?"

Absolutely yes. For a full explanation of the obligations of boats that acquire right-of-way, see the discussion of rule 15 (Acquiring Right of Way).

"Will you be discussing how the rules work in Slam Dunks?"

You bet. That explanation occurs at the end of the discussion of rule 17 (On the Same Tack; Proper Course).

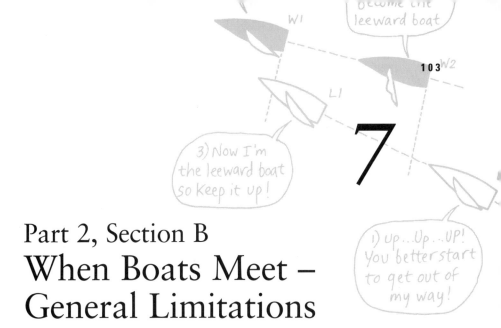

Part 2, Section B
When Boats Meet – General Limitations

In addition to the right-of-way rules, Part 2 also contains rules that **limit** the actions of right-of-way boats (rules 14-17). In other words, a right-of-way boat cannot just go anywhere she wants. These limitations are found in Section B. One example is that a right-of-way boat can be penalized when she's involved in contact that causes any damage (rule 14). Another is that whenever a right-of-way boat changes her course, she is required to give the other boat *room* to *keep clear* (rule 16). Therefore, it is equally important to know what limitations the rules place on right-of-way boats in various situations.

RULE 14 – AVOIDING CONTACT

A boat shall avoid contact with another boat if reasonably possible. However a right-of-way boat or one entitled to *room*

(a) **need not act to avoid contact until it is clear that the other boat is not *keeping clear* or giving *room*, and**

(b) **shall not be penalized under this rule unless there is contact that causes damage.**

This is a very strong rule regarding contact. It talks to all boats in a race, including right-of-way boats, and tells them to avoid any contact whatsoever if reasonably possible. The intent of the rule is to minimize the amount of collisions that occur during a race, and particularly the intentional ones. Collisions can be dangerous, expensive, frustrating to all sailors and particularly intimidating to newcomers and novice sailors. They are not part of the sport.

When two or more boats converge, the possibility of contact exists. The *rules* clearly assign the right-of-way and the requirement to *keep clear* or to give *room* in each situation where boats could hit. A basic principle of navigation is that when one boat is required to *keep clear*, the other shouldn't do anything to make the situation more dangerous. Rule 14(a) makes it clear that the right-of-way boat or the inside boat entitled to *room* can hold her course until it becomes "clear" that the other boat is not going to avoid contact. At that moment, the right-of-way or inside boat must take action herself to avoid the contact if reasonably possible. For instance, take a *port-tack* boat crossing a *starboard-tack* boat. If S holds her course and hits P, with no attempt to avoid or minimize the contact, P has broken rule 10 (On Opposite Tacks) and S has broken rule 14.

However, rule 14(b) states that a right-of-way boat or one entitled to *room* can be penalized under this rule only if the contact causes "damage." Therefore, if the contact causes no physical damage to any boat or person, the right-of-way boat or the one entitled to *room* can be found to have broken rule 14 but will not be penalized for doing so. On the other hand, if there is any damage at all, no matter how slight and regardless of whether the damage has any effect on the speed or handling of the boat, these boats will be penalized if it was found that it was reasonably possible for them to have avoided the contact.

Note that if the give-way boat fails to avoid contact, she technically can be penalized under this rule; however, this is a moot point because she will be penalized under the Section A rule she broke, and a boat can only be penalized once per incident, regardless of the number of rules she may have broken in that incident (rule 44.4(b), Penalties for Breaking Rules of Part 2, Limits on Penalties).

 "If I'm involved in contact that causes damage, can I do a 720 or put up a yellow flag to avoid disqualification?"

Yes! Rule 44 (Penalties for Breaking Rules of Part 2) permits a boat that may have broken any rule in Part 2 while *racing* to take a penalty at the time of the incident. The penalty is the 720-degree Turns Penalty unless the sailing instructions specify the use of some other penalty (rule 44). So if you are a right-of-way boat or an inside boat entitled to *room* and you cause damage to the give-way boat, you can quickly do a "720" and continue in the race. If you are the give-way boat, you can also do a "720" which absolves you of all Part 2 rule breaches you may have committed in the incident. There is one exception, however. Rule 44 goes on to say, "*if [a boat] caused serious damage …she shall retire.*" In other words, you can't absolve yourself with a "720" if the damage was "serious."

See the explanation of rule 44 for a discussion on how to properly do a "720," and what constitutes "serious damage."

"I understand that if I'm the right-of-way boat, I can be penalized for causing any damage at all; what constitutes 'damage'?"

ISAF Case 19 offers an interpretation of the term "damage." "It is not possible to define 'damage' comprehensively, but one current English dictionary says 'harm or injury impairing the value or usefulness of something, or the health or normal function of a person.' This definition suggests questions to consider. Examples are:

1. Was the current market value of any part of the boat, or of the boat as a whole, diminished?

2. Was any item of the boat or its equipment made less functional?

3. Was a member of the crew injured?"

In my opinion, a related question to number 1 above is, "Did the contact result in something needing to be repaired or replaced?"

Clearly, boats will have contact that will cause no damage to either boat or crew. Examples will include two boats having light side-to-side contact while rounding a *mark*, or incidents where the crews fend off and the hulls never touch. On the other hand, there will be contact that clearly causes "damage:" a hole or dent in the boat, a torn sail, a bent stanchion, a nick out of the rudder, a broken finger, etc. The hard calls will be the situations where the gel coat gets scratched, the sailors hear the fiberglass "crunch" though there is no visible sign of "damage" or a crew member gets a temporary soreness from fending off, etc. Protest committees will need to exercise their best judgment in these situations. Notice that the judgment that "damage" occurred is not a "fact found;" it is a conclusion based on the "facts found" and therefore subject to appeal.

 "As I understand the rule, even if I'm involved in contact that causes damage, but it was not reasonably possible for me to avoid the contact, I won't be penalized under this rule; correct?"

Correct. The rule acknowledges that there may be times when it is simply not reasonably possible for a boat to avoid contact. However, this should not be viewed as a rationale for not making every effort to avoid collisions. Ultimately, whether or not it was reasonably possible to have avoided the contact will be decided by the protest committee.

The dictionary defines "reasonable" as "agreeable to reason; possessing sound judgment; not extreme or excessive." In judging whether it was "reasonably possible" for a boat to have avoided contact, it is implicit, to me, that as two boats near each other, the right-of-way boat settle on a straight-line or compass course or risk breaking rule 16 (Changing Course); and the give-way boat begin to take avoiding action. However, when, in her judgment, the right-of-way boat has a reasonable apprehension that contact will occur if she continues to hold her course, she may change her course to avoid the collision (ISAF Case 50). Rule 14(a) reinforces this by telling right-of-way boats and boats entitled to *room* they need not act to avoid contact until it is "clear" that the other boat is not *keeping clear*.

Therefore, as boats approach each other, they must continually assess the situation in terms of "what are the probable chances that I may hit this other boat or vice versa?" This judgment should factor in:

- what the response(s) have been from the other boat,
- whether the other boat is keeping a good lookout,
- what the sailing conditions are like and how well a boat of the class involved maneuvers in such conditions,
- who the sailors in the other boat are, and
- is there anything at all peculiar about the way the other boat is being handled?

In judging whether it was "reasonably possible" for a boat to have avoided contact, I'd consider whether the contact could have been avoided given the sailors' best attempts at avoiding or minimizing the impact of the collision, factoring in the amount of warning they had that a give-way boat might not *keep clear* or give *room*, the time they had to consider what their best attempt might be, and the amount and difficulty of the boat and sail handling involved. Also factored in to a much lesser degree would be the competency of the sailors and the condition of their equipment and boat, i.e. their steering gear, cleats and so on. However, the rules do not make allowances for poor seamanship, and I would be hesitant to excuse a boat due to poor sailing skills or less than adequately functioning equipment. In other words, in my opinion, "reasonable" is defined in terms of what an average sailor possessing average sailing skills could be expected to do in a similar situation.

ISAF Case 87 addresses a situation where a *port-tack* boat (P) and a *starboard-tack* boat (S) are sailing upwind on a collision course. S expected that P would bear off and pass astern of her, but instead P "made no attempt to avoid S and struck her amidships at right angles, causing considerable damage. At the last moment, when S realized that P was not going to keep clear, she changed course to try to minimize the impact of the collision. The protest committee disqualified both boats, P under rule 10 and S under rule 14. S appealed."

In its decision, the appeals committee says, "In S's case...she was required by rule 14 to avoid contact if it was 'reasonably possible' to do so. However, the second sentence of rule 14 allowed S to sail her course in the expectation that P would keep clear as required, until such time as it became evident that P would not do so... For that reason, the time between the moment it became evident that P would not keep clear and the time of the collision was a very brief interval, so brief that it was impossible for S to avoid contact. Therefore S did not break rule 14 and her disqualification is reversed."

ISAF Case 26 concerns a collision where P, a 5-0-5, and S, a Soling, were rounding the same leeward *mark* in opposite directions. Needless to say, the 5-0-5 received most of the damage as the Soling's bow sliced through P's hull and side buoyancy-tank just aft of the mast, the force of the impact knocking P's crew overboard unhurt. The decision reads, "P failed to keep a lookout and to observe her primary duty to keep clear. She was correctly disqualified under rule 10. The main purpose of the rules of Part 2 is to avoid contact between boats. All boats, whether or not holding right of way, should keep a lookout at all times.

"When it became clear that P was not keeping clear, S was required by rule 14 to avoid contact with P if it was reasonably possible...S could have changed course and tried to avoid P. Such action would have constituted an attempt to comply with rule 14 and would not have broken rule 16. Because S did not try to avoid the collision, and damage resulted, she is disqualified under rule 14." (See US SAILING Appeal 52.)

ISAF Case 27 is an illustration of when it was not reasonably possible for a boat to avoid contact. It involves two boats sailing upwind on port tack approaching the starboard-tack layline. "AS, a hull length to leeward and a hull length ahead of BP, tacked as soon as she reached the starboard layline. Almost immediately she was hit and holed by BP traveling at about ten knots." The Decision states, "When AS passed through head to wind, BP became the right-of-way boat and held right of way until AS assumed a close-hauled course on starboard tack. At that moment AS, having just acquired right of way under rule 10, was required by rule 15 to give BP room to keep clear. BP took no action to avoid a collision, but what could she have done? Given her speed and the distance involved, she had perhaps one to two seconds to decide what to do and then do it. It is a long-established underlying principle of the right-of-way rules, as stated in rule 15, that a boat that becomes obligated to keep clear by an action of another boat is entitled to sufficient time for response. Also, while it was obvious that AS would have to tack to round the mark, BP was under no obligation to anticipate that she would break rule 15."

Another scenario in which it may not be reasonably possible for boats to avoid contact is in light air when boats have very little steerageway and large powerboat waves enter the racing area and toss the boats about.

In conclusion, to penalize a right-of-way boat or one entitled to room under rule 14, two things must be decided. One, was the boat involved in contact that caused "damage;" and two, was it "reasonably possible" for the boat to have avoided the contact? If either there was no "damage," or if it is decided that the boat couldn't have reasonably avoided the contact, then the boat should not be penalized under rule 14. As a juror, I would have to be satisfied from the weight of the evidence submitted (in other words there is no onus) that a boat was negligent or had shown very poor judgment or seamanship before I penalized them. On the other hand, I expect jurors would not be very tolerant of situations where the right-of-way boat intentionally hits the give-way boat to prove the foul, causing any damage as a result.

"If I'm on port tack, and a starboard-tacker hits and damages me, and the damage causes me to get a significantly worse finishing position, I realize that I have to do a '720' because I was on port tack; but can I request redress because of the damage?"

Yes! Rule 62.1 (Redress) says that a boat is entitled to request redress when her *"finishing place… has, through no fault of her own, been made significantly worse by… physical damage because of the action of a boat that was breaking a rule of Part 2…"* In the hearing, the protest committee, acting under rule 64.2 (Decisions on Redress) must first decide if S broke rule 14. If so, they must next decide if you contributed to the receiving of damage. That means contributing more than just being in S's way. If you were trying to cross S, and while she was ducking you she hit you causing damage, there is very little you could have done to have prevented that. Finally, the protest committee must decide if the physical damage itself made your finishing place significantly worse. (See US SAILING Appeal 73.)

RULE 15 – ACQUIRING RIGHT OF WAY

When a boat acquires right of way, she shall initially give the other boat *room* to keep clear, unless she acquires right of way because of the other boat's actions.

This rule states one of the oldest and most fundamental principles in the rules, and it makes perfect sense. When a boat takes action that gives her the right of way over you, she must give you the chance to respond and *keep clear* of her. For example, you are sailing on a run on *port tack* with another *port-tack* boat just to *windward*. As the *leeward* boat, you have the right-of-way (rule 11, On the Same Tack, Overlapped) and everything is under control. You have the "sword," so to speak, and the *windward* boat must stay out of "its" way. Suddenly, the *windward* boat gybes. Now she is on *starboard* tack and you are on *port tack*. She now has the right-of-way, i.e. she now has the "sword" (rule 10, On Opposite Tacks), but she can't just gybe and hit you; her actions are limited by rule 15.

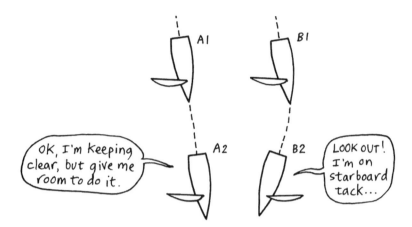

ISAF Case 24 describes a scenario where a boat (B) comes up from astern and becomes overlapped to leeward of the boat ahead. When B becomes overlapped she gains the right of way under rule 11, but also the limitation under rule 15 "which embodies the principle in the rules that when the right of way suddenly shifts from one boat to another, the boat with the newly acquired right of way must give the other boat space and time for response and a fair opportunity to keep clear." (See also ISAF Case 53.)

Note that a right-of-way boat does not have to anticipate that she will lose her right of way. ISAF Case 53 is clear on this point: "Allowing adequate time for response, when rights and obligations change between two boats, is implied in rule 15 by its requirement to allow the newly-obligated boat 'room to keep clear'." Therefore, in the example above, the *leeward* boat need not anticipate her requirement to *keep clear* as a *port-tack* boat before the *windward* boat gybes to starboard.

However, the use of the word "initially" clearly states that the protection of "room to keep clear" is not continuing. In the old video game *Deluxe Asteroids*, a tiny rocket ship tries to blast apart large rocks that will blow up the ship if they hit her. When there are just too many rocks about to hit, the player can press a button, putting a protective force shield around the ship. At first, the rocks bounce off the shield, but after a few seconds the shield begins to fade and disappear.

The *room* to respond to a newly acquired obligation to *keep clear* is a "shield" for the new give-way boat. It is very strong initially, but fades in strength as the seconds go by. Also, for you to be entitled to the protection of the 'shield' you must, at the moment you become the give-way boat, make a prompt and careful attempt to begin to get clear of the right-of-way boat. If you delay at all, you lose the protection of "*room* to *keep clear*" and you run the risk of fouling the right-of-way boat.

Let's look at some common situations on the race course where this principle of transition comes into play:

Becoming overlapped to *leeward* of a boat from *clear astern* (common during pre-start maneuvering and when sailing downwind):

Two boats on the same *tack* are sailing near each other, one clear astern (BL) of the other (AW) and catching up. While BL is approaching AW, she must *keep clear*. When she becomes *overlapped* to *leeward* of AW, rule 12 (*clear astern/clear ahead*) ceases to apply and she **instantly** becomes the right-of-way boat under rule 11 (*windward/leeward*). This is when rule 15 requires her to initially give AW *room* to *keep clear* of her. Remember that AW does not need to anticipate that BL will gain the right of way; therefore she does not need to take any evasive action **before** the *overlap* is created.

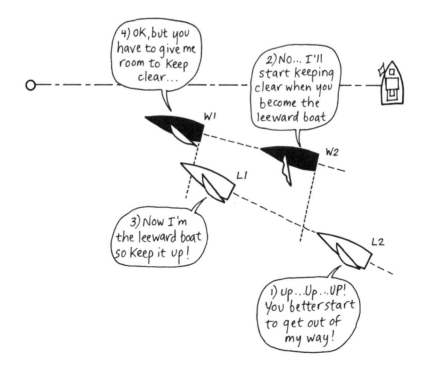

Rule 15 does not change the fact that W is required to keep clear of L. ISAF Case 53 makes the point that the give-way boat must respond immediately: "Since W at once trimmed sails, headed up, and thereafter kept clear, she fulfilled her obligations under rule 11." ISAF Case 7 states, "…L was bound by rule 15 to allow W room to keep clear, but that obligation is not a continuing one, and in this case the overlap had been in existence for a considerable period during which nothing had obstructed W's room." (See ISAF Case 24 and US SAILING Appeal 43.)

Tacking into a right-of-way position to leeward of a right-of-way boat (commonly known as "lee-bowing"):

While a boat is tacking near another boat, rule 13 (While Tacking) requires her to *keep clear* of the other boat from the time she passes head to wind until she is on a close-hauled course. But, once she is on a close-hauled course, and if she has become the right-of-way boat, rule 15 applies. For a good analogy (though this may not be the actual highway law), picture yourself coming up the entrance ramp to a three-lane highway. Cars driving down the right-hand lane must stay clear of other cars in the right-hand lane in front of them. While you're on the ramp you cannot interfere with cars driving in the right-hand lane. If, while you are moving across the white line into the right-hand

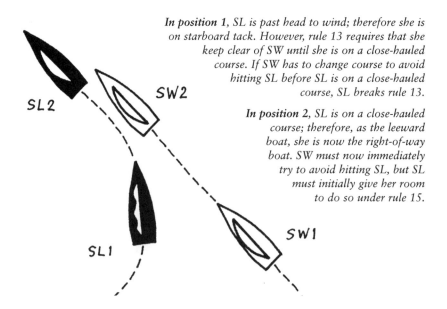

In position 1, SL is past head to wind; therefore she is on starboard tack. However, rule 13 requires that she keep clear of SW until she is on a close-hauled course. If SW has to change course to avoid hitting SL before SL is on a close-hauled course, SL breaks rule 13.

In position 2, SL is on a close-hauled course; therefore, as the leeward boat, she is now the right-of-way boat. SW must now immediately try to avoid hitting SL, but SL must initially give her room to do so under rule 15.

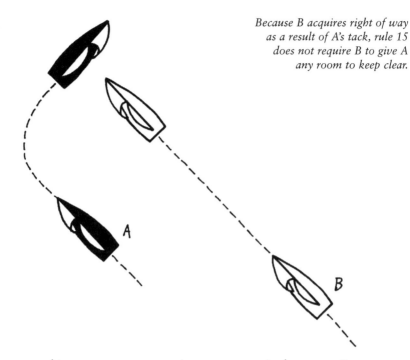

Because B acquires right of way as a result of A's tack, rule 15 does not require B to give A any room to keep clear.

lane, a car hits you or swerves to miss you, you are in the wrong. But once you get **all four wheels** across the line, you are now technically in the right-hand lane yourself and cars coming up from behind have to keep clear of you. However, these cars are not required to begin to avoid you or even to **anticipate** avoiding you until you are completely in the lane. Once you are in the lane they have to try reasonably hard to miss you. If they can't, then you've moved on too close in front of them.

The same is true in sailboats. Let's say I'm on *starboard tack*, you're approaching me on *port tack*, and you want to tack on my lee-bow or in front of me. If I could hit you before you passed head to wind (i.e. before you began to cross the white line), you'd be wrong under rule 10 (*port/starboard*). If I could hit you after you'd passed head to wind but before you were aiming on your close-hauled course (i.e. while you were crossing the line), you'd be wrong under rule 13 (a boat past head to wind must *keep clear*). However, the moment you get to your close-hauled course (i.e. completely in my lane) and you are either *clear ahead* or to *leeward* of me, you have the right of way under either rule 12 (*clear astern/clear ahead*) or rule 11 (*windward/leeward*) and I have to promptly take action to *keep clear* of you. This is when rule 15 requires you to initially give me the *room* I need to *keep clear* of you. Of course, in most situations it will take me only a second or two to react enough to luff or bear away slightly to avoid a collision.

"In protests involving the situation where P tacks very close to leeward of S, it seems that P and S may often disagree on whether P was actually on a close-hauled course before S changed course to avoid her; or whether P, after acquiring right of way, actually gave S room to keep clear. Are there any onuses to help resolve these disagreements?"

No. In resolving these disagreements, most protest committees apply the principle in ISAF Case 50 (see rule 10 discussion), which is that they first put responsibility on S to satisfy the committee that the boats were close together. They then put the responsibility on P to satisfy them that P was on a close-hauled course before S changed her course; and that once she was on a close-hauled course, she gave S *room* to *keep clear*. This responsibility on P is often difficult to win against. Hails to the effect of "My tack is completed-2-3-4, now you're changing course" and a witness are very helpful.

US SAILING Appeal 78 describes a situation where three *port-tack* boats (call them L, M and W) were sailing upwind and L (the leeward-most boat) tacked to *starboard* thereby acquiring the right of way. The middle boat (M) tacked to *starboard* and kept clear of L, but she tacked so close to the windward boat (W) that she and W could not avoid colliding. The Appeals Committee said this, "If a boat maneuvers in a way that causes her to collide with another boat, her maneuver is not seamanlike. [L], by depriving [M] of the space necessary to maneuver in a seamanlike way, failed to give [M] room to keep clear (see the definition Room)... the results are that [L] broke rule 15 against [M] and is disqualified..." M was exonerated from breaking rule 15 against W under rule 64.1(b) (Penalties and Exoneration).

Gy113ng into a right-of-way position:

The same is true when gybing. If two boats are running side by side on *port tack* and the *windward* boat gybes, the moment the foot of the mainsail crosses her centerline she is on *starboard tack* and the other boat (P) must promptly maneuver to get clear. However, S must plan to initially give P the *room* she needs to *keep clear*.

Completing penalty turns or starting after being over early:

Again, the principle applies when a boat is completing penalty turns for fouling another boat (rule 44, Penalties for Breaking Rules of Part 2) or touching a *mark* (rule 31, Touching a Mark). While making her penalty (turns), she is required to *keep clear* of boats not doing so (rule 20, Starting Errors; Penalty Turns; Moving Astern). The moment she completes her last "360," she is no longer bound by rule 20. If she suddenly acquires the right of way over a nearby boat, she must give this boat *room* to respond. The same applies when she returns to the correct side of the starting line to *start* after being on the course side of the starting line at the gun (rule 20).

"What is the reason for the last phrase of the rule, 'unless she acquires right of way because of the other boat's actions'?"

This is to protect boats that suddenly become right-of-way boats because of an action by the other boat. For instance, you are sailing upwind on *starboard tack* just to windward and slightly behind a boat to leeward. Suddenly, the leeward boat tacks and is now directly in front of you on *port tack*! Without the last phrase in rule 15, you would be required to give the boat that tacked *room* to *keep clear* of you, because you have just acquired the right of way! Clearly this would be unacceptable, hence the phrase. Therefore, in the example above, assuming you had to take action to avoid contact, the boat that tacked broke rule 10 (*port/starboard*), and rule 15 did not apply to you.

Another situation where this applies is when a boat *clear ahead* (A) bears away and creates an *overlap* with the boat *clear astern* (B). The moment the boats are *overlapped*, B becomes the right-of-way boat under rule 11 (*windward/leeward*). In this case, B was holding her course and it was A's action that gave B the right of way. Therefore rule 15 does not apply to B, and if A were to suddenly luff and strike B's bow with her port stern quarter, A would be penalized for breaking rule 11 (On the Same Tack, Overlapped).

RULE 16 - CHANGING COURSE

Rule 16.1

When a right-of-way boat changes course, she shall give the other boat *room* to *keep clear*.

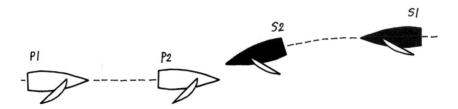

S has the right of way over P. But rule 16 requires that S not change her course so close to P that P does not have room to keep clear; and after the starting signal, S cannot change course so close to P that P is forced to immediately take avoiding action as a result.

Rule 16 contains one of the most fundamental principles in the rules. Simply put, before a right-of-way boat changes her course near a give-way boat, she must be aware of the space and time the give-way boat will need to stay clear of her, assuming the give-way boat reacts and maneuvers promptly in a sea-manlike way; and she must be sure to give her that **space** and **time**.

Let's get into this extremely important rule. Rule 16 is clearly talking to right-of-way boats (see ISAF Case 52). When two boats are about to collide, the give-way boat has the obligation to *keep clear*. The only way she can decide how to do this is if she can accurately figure out where the right-of-way boat is going. It would be chaos if just as a *port-tack* boat was reaching by a *starboard-tack* boat, S could suddenly and unexpectedly turn and hit P. The purpose of rule 16 is to protect give-way boats from unpredictable or last-second changes of course by right-of-way boats which, in essence, prevent the give-way boat from being able to *keep clear*.

 "So if I'm on starboard tack near a port-tack boat, rule 10 doesn't allow me to steer any course I want to?"

Absolutely not. That is exactly what rule 16 is designed to prevent. ISAF Case 60 says, "Tactical desires do not relieve a boat from her obligations under the rules. A (the right-of-way boat in the case) was free to adopt any course she chose to reach the leeward mark, but she did not have the right to luff into the path of B (the give-way boat) so close to B that B could not keep clear."

However, rule 16 does not shift the right-of-way between two boats; it is simply a common-sense "limit" on the right-of-way boat requiring her to limit her course changes when a give-way boat is close by and trying to *keep clear*.

Notice that rule 16 only applies to a "change of course." It in no way applies to a change in your boat's speed or its angle of heel. When P reaches by just to *windward* of S such that S momentarily loses her wind, thereby straightening up and hitting P's mast, P is wrong under rule 10 (On Opposite Tacks). Of course, rule 2 (Fair Sailing) is available to P if she suspects that S deliberately tried to hit her in an unfair manner.

"If I'm making a smooth turn toward a give-way boat, am I considered to be 'changing course' if I continue the arc of my turn?"

US SAILING Appeal 33 says, "Yes, it is a change of course for a boat to sail the arc of a circle or any other course where she is changing direction, whether or not she moves her helm. To change course means to change compass direction."

That tells us that "course" in rule 16 refers to the boat's straight-ahead or "compass" course. Therefore, whenever a boat is turning, it is changing "course." It also refers to its fore and aft or "directional" course; i.e. when a boat that was moving forward begins to move astern, it has also changed "course" (see also rule 20, Starting Errors; Penalty Turns; Moving Astern).

"Okay, so if I'm a right-of-way boat and want to change course near another boat, what exactly does rule 16.1 require that I give her?"

You need to give her *"room* to *keep clear"* of you. She is *keeping clear* of you when you can sail your straight-ahead course with no need to take action to avoid hitting her. The *room* you have to give her is the "space" and "time" she needs to get far enough away from you so that you can sail your course, assuming she acts promptly in a seamanlike way (see definition *Room*).

Note that "promptly" means "performed readily, quickly, immediately" which builds in the time element. Therefore when a right-of-way boat changes course, rule 16.1 requires nearby boats to respond "promptly" or risk losing the protection of *room*.

However, "seamanlike" means "responsible, prudent, safety conscious." Therefore, you have to be sure that your course change doesn't force the give-way boat to put their or your boat's crew, boat or equipment at risk of injury or damage by the need to make a sudden, hurried or extreme maneuver. For instance, forcing a *windward* boat to sail head to wind with a spinnaker up in heavy air may be considered "unseamanlike" as it may put their spinnaker in great risk of tearing.

 "Well, if I'm the right-of-way boat, how close to the give-way boat can I be and still change my course without breaking rule 16?"

Before I can answer that important question, we have to look at rule 16.2.

Rule 16.2

In addition, when after the starting signal boats are about to cross or are crossing each other on opposite *tacks*, and the *port-tack* boat is keeping clear of the *starboard-tack* boat, the *starboard-tack* boat shall not change course if as a result the *port-tack* boat would immediately need to change course to continue *keeping clear*.

So, there are basically two questions the right-of-way boat will need to consider before changing course near another boat (these will be the same two questions the protest committee will have to answer in a protest involving rule 16):

1) When I change my course, will the other boat have enough "space" and "time" to get away from me "promptly" but without having to make an "unseamanlike maneuver" to do so?

2) If it is after the starting signal, and if I am on *starboard tack* converging with a *port-tack* boat that is about to safely cross ahead of or behind me (upwind or downwind), will I be able to change my course without making the port-tacker have to make an "immediate" course change to continue crossing safely past me?

If the answer to either of these questions is "No," then the right-of-way boat will break rule 16.1 and/or rule 16.2 if she changes course near the other boat.

Clearly, the questions must be answered depending on the circumstances at the time, and for that reason it is impossible to project a hypothetical distance apart. The major considerations will be:

1) the distance between the boats;

2) the speeds and sizes of the boats;

3) the angles at which they are converging;

4) the visibility between the boats;

5) the amount of course change by the right-of-way boat;

6) the amount and difficulty of the boat handling required by the give-way boat to *keep clear*; and

7) the reasonableness of the give-way boat's attempt to *keep clear*.

Having said all this, I will say that as a conservative and safe rule of thumb in most boats, any course change by the right-of-way boat when closer than two lengths from the give-way boat is risky.

Let's look at some common situations when rule 16 will come into play.

When a *port-tack* boat (P) and a *starboard-tack* boat (S) are converging on a beat:

Situation 1: P will cross S by half a boat-length or so. When about two lengths apart, S hails "Starboard" and makes a medium fast luff toward P. P, who has been watching S, continues for a couple of seconds, then makes a routine tack to *starboard tack* on S's lee-bow. S could continue straight-ahead, but decides to tack away to avoid P's bad air.

Resolution: When the boats are converging, P is required to *keep clear* under rule 10 (On Opposite Tacks). When S changes her course near P, she is required to give P *room* to *keep clear* (rule 16.1), and not to make P make an immediate course change to continue *keeping clear* (rule 16.2). P does not make an immediate course change, and she is able to tack in a seamanlike way to continue *keeping clear* of S. S is able to sail her course without concern of hitting P. Therefore P *keeps clear*, S does not make P make an immediate course change to continue *keeping clear*, and S gives her the *room* she needs to *keep clear*. Neither boat breaks a *rule*.

NOTE: in the same scenario, if when S changed course, P had to tack immediately to continue *keeping clear* of her, then S would have broken rule 16.2.

Situation 2: P will cross S by half a boat-length or so. When about one-and-a-half lengths apart, S hails "Starboard" and makes a medium fast luff toward P, putting the two boats on a collision course. P holds her course to get across S as quickly as she can (tacking would make matters worse because she would be turning directly in front of S). Just before contact, S bears away and protests.

Resolution: The first job of the protest committee will be to determine if P actually *keeps clear*. Clearly she doesn't because S needs to take action to avoid hitting her (see definition *Keep Clear*). Therefore, P breaks rule 10 (On Opposite Tacks). Their next task is to decide if, when S changes course, she gives P *room* to *keep clear*. Clearly she doesn't because there is nothing P can do to get out of S's way. Therefore S breaks rule 16.1; and because it was her "illegal" course change that compelled P to break rule 10, P is exonerated under rule 64.1(b) (Penalties and Exoneration).

NOTE: there does not have to be contact in order for a boat to break rule 16. Anytime a right-of-way boat changes course near a give-way boat, rule 16 comes into effect. If it is determined that there would have been a collision if the right-of-way boat had not taken subsequent avoiding action, then that establishes that the give-way boat did not *keep clear*. At that point, either the give-way boat will be disqualified under the appropriate Section A – Right of Way rule, or the right-of-way boat will be disqualified under rule 16 (and the give-way boat exonerated under rule 64.1(b)). (See ISAF Case 60.)

Situation 3: P bears away to "duck" (pass astern of) S. When a length and a half away, S bears away towards P and P immediately bears away further to avoid S. S luffs back up to close-hauled and P passes close astern of her. P protests.

Resolution: By bearing away, P is *keeping clear* of S. When S changes her course, P needs to immediately bear away further to keep clear of S. By causing P to have to immediately change her course to continue *keeping clear*, S breaks rule 16.2. (See ISAF Case 92.)

BOTTOM LINE: Rule 16 is very strict, and S must be very careful with her course changes when near P. Again, course changes when closer than two lengths from the give-way boat are risky.

 "I assume from all this that if I get a wind shift on a beat, I can't follow the shift and hit a port-tack boat that is just crossing my bow?"

That's absolutely right. Rule 16 applies to any course change, regardless of the reason. If you find yourself in the situation where P is crossing you and you get a favorable wind shift and want to head up and pass close astern of

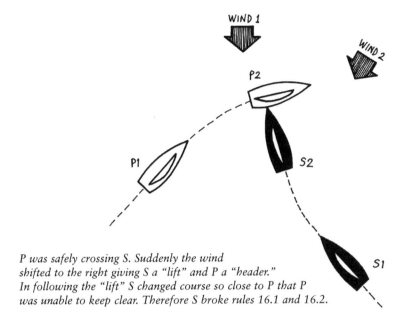

P was safely crossing S. Suddenly the wind shifted to the right giving S a "lift" and P a "header." In following the "lift" S changed course so close to P that P was unable to keep clear. Therefore S broke rules 16.1 and 16.2.

P, but you know that P doesn't have *room* to tack away after you do head up, simply let P know, with a hail or a wave, that she can continue on across you as you head up to pass close astern of her.

"Do I have to hail before changing my course? And if I do warn the other boat with a hail that I am about to change course toward them, does that count as 'giving room' ?"

No and No. First, the rule does not require a hail. Second, the rule is about "changing course," which means that the test of whether you gave *room* will begin at the moment you actually changed your course. However, a clear hail alerting the give-way boat that you are about to change course is strong evidence that you intend to give her *room* to *keep clear* when you change course, and is therefore strongly recommended.

When a *port-tack* boat (P) and a *starboard-tack* boat (S) are on a downwind leg:

Situation 1: P will cross S by half a boat-length or so. When one length away, S bears away such that the boats are now on a collision course. P immediately bears away to *keep clear* of S, and protests.

Resolution: When S changes her course, P needs to immediately bear away to *keep clear* of S. By causing P to have to immediately change her course to continue *keeping clear*, S breaks rule 16.2.

Situation 2: P and S are sailing parallel courses dead downwind about one length apart. S changes course towards P and P immediately bears away and gybes in a seamanlike way to *keep clear* of S, and protests.

Resolution: Rule 16.2 does not apply because P and S are not about to cross or are not crossing each other; they are sailing parallel courses. When S changes her course, P is able to get out of her way in a seamanlike way. Neither boat breaks a rule. (See ISAF Case 18.)

NOTE: some have complained that in this dead downwind situation, the *rules* are flawed because P can parallel herself so close to S that S can't change course without breaking rule 16.1. My opinion is (a) P runs a great risk by getting that close to S because if S feels any apprehension of contact, she would be justified in protesting under rule 10 (On Opposite Tacks); and (b) S can see the situation developing and turn toward P **before** P gets that close to her.

When a *leeward* boat (L) and a *windward* boat (W) are sailing on the same tack:

Situation 1: L is sailing along on a reach. W catches up and *overlaps* her to *windward*, but far enough away so that L can change her course toward her (luff) without immediately hitting her. L begins to luff medium fast and W promptly responds and *keeps clear*. At some point during the luff, L gets closer to W (either because W slows down her response rate, or L increases her luffing rate or because of the boats simply getting closer as they rotate up). L realizes that if she continues her luff she will get so close to W that she could then immediately hit W if she luffed even more. She stops her luff and protests.

Resolution: When W gets near L she must be prepared for L to luff (change course toward her). And when L luffs, W must respond "promptly" (i.e. very quickly) and make her best effort to get out of L's way. Furthermore, L can luff as quickly as she chooses **provided** she allows W the space and time needed to get out of her way assuming W is responding promptly. However, L can never luff so suddenly or fast that, despite W's best efforts, W physically cannot *keep clear* of her.

The first job of the protest committee will be to determine if W actually *keeps clear* of L. Clearly she does because L can always sail her course, i.e. her straight-ahead course, with no apprehension of collision. Furthermore, throughout the incident L can always change course in either direction without making immediate contact with W. Once it is decided that W has *kept clear* throughout the incident, it then means that L has complied with rule 16.1. Neither boat breaks a rule.

NOTE: If L had allowed herself to get so close to W that L could not change course any more without immediately making contact with W, it would have been a much different situation. First, by definition W was not *keeping clear* (see last line in definition *Keep Clear*), and she breaks rule 11 (On the Same Tack, Overlapped). Therefore, either W will get disqualified for breaking rule 11, or L will get disqualified for breaking rule 16 (and W will get exonerated under rule 64.1(b), Penalties and Exoneration). This *protest* will be resolved by the protest committee's determination of whether W was maneuvering promptly in a seamanlike way or not (an admittedly difficult protest at best). If yes, then L failed to give her enough *room* to continue *keeping clear* and is disqualified under rule 16; if no, then W failed to *keep clear* by her own actions and is disqualified under rule 11.

"If L luffs, then stops luffing to give W more room to respond, is L still bound by rule 16.1 to give W room to keep clear when L begins luffing again?"

Yes. Rule 16.1 applies to L whenever she changes her course. The use of the word "initially" in rule 15 (Acquiring Right of Way) makes the requirement in rule 15 a temporary one at the outset of the overlap. However, rule 16.1 does not contain the word "initially." Therefore, each time L stops and then changes her course again, she must give W *room* to *keep clear* once again. W, on the other hand, will put herself at great risk by remaining too close to L over an extended period of time, and should make every effort to get well clear when L first luffs.

"What if, despite the fact that L has given W plenty of room, W allows herself to get so close to L that L can't change course at all without hitting W?"

The last phrase in the definition *Keep Clear* tells W that she is not *keeping clear* if she allows herself to get so close to L that L can't change course in **both directions** at that moment without **immediately** making contact with her. Note that the second "if" in the definition suggests that L does not need to actually hit W to prove she couldn't change course without contact. If the protest committee decides that L couldn't have changed course without immediately hitting W, then W has broken rule 11 (On the Same Tack, Overlapped) simply by her extreme close proximity to L.

Furthermore, any time L has a reasonable apprehension that contact with W may occur if she holds her course, W fails to *keep clear* and breaks rule 11; and when W allows herself to get that close to L, L will generally be justified in being concerned about the masts touching, the boats being tossed together by waves, etc., etc.

However, when L is luffing and her bow is getting closer to W's stern quarter, there will come a point that, due to the way boats rotate, it will become impossible for W to *keep clear* if L continues to luff. At that point, L must cease her luff and allow W the room she needs to move away from L before she continues her luff again.

 "Is it true that the rules regarding the rate of L's luff are the same before and after starting?"

Yes. Rule 16.1 is the rule that deals primarily with the rate of L's luff, and there is absolutely no difference in the application of rule 16.1 before or after *starting*.

 "What if a boat to windward of W, or some other object, restricts her ability to respond to a luff by L?"

This is commonly the situation as boats begin to tightly line-up in the final minutes before a start or as they approach a crowded downwind *mark*. The *room* that rule 16.1 requires L to give W often must include time for W to wait for boats to *windward* of her to respond; or for W to sail past an object

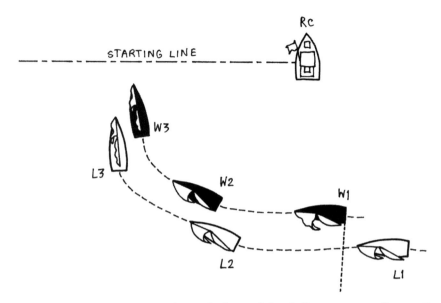

When L becomes overlapped to leeward of W and then luffs, L must initially give W room to keep clear when she first becomes overlapped; and then L must give W any additional room she needs to keep clear when she luffs.

(e.g. something in the water) that prevents her from *keeping clear* of L. A hail by W to the effect, "I am trying to *keep clear* but I have these other boats, or this object, to windward of me!" will be useful and is strongly encouraged.

Situation 2: W is slowly sailing along the starting line about a minute before starting. L catches up from *clear astern* and becomes *overlapped* to *leeward* of W. After about five seconds, L begins to slowly luff toward W.

Resolution: Prior to the *overlap*, W, as the boat *clear ahead*, is the right-of-way boat under rule 12 (On the Same Tack, Not Overlapped); therefore she doesn't need to take any action in anticipation of L's *leeward overlap*. When L becomes *overlapped*, L is required by rule 15 (Acquiring Right of Way) to initially give W *room* to *keep clear*. This includes the "space" and "time" necessary for W to trim her sails and otherwise get steerageway to get away from L. After W has had *room* to *keep clear*, L may luff, provided she gives W any **additional** *room* W needs to *keep clear* under rule 16.1. The bottom line is that when *leeward* boats "come in the back door" (i.e. establish *leeward over-laps* from *clear astern* on *windward* boats) and then want to luff, they must plan to be very patient. (See ISAF Case 7.)

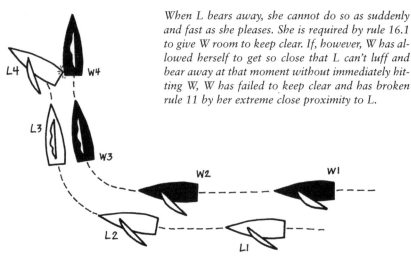

When L bears away, she cannot do so as suddenly and fast as she pleases. She is required by rule 16.1 to give W room to keep clear. If, however, W has allowed herself to get so close that L can't luff and bear away at that moment without immediately hitting W, W has failed to keep clear and has broken rule 11 by her extreme close proximity to L.

   "Can L ever bear away with no limitation and hit W with her trasom?"

No. When L bears away near W, L must comply with rule 16.1 as well, i.e. she must bear away in a way that gives W *room* to *keep clear*. Normally, if L bears away slowly and with some caution not to swing her stern into W's *leeward* side, L will not break rule 16.1. And if W has left herself so close to *windward* of L that L can't luff and bear away without immediately hitting her, W has failed to *keep clear* and has broken rule 11 (On the Same Tack, Overlapped).

"Sounds like there could be some difficult protests involving rule 16.1; are there any onuses to help resolve these disputes?"

No. In a dispute over whether W *kept clear* or whether L provided enough *room* to *keep clear*, neither the rules nor the appeals place any "onus" on either boat. The protest committee will have to determine the facts and use its best judgment. Remember that a *windward* boat's right to "*room* to *keep clear*" under rule 16.1 is a shield and not a sword for W. Also, to be entitled to the protection of *room*, W must respond as soon as she can to L's change of course and make a reasonable attempt to get clear. From there it will be up to the protest committee to decide from the weight of the evidence on (a) the wind and sea conditions, (b) the nature of the incident, and (c) the exact actions of both boats, as to whether or not W had '*room* to *keep clear*'. Hails by both boats at the time will be very helpful in resolving such conflicts and are strongly encouraged. And to be safe, I always assume that the benefit of any doubt will go to the right-of-way boat (L).

"Are there any exceptions to rule 16?"

Well, in fact, there is one exception to rule 16, and that is found in rule 18.2(d) (Changing Course to Round or Pass). This will be discussed in detail in the discussion of rule 18 (Rounding and Passing Marks and Obstructions) in Chapter 8 (beginning on page 149). But in a nutshell, rule 18.2(d) says that rule 16 does not apply to a right-of-way boat that is changing course to round or pass a *mark*.

RULE 17 – On The Same Tack; Proper Course

Rule 17.1

If a boat *clear astern* becomes *overlapped* within two of her hull lengths to *leeward* of a boat on the same *tack*, she shall not sail above her *proper course* while they remain *overlapped* within that distance, unless in doing so she promptly sails astern of the other boat. This rule does not apply if the *overlap* begins while the *windward* boat is required by rule 13 to *keep clear.*

Rule 16 (Changing Course) is about limiting **how fast** a right-of-way boat can turn near a give-way boat; rule 17.1 is about limiting **where** a *leeward* boat can sail when near a give-way boat. Note that rule 17.1 simply puts a "limit" on where a *leeward* boat can sail when near a *windward* boat in certain situations. It does not shift any right-of-way to the *windward* boat. When near each other, W must remember that rule 11 (On the Same Tack, Overlapped) requires her to *keep clear* of L.

The concept in rule 17.1 is simple: either L is "limited" to sailing no higher than her *proper course* or she is "free" to sail up to head to wind if she pleases; it is always one or the other for L whenever L and W are *overlapped* and within two of L's lengths of each other.

Whether L is "limited" or "free" depends on the following five factors:

1) whether the boats are *overlapped*;

2) whether the boats are within two of L's hull lengths of each other;

3) whether L became *overlapped* from *clear astern* within two of her hull lengths of W;

4) whether W was subject to rule 13 (While Tacking), i.e. past head to wind but not yet close-hauled, when L became *overlapped*; and

5) whether the starting signal has been made.

*(It is important to point out that when boats are rounding or passing **marks** and **obstructions**, rule 18, Rounding and Passing Marks and Obstructions, may impose some conflicting obligations or limitations on L, in which case they would take precedence over those in rule 17.1. See the explanation of rule 18 for a full discussion.)*

A few clarifying points on the five factors listed above:

- When L is not "limited" under rule 17.1, she is "free" to sail up to head to wind if she pleases, provided she gives W *room* to *keep clear* in a seamanlike way (rule 16.1, Changing Course). To clarify, even if L is only *overlapped* with W by two feet, L can sail up to head to wind. US SAILING Appeal 17 says, "A boat is head to wind when her bow is facing the wind, and the centerline of her hull is parallel to it, irrespective of the position of her sails." This clarification is helpful because often when a boat is head to wind her sails will blow momentarily to the other side giving the **illusion** that she is past head to wind and therefore subject to rule 13 (While Tacking).

Remember that when L is head to wind, it is quite possible that W will be required to go **beyond** head to wind in order to *keep clear* under rule 11 (On the Same Tack, Overlapped). If this is the case, W must do so. If it's not possible for W to *keep clear* without fouling other boats to *windward* of her, W should clearly alert L that she needs more *room* to *keep clear* (as required by rule 16.1).

- The "limit" in rule 17.1 only applies to boats that are "*overlapped.*" The terms *clear ahead, clear astern* and *overlap* do not apply to boats on opposite *tacks* (unless they are about to round or pass a *mark* or *obstruction* and rule 18 applies). So when a *starboard-tack* boat and a *port-tack* boat are half way down a leg and they are sailing side by side, they are not considered *overlapped*; and if P catches up from astern and sails in alongside of S, P has not become *overlapped* to *leeward* from *clear astern* on S.

On the other hand, a boat is always on a *tack*. Therefore, when P and S are converging on a beat and S tacks in front of P, the moment S passes head to wind she is on *port tack* (though she still must *keep clear* until she's on a close-hauled course under rule 13, While Tacking). Even when P becomes *overlapped* the moment S passes head to wind, the boats are considered *overlapped*. (See the discussion of definition *Clear Astern* and *Clear Ahead; Overlap.*)

- The "limit" only applies when L and W are **within two lengths of each other.** The "two lengths" distance is determined by two of L's **hull** lengths, i.e. the length of L's hull, and not the additional length of any bowsprits, overhanging mizzen booms, etc. This is particularly important when boats of different sizes are near each other.

- The only time L is "limited" is when she becomes *overlapped* **to leeward of W from *clear astern* within two of her lengths** of W. That's it! The "limit" does not apply when L *overlaps* W when more than two lengths apart, or when W becomes *overlapped* to *windward* of L or when L is to leeward of W on the opposite *tack* and then gybes. Furthermore, once the *overlap* begins with no "limit" on L, there is no way for W to thereafter put the "limit" on during that *overlap*.

- Note that rule 17.1 uses the phrase "becomes *overlapped*." This means that any time a boat that was *clear astern* crosses a line perpendicular to the *clear ahead* boat's centerline drawn through the boat's aftermost point in normal position, it is considered that the boat has "become *overlapped*" to *leeward* of the boat that was *clear ahead*, regardless of how that line came to be in front of the boat *clear astern*. So even in the situation where a boat *clear astern* is holding her course and a boat *clear ahead* and to windward turns down and creates an *overlap*, it is considered that the *leeward* boat has become *overlapped* with the *windward* boat.

- The "limit" in rule 17.1 is that L **cannot sail above her** *proper course*. Because a boat does not have a *proper course* until the starting signal is made, there is never any "limit" on L **before** her starting signal (see the discussion of definition *Proper Course*). Therefore, before the starting signal, L can sail up to head to wind at all times.

But at the starting signal, L will become "limited" or "free" depending on how the *overlap* began (whenever it began). Note that this applies regardless of whether the boats have actually *started*, i.e. have crossed the starting line or not. If with 20 seconds to go before the starting signal L becomes *overlapped* from *clear astern* within two lengths of W, then at the starting signal L is "limited" and must sail no higher than her *proper course*. If with 20 seconds to go W *overlaps* L to *windward*, then at the starting signal L continues to be "free" to sail up to head to wind if she pleases.

"So it sounds like the starting signal is the key moment in time for determining whether L is 'limited' or 'free;' and that it is pretty important for overlapped boats to remember how they first became overlapped as the starting signal approaches!"

Exactly right. Before the starting signal, L is not "limited" in any way, i.e. she can sail head to wind if she pleases; after the starting signal, L is "limited" to sailing no higher than her *proper course* if she originally became *overlapped* from *clear astern*. The advantage of having L's limitation begin at the starting signal is that it is a precise and predictable moment in time.

And the moment the starting signal is made, L instantly gets a *proper course* (see the definition *Proper Course*). At that moment it is critical for L and W to

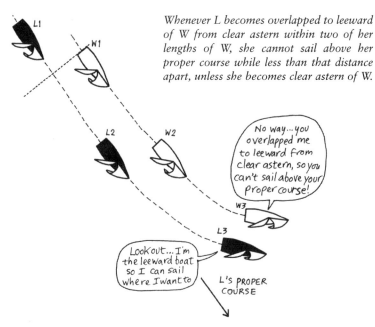

Whenever L becomes overlapped to leeward of W from clear astern within two of her lengths of W, she cannot sail above her proper course while less than that distance apart, unless she becomes clear astern of W.

No way...you overlapped me to leeward from clear astern, so you can't sail above your proper course!

Look out...I'm the leeward boat so I can sail where I want to

L's PROPER COURSE

remember how they became *overlapped*! Hails when the *overlap* first begins and throughout the *overlap* are going to be critical for producing orderly starts and reducing disputes!

"Do I have to bear away to my proper course before the starting signal is made; i.e. do I have to anticipate my obligation not to sail above my proper course after the starting signal?"

No. You do not have a *proper course* before the starting signal, and therefore you are not "limited" as to where you can sail. When the starting signal is made, and if you are now "limited" because you originally became *overlapped* from *clear astern*, you are required to sail no higher than your *proper course*. The course you will sail to *finish* as soon as possible will include the course you are on at the moment the starting signal is made. If you must then bear away to a lower course to get to the next *mark* and ultimately the finishing line as soon as possible, you must do so immediately. For instance, if you are head to wind before an upwind start, your *proper course* will be to bear away to a close-hauled course or even slightly lower to build speed and sail upwind.

"What is the purpose of the last sentence in rule 17.1, the one about rule 13?"

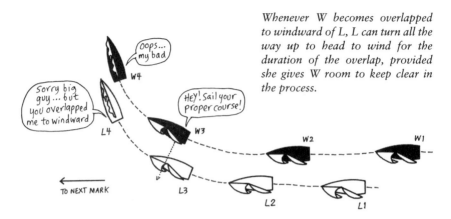

Whenever W becomes overlapped to windward of L, L can turn all the way up to head to wind for the duration of the overlap, provided she gives W room to keep clear in the process.

This sentence specifically addresses the tactic known as the "Slam Dunk." (For a detailed analysis of the Slam Dunk, see page 143.) Consider two close-hauled boats on opposite *tacks* (S and P) converging. P bears away to pass astern of S. When P gets near S's stern, S tacks. At some point during S's tack, P becomes *overlapped* to *leeward* of S. Is P "limited" or "free" under rule 17.1?

Well, once S passes head to wind and until she is on a close-hauled course, S is required by rule 13 (While Tacking) to keep clear of P. And the last sentence in rule 17.1 says that if P becomes *overlapped* to *leeward* of S while S is required by rule 13 to *keep clear* of her, then rule 17.1 doesn't apply. So in this case, P would be "free" for as long as the boats remained *overlapped*, i.e. she could sail up to head to wind, subject of course to rule 16.1 (Changing Course). If S was already down to a close-hauled course before P became *overlapped*, then P would be "limited" under rule 17.1 throughout the *overlap*. The net effect of this rule will be to discourage Slam Dunks, which are very aggressive and often contentious.

 "What happens in the situation where L and W are both sailing their proper courses and the two boats are converging; who has to keep clear?"

W must *keep clear* of L under rule 11 (On the Same Tack, Overlapped). Rule 17.1 only requires that L not sail **above** her *proper course*. When L **is** on her *proper course*, W must *keep clear*. Note that the phrase in rule 17.1 "her *proper course*" clarifies that it is L who gets to sail **her** *proper course*. Therefore, when L is sailing on her *proper course*, W must *keep clear* under rule 11, even when W's *proper course* may be a **lower** course than L's. (See ISAF Cases 7 and 14.)

Remember that a *proper course* is essentially any course a boat chooses to sail in order to get to the next *mark* and ultimately to *finish* as quickly as possible. Therefore it is possible that there may be several *proper courses* at any given moment depending upon the circumstances involved. It is also obvious that two *overlapping* boats sailing for the same *mark* will converge. Note also that a boat's *proper course* is not necessarily a straight-line course. It can change with changes in the breeze, current or waves, or with a change in the boat's strategy (see the discussion of definition *Proper Course*). However, whenever L wants to change her course to a new *proper course*, she must give W *room* to *keep clear* under rule 16.1 (Changing Course). A hail that she intends to change course is strongly recommended.

"What happens when L wants to luff two or more boats and one of the middle boats is 'limited' to where she can sail?"

Good question! Let's take the situation where L and W are sailing down a reach about two lengths or so apart. A boat from astern (M) catches up and becomes *overlapped* between them. When M becomes *overlapped* on W, there was clearly *room* for her to pass between L and W such that she is entitled to *room* from W to pass L (rule 18.2(a), Rounding and Passing Marks and Obstructions and rule 18.5, Passing a Continuing Obstruction). Now L begins to luff toward M and W. M responds by luffing. W must *keep clear* of M

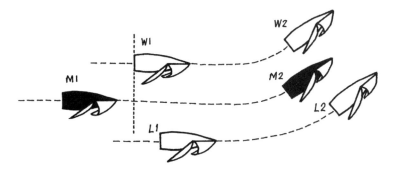

Because M becomes overlapped to leeward of W from clear astern, she is "limited" to sailing no higher than her proper course. When L luffs, M is required to keep clear of her under rule 11. Even in the absence of W, M would luff to keep clear of L. Therefore, M is not sailing above her proper course and W must keep clear of M under rule 11 and give her room under rule 18.2(a).

under rule 11 (On the Same Tack, Overlapped) and give her *room* under rule 18.2(a). And M is not breaking rule 17.1 because in fact M is **not** sailing above her *proper course*. Here's the reason. Take the two boats involved, M and W. M became *overlapped* on W to leeward from *clear astern*. Rule 17.1 requires M, therefore, not to sail above her *proper course*. In determining her *proper course*, the definition of *proper course* instructs us to remove the boats referred to in the rule using the term *"proper course."* In this case, rule 17.1 uses the term and refers to the *windward* boat W, so we remove W. As M was sailing a course to keep clear of L, she would have been sailing the same course in the absence of W; therefore, M was sailing her *proper course* and not above it.

 "What's the purpose of the phrase in rule 17.1, '…unless in doing so she promptly sails astern of the other boat'?"

This is to close a very subtle, undesirable loophole in the rule. Here's a potential scenario: on a beat to windward, a boat crosses you and tacks just ahead and about half-a-length to windward of you. Due to your greater speed you become *overlapped* to *leeward* from *clear astern*, but you realize that you won't be able to sail past them enough to get your air clear. You want to tack out of there. Assuming that when sailing upwind your *proper course* is a close-hauled course, without an exception to the rule the question would be: "Could you sail above close-hauled and tack while you're *overlapped* to *leeward* of W; or would you have to wait until you were no longer *overlapped* so you didn't break rule 17.1?" Rule 17.1 clarifies that you can certainly luff and tack (i.e. sail above your *proper course*) provided you break the overlap with W at some point during your turn. If you luff and then realize that your bow won't clear W's transom and have to pull your bow back down, you risk breaking rule 17.1.

Rule 17.2

Except on a beat to windward, while a boat is less than two of her hull lengths from a *leeward* boat or a boat *clear astern* steering a course to *leeward* of her, she shall not sail below her *proper course* unless she gybes.

This rule is saying that if you are sailing downwind and there's a boat within two lengths and either *clear ahead* or to *windward* of you, and you are steering a course to leeward of them, she **cannot** sail below her *proper course*. This is only fair, because when you try to pass a boat to *windward*, she can prevent you by luffing. It would give that boat too much of an advantage if, when you tried to pass her to *leeward*, she could bear away on your wind too.

This is possibly the most infringed rule in Part 2, partially because many sailors don't know it and partially because it is very difficult to prove a breach. It is commonly broken as boats near *marks* and the boats ahead try to prevent or discourage the boats behind from getting an inside *overlap*.

Note that this rule does not apply to a boat that is "on a beat to windward." Therefore, on a "beat to windward" it is legal to bear off to get closer to a boat to *leeward* or *clear astern* of you, though this is not commonly done except in team racing.

"On a beat to windward" is not interpreted by any appeal. My opinion is that a boat is "on a beat to windward" if her *proper course* to the next *mark* at the time is to sail close-hauled. All other legs are considered "free legs." Therefore, any leg on which your *proper course* to the next *mark* is below close-hauled is a "free leg" for you, and rule 17.2 applies. For instance, if you are on a beat sailing close-hauled near the starboard-tack layline and the wind shifts 20 degrees to the right such that now you are "overstanding" (i.e. can get to the *mark* by sailing a lower than close-hauled course), **you** are now on a "free-leg," whereas the boats on the left side of the leg may still be on a "beat to windward." The same logic applies to an off-wind leg. If you can get to the next *mark* by sailing a course lower than close-hauled, it is a "free leg" for you. But if the wind shifts such that you must now sail close-hauled to get there, the leg is now a "beat to windward" for you.

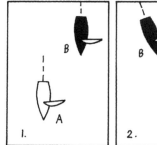 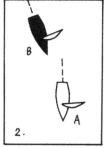 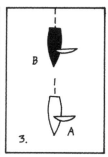 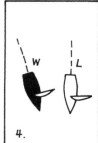

Rule 17.2 applies to A in positions 1 and 2, but not to A in position 3. It applies to W in position 4.

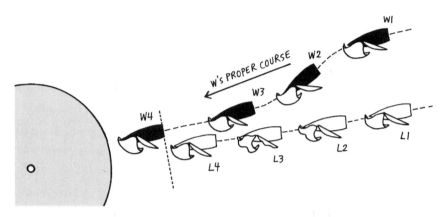

In position 2, W sails below her proper course in order to get closer to L, slow her down and prevent her from maintaining an inside overlap. W would not have borne away in the absence of L. This is a common breach of rule 17.2.

Note the phrase "steering a course to *leeward* of her." In my opinion, a boat *clear astern* is considered to be steering a course to *leeward* of the boat *clear ahead* any time her course will take her to the *leeward* side of the boat *clear ahead*, including when the boat *clear astern* is up to windward of the boat *clear ahead*'s wake.

An example of a boat *clear astern* **not** "steering a course to *leeward*" is when the boat *clear astern* is aiming at, or to *windward* of, the boat *clear ahead*'s transom and is sailing a course parallel to or higher than her.

Finally note that the rule only applies when boats are within two hull lengths of each other.

 "Are there any exceptions to this rule?"

Rule 17.2 contains one exception, "...unless she gybes." This parallels the exception in rule 17.1. A common scenario is W, sailing downwind and close to L, wants to gybe. Because she is a *windward* boat within two lengths of a *leeward* boat, she technically infringes 17.2 (in the absence of the exception). The rule now clarifies that W can certainly bear away and gybe, provided she doesn't hit L or cause L to take avoiding action, and provided she continues right into her gybe following her bearing away. If she bears away and then realizes her bow won't clear L's transom and has to pull her bow back up, she risks breaking rule 17.2.

Section A and B Rules In Action

Now that we've had a thorough explanation, let's look at how the rules in Section A and B work in various common situations on the race course.

STARTING MARK SITUATIONS

(For the purposes of these following explanations, it will be assumed that the starting *mark* is surrounded by navigable water, and that the boats are approaching the starting *mark* to *start*. For a full explanation of the rules at starting *marks*, see the discussion of rule 18.1(a), Rounding and Passing Marks and Obstructions, When This Rule Applies.)

UPWIND STARTS (including a discussion on "Barging")

When boats are on their final approach to *start*, rule 18 (Rounding and Passing Marks and Obstructions) does not apply (rule 18.1(a)), meaning that a *leeward*/outside boat (LO) does not have to give a *windward*/inside boat (WI) *room* to pass to *leeward* of the starting *mark* (say a race committee boat). If W tries to squeeze between L and the *mark* and hits L or forces L to bear away to avoid a collision, W has broken rule 11 (On the Same Tack, Overlapped). This is what is called "Barging."

   (Note: the term "Barging" applies to action at the starting *mark*. If, half-

If Barger tries to squeeze in between the race committee boat and L, and hits L or causes L to bear off to avoid a collision, Barger breaks rule 11.

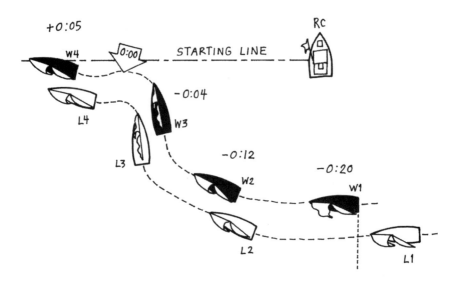

Before the starting signal, even though L becomes overlapped to leeward from clear astern she is permitted to sail up to head to wind provided she gives W room to keep clear. However, after the starting signal, L may not sail above her proper course which, when sailing to windward, is normally close-hauled.

way down the line, a *windward* boat bears off on a *leeward* boat in an attempt not to be over the line early, the windward boat has not "Barged" on the *leeward* boat. They have simply broken rule 11, On the Same Tack, Overlapped.)

> *"I understand that when I'm the windward boat, a leeward boat doesnot have to give me room to pass to leeward of the race committe boat; but does that mean she can do anything she pleases to 'shut the door' on me?"*

Absolutely not. As we've discussed above, the rules in Sections A and B apply. There are no other special rules that apply at this starting *mark*. Therefore, L must behave in exactly the same way that she must behave anywhere else on the race course. Rule 11 (On the Same Tack, Overlapped) gives L the right of way; and L can sail up to head to wind if she pleases, even when only *overlapped* with W by two feet.

However, rule 16.1 (Changing Course) tells L when and how fast she can luff near other boats, i.e. she must give them *room* to *keep clear* whenever she changes course near them. Consider L and W approaching the race commit-tee boat. If L holds her course W will be able to pass between L and the com-

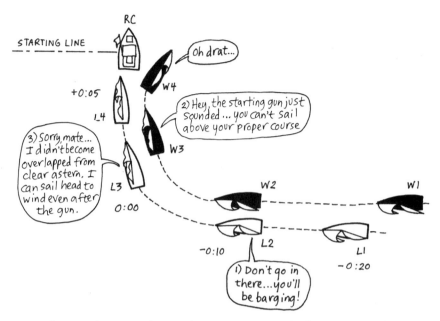

mittee boat without touching either. Just as W sticks her bow in behind the race committee boat, L luffs slowly, but W is unable to *keep clear* due to her proximity to the race committee boat and hits both it and L. L has broken rule 16.1 by changing course (luffing) without giving W *room* to *keep clear*, and rule 14 (Avoiding Contact) by not avoiding a collision with W. If L wants to prevent W from passing between her and the committee boat, she must put herself on a course to "shut the door" before W gets her bow stuck in to leeward of the committee boat.

So the answer to the question is "no," L may not do anything she pleases to "shut the door;" she must comply with the rules of Section A and B fully.

"Now, what about after the starting signal?"

If L is not "limited," then she can continue to sail where she pleases. She is under **no obligation** to turn down to her *proper course* at the starting signal. Therefore, L can sail head to wind after the gun, even if it forces W onto the wrong side of the race committee boat, before turning down to *start* herself!

Now if L is "limited," then she must not sail above her *proper course* after the starting signal. Therefore, if she is "limited," and sailing above close-hauled before the starting signal, she must immediately turn down to her *proper*

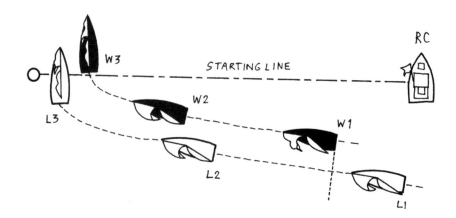

L becomes overlapped to leeward from clear astern on W. Before the starting signal she may sail up to head to wind whenever she pleases. After the starting signal she cannot sail above her proper course, which, when sailing to windward, is normally close-hauled. However, in order to pass the starting mark L's proper course may be to momentarily luff up to head to wind. In this case W must keep clear but L must give her room to do so.

course when the starting signal is made. She does not have to anticipate this obligation; she need only react when the signal is made. However, if LO is sailing her *proper course* after the starting signal, and there is no *room* for WI to squeeze in between her and the committee boat, tough luck on WI; WI is not allowed to go in there.

"Anything special I should know when I'm starting near the leeward end of the starting line?"

Well, one thing that often happens at the leeward end of the starting line for an upwind start is that L gets into a position where she cannot make it around the starting *mark* after the starting signal goes off without sailing above close-hauled.

Remember that in this situation, sailing above close-hauled to get around the *mark* can certainly be considered L's *proper course*, and W must keep clear regardless of how the *overlap* began. However, L has to remember that her luff is limited by rule 16.1 (Changing Course) in that she must give W *room* to *keep clear* when she changes her course. This may be difficult when W is close by or when there is a pack of boats to *windward* of her.

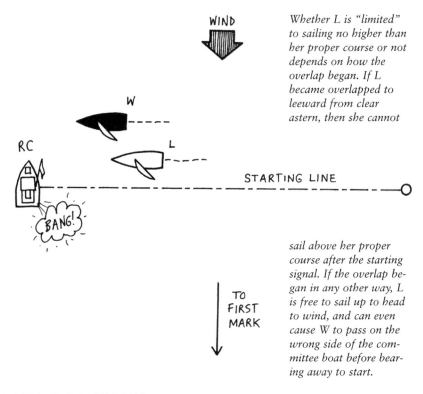

Whether L is "limited" to sailing no higher than her proper course or not depends on how the overlap began. If L became overlapped to leeward from clear astern, then she cannot sail above her proper course after the starting signal. If the overlap began in any other way, L is free to sail up to head to wind, and can even cause W to pass on the wrong side of the committee boat before bearing away to start.

DOWNWIND STARTS

On downwind starts, it is especially critical that boats remember how they became *overlapped*! If L is not "limited," she may sail where she pleases; i.e. she is under no obligation to head for the first *mark* or sail her *proper course* at the gun. W must beware, especially before setting her spinnaker if L has not set her spinnaker yet!

As *overlapped* boats approach one of the starting *marks* (which can include the race committee boat) and the starting gun goes off, remember that L is under **no obligation** to give W *room* at the starting mark! If L is not "limited," then L can force W onto the wrong side of the *mark* before turning down to start herself. And if L **is** "limited," then she need only turn down to her *proper course* (not to the compass course to the first *mark*). As *proper course* is so subjective, especially around a starting line, *windward* boats will be well advised to try and avoid becoming *overlapped* to *windward* of *leeward* boats near the starting *marks*. If ever W feels L is sailing above her *proper course*, she is well advised to *keep clear* and protest.

ON UPWIND LEGS ("Beats")

Again, coming off the starting line it will be essential that L and W remember how they became *overlapped*. If L originally became *overlapped* from *clear astern*, then she is "limited" and cannot sail above her *proper course* (most likely close-hauled). If she is not "limited," she can turn all the way to head to wind and W must *keep clear*.

A common situation on beats is when a *port-tack* boat (PL) tacks on the lee-bow of a *starboard-tack* boat (SW). Because PL did not become *overlapped* from *clear astern*, she is not "limited" and therefore can luff up to head to wind at any time during the *overlap*, even when only *overlapped* with SW by a couple of feet. *Windward* boats will have to be a bit more cautious when rolling over *leeward* boats in this situation.

If P tacks in front of S, and S chooses to *overlap* her to leeward, then S must comply with rule 15 (Acquiring Right of Way) and furthermore must not sail above her *proper course* during the *overlap* unless she chooses to luff and pass astern of P (rule 17.1, On the Same Tack; Proper Course).

 "Can you walk me through how the rules apply to a Slam Dunk?"

Sure. The Slam Dunk is an aggressive and often contentious tactic used upwind by S to gain control over P. It is more commonly used in match and team racing than in fleet racing. The relationship between S and P is rapidly changing in this maneuver such that the rules analysis gets quite complicated. However, the addition of the last sentence in rule 17.1 (On the Same Tack; Proper Course) in the 2001-04 RRS will greatly discourage S from using this tactic (see pertinent discussion of rule 17.1 on page 132). See the illustration opposite for a detailed analysis of the "Slam Dunk."

ON DOWNWIND LEGS (Reaches & Runs)

L and W are sailing down a reach. L did not become *overlapped* from *clear astern* and therefore L is free to sail where she pleases, subject to rule 16.1 (Changing Course). W begins to pass L and L luffs to prevent her from doing so. W turns more quickly and "breaks" the *overlap*. W then turns back down, thereby creating an *overlap* once again (being sure to *keep clear* under rule 11, On the Same Tack, Overlapped, and remembering that her actions have

THE SLAM DUNK

POSITION 1: *P has borne away to pass astern of S. The moment P is steering a course to clear S's transom, S luffs to begin tacking. As long as when she luffs, S does not cause P to have to immediately change her course to continue to keep clear, S does not break rule 16.2.*

POSITION 2: *S is not past head to wind and is therefore still on starboard tack; P must still keep clear of her under rule 10.*

POSITION 3: *S has just passed head to wind. She is now on port tack, i.e. the same tack as P, and P is clear astern. S must keep clear of P under rule 13 until she is close-hauled, and then under rule 11 as the windward boat. P, now the right-of-way boat, does not need to give S room to keep clear under rule 15 if she maintains her straight-line course because she acquired the right of way by S's actions. However, if P changes course toward S, she is required by rule 16.1 to give S room to keep clear (i.e. not to prevent S from being able to keep clear or cause her to make an unseamanlike maneuver to do so).*

Furthermore, if P becomes overlapped to leeward of S before S is down to a close-hauled course, P is not "limited" under rule 17.1, because S is required by rule 13 to keep clear of her. Therefore P can sail up to head to wind, provided she complies with rule 16.1. If S is on a close-hauled course when P becomes overlapped, then P is "limited" to sailing no higher than her proper course (most likely a close-hauled course) for the duration of the overlap because she became overlapped from clear astern.

POSITION 4: *P has become overlapped with S before S is on a close-hauled course; and P has luffed above her proper course towards S. Rule 17.1 does not apply. Whether or not she broke rule 16.1 will be decided by the protest committee based on their determination of whether P gave S enough space and time to cease her turn towards P and begin her turn away from P in a seamanlike way. If the collision was avoidable, P and/or S may be found to have broken rule 14; and if there was damage, P could get penalized under rule 14(b).*

NOTE: *If, in position 3, P and S were overlapped the moment S passed head to wind, then P would not be "limited" under rule 17.1, and would be permitted to sail up to head to wind provided she gave S room to keep clear under rule 16.1. Again rule 15 wouldn't apply to P; but P could still be penalized under rule 14(b) if the contact caused damage.*

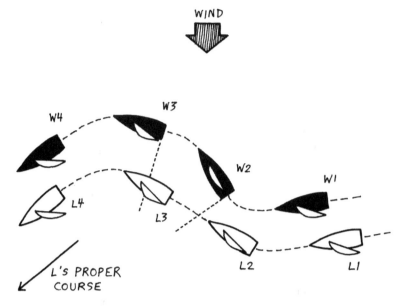

In this situation it is W's luffing that breaks the overlap and her bearing away that caus-es the overlap to begin again. When L acquires the right of way at position 3, she does not need to give W room to keep clear because she acquires right of way as a result of W's actions. However, rule 17.1 is not concerned with how the overlap was established. Therefore, because L became overlapped from clear astern, she must immediately bear away and sail no higher than her proper course during the overlap.

given L the right of way such that rule 15, Acquiring Right of Way, does not require L to "give" W *room* to *keep clear!*). Now, L has become *overlapped* to *leeward* from *clear astern* and therefore is required to immediately comply with her rule 17.1 (On the Same Tack; Proper Course) "limitation" and turn back down to her *proper course*, which includes gybing when that is neces-sary for L to sail her *proper course* to the next *mark*.

Anytime a boat becomes *overlapped* to *leeward* from *clear astern* within two of her lengths of a *windward* boat, she is not permitted to sail above her *proper course*. However, prior to becoming *overlapped*, L is free to sail where she pleases. Therefore, the moment the *overlap* begins, the course she will sail to *finish* as soon as possible will include the course she is on at that moment. If she must then bear away to a lower course to get to the next *mark* and ulti-mately the finishing line as soon as possible, she must do so immediately. Rule 15 (Acquiring Right of Way) builds in a cushion to protect W while L is bear-ing away.

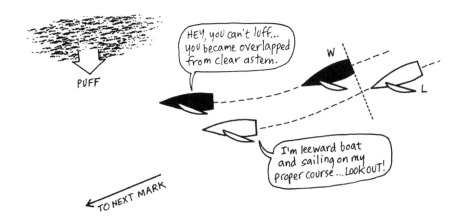

L is slowly luffing up to a new proper course in order to get to a puff of wind sooner. Because she is not sailing above her proper course, she is not breaking rule 17.1; and because she is giving W room to keep clear, she is not breaking rule 16.1. W must keep clear under rule 11.

Here are three common situations where a boat can catch up from astern and sail in to *leeward* of a boat ahead and be "free" to sail up to head to wind if she chooses, subject to rules 15 (Acquiring Right of Way) and 16.1 (Changing Course):

1) The boat behind (BL) *overlaps* the boat ahead (AW) more than two of her lengths to *leeward* of AW. Rule 17.1 (On the Same Tack; Proper Course) does not apply because the *overlap* did not begin when BL was within two of her lengths of AW. Now BL turns toward AW and maintains her *overlap* as she gets within two lengths. BL is not "limited" and can sail up to head to wind, even when she may be *overlapped* with AW by just two feet. As a defense, AW can "break" the *overlap* by heading up just before BL comes within two lengths of her; and then "create it" again by bearing off thereby causing BL to "become **overlapped** within two of her hull lengths" of AW.

2) BL overlaps AW to *leeward* within two of her lengths. At that point BL is "limited" to sailing no higher than her *proper course*. BL then gybes and gybes right back, maintaining her "overlap" throughout the maneuver. Now, BL is not "limited" and can sail up to head to wind, even when she may be *overlapped* with AW by just two feet. The reason is that when

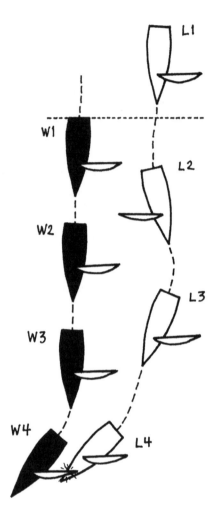

In position 1, L is clear astern of W. When L becomes overlapped on W she is "limited" under rule 17.1 to sailing no higher than her proper course.

In position 2, L gybes so that the two boats are on opposite tacks and rule 17.1 no longer applies.

In position 3, L gybes back, becoming overlapped again on W, but this time not from clear astern; therefore L is not "limited" and can sail up to head to wind if she pleases.

In position 4, L luffs, giving W room to keep clear under rule 16.1. W fails to keep clear thereby breaking rule 11.

BL gybed the first time, she became on opposite *tacks* with AW and therefore the term "*overlap*" did not apply (see the definition *Clear Astern* and *Clear Ahead; Overlap*). When she gybed back onto the same tack as AW, she was instantaneously *overlapped*, i.e. she did not become *overlapped* from *clear astern*. Therefore she was not "limited" by rule 17.1 (On the Same Tack; Proper Course). However, BL did acquire the right of way by her own actions, so she must initially give AW *room* to *keep clear* under rule 15 (Acquiring Right of Way); and when she changes her course toward AW, she must give AW **additional** *room* to *keep clear* under rule 16.1 (Changing Course).

3) Halfway down a run, a *port-tack* boat (PL) is converging with a *starboard-tack* boat (SW). PL, after passing very close astern of SW, turns down thereby creating an "overlap" on SW's *leeward* side (note the terms *clear ahead*, *clear astern* and *overlap* do not apply because SW and PL are on opposite tacks and not near a *mark*). Maintaining her "overlap," PL gybes. When her boom crosses her centerline and she is on the same *tack* as SW, the two boats are instantaneously *overlapped*. Therefore PL is not "limited" and can sail up to head to wind, even when she may be *overlapped* with SW by just two feet. However, the same "limitations" under rules 15 (Acquiring Right of Way) and 16.1 (Changing Course) apply to PL as in the example above; and SW can employ the same tactic as in #1 above of breaking the *overlap* with PL just as PL is about to gybe and then re-creating it the moment PL gybes.

8

Part 2, Section C
When Boats Meet at Marks and Obstructions

SECTION C contains the rules that apply when boats are rounding or passing *marks* and *obstructions* on the race course (rules 18 and 19). The purpose of these rules is to allow for safe and orderly sailing when boats converge at *marks* and *obstructions*. In order for that to happen, there are times when a right-of-way boat may find herself with a **limit** on her right of way or a temporary requirement to give *room* to a give-way boat. An example is when a *leeward* boat is on the outside of a *windward* boat while rounding a *mark*; the *leeward*/outside boat may have to give that *windward*/inside boat room to round the *mark* (rule 18.2(a), Giving Room; Keeping Clear). Another example is when a *starboard-tack* or *leeward* boat is on the inside at a *mark*, and she must gybe to sail her *proper course*, she cannot sail any farther from the *mark* than needed to sail her *proper course* (rule 18.4, Gybing). Finally, there are times when a boat may need to tack to avoid hitting an *obstruction*, but other boats are too close for her to tack without fouling them. Rule 19 (Room to Tack at an Obstruction) gives **special permission** in certain circumstances that permit the boat to tack.

PREAMBLE TO SECTION C

To the extent that a Section C rule conflicts with a rule in Section A or B, the Section C rule takes precedence.

Part 2 is clearly constructed so that in the event one rule conflicts with another it is easy to know which one takes precedence. When a Section C rule is not in conflict with a Section A or B rule, then the A and B rules continue to apply along with the C rule. However, when a Section C rule explicitly provides a requirement that conflicts with a requirement in a rule in Section A or B, the C rule takes precedence. Also, some Section C rules simply state that some A or B rules do not apply while the C rule does.

For instance, a *leeward* boat (L) and a *windward* boat (W) on *port-tack* are approaching a *mark* to be left to port. When 20 boat-lengths from the *mark*, the boats are not yet "about to round or pass" the *mark*, and therefore rule 18 (Rounding and Passing Marks and Obstructions) in Section C is not yet in effect. W must *keep clear* of L under rule 11 (On the Same Tack, Overlapped) which is in Section A. When the boats are within two lengths of the *mark*, they are now "about to round or pass" it and rule 18 (in Section C) now applies. Rule 18.2(a) (Giving Room; Keeping Clear) requires L, as the outside boat, to give W *room* to round or pass the *mark* because she's the inside boat. This requirement clearly conflicts with rule 11 (in Section A) and therefore it takes precedence for as long as it applies.

RULE 18 – ROUNDING AND PASSING MARKS AND OBSTRUCTIONS

In rule 18, *room* is *room* for an inside boat to round or pass between an outside boat and a *mark* or *obstruction*, including *room* to tack or gybe when either is a normal part of the manoeuvre.

Rule 18.1 – When This Rule Applies

Rule 18 applies when boats are about to round or pass a *mark* they are required to leave on the same side, or an *obstruction* on the same side, until they have passed it.

This is the rule that governs boats when they are rounding or passing *marks* or *obstructions*. It is commonly called the "buoy room" rule, but that is only half right. Rule 18 applies whether you are rounding or passing a racing *mark*, a breakwater, a right-of-way boat in your race such as a *starboard-tack* boat or even an iceberg that has floated onto the course. (See ISAF Cases 11 and 41 and US SAILING Appeals 6, 7 and 36.)

Though rule 18 is the longest rule in Part 2, it is very clearly written and fits very sensibly with the basic right-of-way rules in Section A. Again, the key to understanding it is not to try to memorize its every detail, but to stand back and see how the rule is trying to create orderly sailing when boats converge at *marks* and *obstructions*.

RULE 18 is broken into the following four distinct sections:

18.2(a) .... when the boats are *overlapped* at the *mark* or *obstruction*.

18.2(c) .... when the boats are not *overlapped* at the *mark* or *obstruction*.

18.3 and 18.4 when the boats tack or gybe at the *mark* or *obstruction*.

18.5 .... when the *obstruction* is a continuing one.

"How do I know on which side the mark or obstruction is to be left?"

Good question. First of all, "side" in rule 18.1 refers to the boat's side, not the *mark's* or *obstruction's* side. Therefore, when two boats are rounding or passing a *mark* going in the opposite direction (as they might when they are in different races using the same *mark* but leaving it on opposite sides as in ISAF Case 26), or are passing an *obstruction* going in the opposite direction (as they might when they are circling around a race committee boat or spectator boat during pre-start maneuvering), rule 18 does **not** apply, and the rules of Section A and B apply.

As for which way to "leave" a *mark*, the sailing instructions must indicate that (definition *Mark*, rule 28.1, Sailing the Course and rule J2.1(5), Sailing Instruction Contents). As for which way an *obstruction* will be "left," that will become increasingly more evident by the courses of the boats as they approach the *obstruction* at the time of the incident.

"To whom is rule 18 talking?"

Rule 18 is "talking" to all the boats involved in the rounding or passing maneuver, but fundamentally it is talking to the outside or *clear astern* boats. As boats get closer to a *mark* or *obstruction*, the "force" of rule 18 begins to reach out to them. Outside and *clear astern* boats, whether on *port tack* or *starboard tack* and whether *leeward* or *windward* boats, must start preparing for their upcoming obligations to the inside or *clear ahead* boats.

Remember, rule 18 is a rule of exception. In some situations at *marks* and *obstructions*, an outside boat otherwise holding right of way must nonethe-

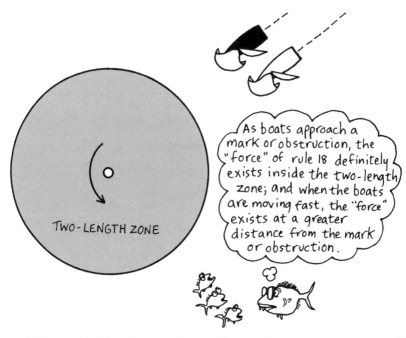

As boats approach a mark or obstruction, the "force" of rule 18 definitely exists inside the two-length zone; and when the boats are moving fast, the "force" exists at a greater distance from the mark or obstruction.

TWO-LENGTH ZONE

less yield to an inside give-way boat and even change course to move far enough away from the *mark* or *obstruction* to give the give-way inside boat the *room* she needs to round or pass it. A *starboard-tack* boat with a *port-tack* boat inside and a *leeward* boat with a *windward* boat inside are examples of this sort of situation that put a "limit" on the right-of-way boat. So, even though you are the right-of-way boat approaching a *mark* or *obstruction*, when the "force" of rule 18 begins to reach you, your right of way may be temporarily "limited."

 "As I approach a mark or obstruction, when does the 'force' of rule 18 begin to apply to me?"

The "force" of rule 18 begins to apply when you are "about to round or pass" the *mark* or *obstruction*. ISAF Case 84 reads, "The phrase 'about to round or pass' has never been defined precisely, nor can it be. In approaching a mark, there is no exact point at which a boat becomes 'about to round or pass' it. Almost always, a boat two hull lengths from a mark is about to round or pass it, but this is sometimes so at a greater distance too. Not only is the distance from the mark a factor, but the boat's speed is also important, and other factors such as the conditions of wind and current and the amount of sail han-

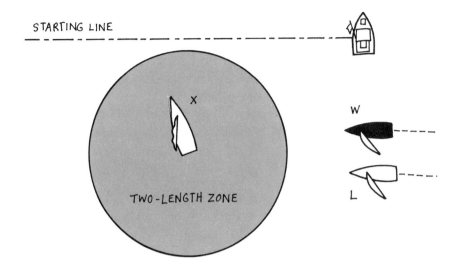

X is clear ahead of both L and W; therefore, as a right-of-way boat, she is an obstruction to both. The "force" of rule 18 exists within the two-length zone around X, but it is L who gets to choose on which side of X she will pass. If she chooses to pass to leeward of X, rule 18.2(a) requires her to give W room to do likewise if W also wants to pass to leeward of X.

dling required before or during the rounding may also be relevant. Moreover, the nearer the boat is to the mark the more definitely she is about to round or pass it. The answer to the question depends upon the particular circumstances of each situation." (See ISAF Case 94.)

So the "force" of rule 18 is "on you" when you are two of your hull lengths from the *mark* or *obstruction*, and at times even farther away, e.g., if you are on a catamaran going 20 miles per hour or on an offshore boat with a huge spinnaker to get down. Remember, before you are "about to round or pass," you have your basic right-of-way rights; i.e. if you are a *leeward* boat, a *windward* boat must *keep clear*, etc.

Though a boat is "about to pass" an *obstruction* when two lengths away, the "force" of rule 18 does not grow strong until it is evident on which side of the *obstruction* the right-of-way boat chooses to go. So on a starting line for example, as two *overlapped* boats approach a boat *clear ahead* (an *obstruction*), rule 18 begins to apply when the first boat gets to two of her lengths from the *obstruction*. At that point the boats need to be *overlapped* in order for either one to be entitled to *room* to pass the *obstruction*. But the *leeward* boat, as right-of-way boat, gets to **choose** on which side she wants to pass the *obstruction*. The moment it's evident that L will pass to *leeward* of the *obstruction*, the full force of rule 18 is on and W is entitled to *room* to pass to leeward also, if she chooses. (See US SAILING Appeal 7, 36 and ISAF Case 41.)

WHEN THE BOATS ARE OVERLAPPED

 "When the 'force' is on the boats, what rights and requirements do the inside and outside boats have?"

That's the key question, and it's covered in rule 18.2(a). Let's get into it.

Rule 18.2 – Giving Room; Keeping Clear

Rule 18.2(a) – Overlapped – Basic Rule

When boats are *overlapped* the outside boat shall give the inside boat *room* to round or pass the *mark* or *obstruction*, and if the inside boat has right of way the outside boat shall also *keep clear*. Other parts of rule 18 contain exceptions to this rule.

To possibly make it easier to understand the various rights and requirements contained in this rule, I have broken it out below.

The rule is "talking" only to overlapped boats:

Rule 18.2(a) starts off, *"When boats are **overlapped**..."* Therefore, rule 18.2(a) deals only with boats that are *overlapped*. (Rule 18.2(c) deals with boats that are not *overlapped*.)

Remember, a boat is *overlapped* with another if her bow is on or across a line drawn abeam through the aftermost point of the other boat's hull and equipment in normal position. Also, two boats that otherwise are not *overlapped* suddenly become *overlapped* when a boat **in between them** *overlaps* both of them. So if you are approaching a *mark* to be left to port and are just *overlapped* on the port transom of the boat ahead of you, and she is just *overlapped* on the port transom of the boat ahead of her, you are technically *overlapped* with the boat ahead of her. Therefore you are entitled to *room* under rule 18.2(a) from both boats if you are *overlapped* when the **farthest boat ahead** arrives at the *two-length zone*.

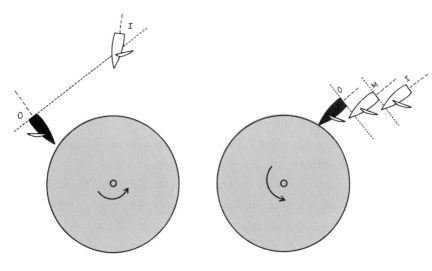

Even though I is well behind O, I has an inside overlap when O reaches the two-length zone; therefore O must keep clear of I and give I room until both boats have passed the mark.

M is in between O and I and overlaps both of them; therefore, I is technically overlapped with O when O reaches the two-length zone. O and M must keep clear of I and give I room until all three boats have passed the mark.

Also remember that, by definition, two boats *overlap* when the bow of one is over the line drawn through the aftermost part of the other, even when the boats are a quarter of a mile apart; and that when rule 18 applies, the boats are considered *overlapped* even when they are on opposite *tacks*. This becomes important as boats approach the leeward *mark* on opposite *tacks* and widely differing angles. (See definition *Clear Astern* and *Clear Ahead*; *Overlap*.)

"Are there any limitations on obtaining an overlap and becoming entitled to the rights in rule 18.2(a)?"

Yes, and rule 18.2(a) announces that by saying, *"Other parts of rule 18 contain exceptions to this rule."* There are three:

1) the boat astern cannot obtain an inside *overlap* if the boat ahead reaches the *two-length zone clear ahead* of the boat astern (18.2(c));

2) the outside boat must be physically able to give the inside boat *room* (18.2(e)); and

3) at a continuing *obstruction*, there must be *room* for the boat astern to

pass between the other boat and the *obstruction* at the moment the *overlap* begins (18.5).

Up to 1965, a boat *clear astern* could get a legal inside *overlap* as long as it was (a) in time to enable the outside boat(s) to give *room*; (b) before the boat ahead changed her course in the act of rounding; and (c) before any part of the boat ahead came abreast of the *mark* or *obstruction*. Things were often a tad out of control as boats came barreling up from astern yelling for "buoy room" at the last second.

In 1965 the rule writers took a creative step. Realizing that there ought to be some cutoff "point" after which a boat *clear astern* could not obtain an inside *overlap*, they devised a safety zone now called the *two-length zone*, which has proved to work very effectively. And because the "point" can be in any direction from the *mark* or *obstruction*, the *two-length zone* is an imaginary area with the *mark* or *obstruction* in the center and having a radius of two of the **nearer boat's hull lengths;** for instance, 48 feet in a J/24 (see the definition *Two-Length Zone*). Note the fact that it is the nearer boat's hull lengths. This becomes important when the boats are different sizes.

Rule 18.2(c) starts off, "*If a boat is **clear ahead** at the time she reaches the **two-length zone**, the boat **clear astern** shall thereafter **keep clear.**"* So the game ends at the *two-length zone*. If you are catching up from astern but don't get the inside *overlap* before the boat ahead of you gets to two of her hull lengths from the *mark*, then you are not entitled to the rights in rule 18.2(a) and must *keep clear* of her under rule 18.2(c). If you do get the *overlap* before she gets to the *two-length zone*, then you are entitled to the rights in rule 18.2(a) and 18.2(b).

 "What if I physically can't give room to the boat that just obtained the inside overlap on me?"

That's the second exception to rule 18.2(a). When a boat obtains an inside *overlap* from *clear astern*, the boat ahead has a "protective shield" if she needs it. When a boat gets an *overlap* at the zero-moment before you enter the *two-length zone*, she becomes entitled to *room* under rule 18.2(a) as an inside boat. However, you are not required to anticipate her arrival. There are times when you may be physically unable to give her the *room* she needs to round or pass the *mark* based on your situation at that moment.

Rule 18.2(e) (Overlap Rights) says, *"If the outside boat is unable to give room when an overlap begins, rules 18.2(a) and 18.2(b) do not apply."* In this situation, she is not entitled to *room* and the applicable rules of Section A and B apply. If she is a right-of-way boat, she must comply with rule 15 (Acquiring Right of Way) which means she won't get inside at the *mark* because if the outside boat could have created enough *room* to do so, she would have done so in the first place. And if she is a give-way boat, she must *keep clear.*

One example of where this situation might occur is a tightly packed *mark* rounding in light air where a boat astern gets an inside *overlap* on a boat that is two-and-a-half boat-lengths from the *mark*, but there's just no way the outside boat can get everyone else outside of her to move away from the *mark* in time to create *room* for the new inside boat. Another example is when two boats are going so fast that by the time the outside boat can react to her new obligation and make the *room*, the inside boat is already past the *mark* on the wrong side. Twelve knots of boat-speed equals about 20 feet per second, so on a windy reach a Hobie 18 will chew up two boat-lengths in less than two seconds!

"What if at a windward mark the boat ahead of me, or overlapped outside of me, didn't reach the two-length zone clear ahead of me, but instead they approached me on the opposite tack and then tacked inside the two-length zone?"

If a boat tacks inside the *two-length zone* and is *clear ahead* of you when she completes her tack, you can obtain an inside *overlap* and become entitled to *room* under rule 18.2(a) provided the outside boat can physically give you *room* (rule 18.2(e), Overlap Rights). And if a boat tacks within the *two-length zone* into an outside *overlap* on you, it must give you *room* at the *mark* under rule 18.2(a) as well.

A possible scenario is two boats (P and S) approaching a windward *mark* to be left to port on opposite tacks. S is about two lengths below the *starboard-tack* layline; P is close to the *port-tack* layline. When S nears the *port-tack* layline she tacks. When she passes head to wind she is within the *two-*

length zone. She completes her tack *clear ahead* of P. P, moving faster, *overlaps* S to windward about one length from the *mark.* Or in a similar approach, when S completes her tack she is *overlapped* to *leeward* of P. In both scenarios, S is required to give P *room* at the *mark.*

The reason is that rule 18.2(a) makes no reference to the *two-length zone.* It just talks about *overlapped* boats. (Rules 18.2(b) and 18.2(c) contain references to the *two-length zone* but they do not apply in the scenario described here.) S and P are *overlapped* with S on the outside, rule 18.2(a) requires the outside boat to give the inside boat *room,* and, provided S can physically give P *room,* no exceptions in rule 18 apply.

Let's look at what specific rights and requirements the inside and outside boats have under rule 18.2(a):

When the inside boat has the right of way, rule 18.2(a) (Overlapped – Basic Rule) requires the outside boat to both give the inside boat *room* and to *keep clear.*

"Why does rule 18.2(a) require an outside give-way boat to both 'give room' and 'keep clear;' it seems redundant?"

I agree that on first read it appears redundant. But the reason is that when I have to *keep clear* of you, all I have to do is make sure you have enough space to sail your "straight-ahead" course with no apprehension of hitting me. But when you are rounding a *mark* you are going to need **more** space than that in order for your boat to turn without hitting me. The preamble to rule 18 states that "***room* is *room* for an inside boat to round or pass between an outside boat and a *mark* or *obstruction*...**" Therefore it is necessary for the rule to require outside give-way boats to both *keep clear* and give *room.*

"I understand that when the inside boat also has the right of way, the outside boat must both 'give her room' and 'keep clear' of her, but does that mean that the inside boat can sail wherever she pleases?"

No. It means that the inside right-of-way boat can sail her course around or past the *mark* without the need to avoid the outside boat, subject to either of the two "limits" she may have on sailing above her *proper course.*

When boats are about to round or pass a mark, i.e. when rule 18 applies, the term "overlap" applies to boats on opposite tacks. Therefore, X and Y are "overlapped" at the mark. When the inside boat has the right of way and when she must gybe to sail her proper course, rule 18.4 requires her not to sail any farther from the mark than needed to sail her proper course until she gybes. By not gybing, i.e. sailing her proper course, X breaks rule 18.4.

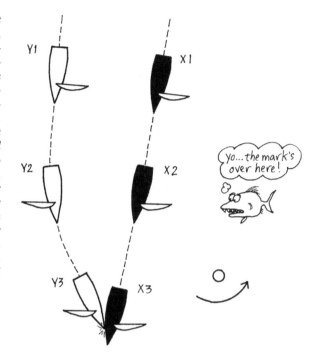

Let's look at those two "limits."

- One such "limit" is in rule 17.1 (On the Same Tack; Proper Course) which limits L to sailing no higher than her *proper course* when she becomes *overlapped* from *clear astern*. Therefore, at a windward *mark*, if LI (*leeward*/inside) becomes *overlapped* on the inside of a boat that has just tacked in front of her inside the *two-length zone*, LI must sail her *proper course* around the *mark*. Note that, in this situation, her *proper course* may be to sail head to wind momentarily to get up and around the *mark*.

- The other "limit" is in rule 18.4 (Rounding and Passing Marks and Obstructions, Gybing) which says that if an inside *overlapped* right-of-way boat must gybe to sail her *proper course* around the *mark*, she is required to sail no higher than her *proper course* until she gybes; i.e. she can't continue on straight past the *mark* or luff away from the *mark* if that takes her farther from the *mark* than necessary to sail her *proper course*. (For a full discussion see the explanation of rule 18.4.) This "limit" commonly arises at offwind *marks* whenever L or S is on the inside and her *proper course* is to gybe around the mark.

In fact, when rounding a *mark*, the only time an inside right-of-way boat can sail higher than her *proper course* is when she is a *leeward* boat rounding a *mark* that she **doesn't** have to gybe around to sail her *proper course* (typically a windward *mark* or a gybe *mark* going onto a very broad reach or run), **and** she did not become *overlapped* to *leeward*/inside from *clear astern* within two boat-lengths of WO (the *windward*/outside boat).

On the other hand, an inside right-of-way boat is allowed to swing wide and then cut close around the *mark* (often called a "tactical rounding"). The reason is because inside right-of-way boats **always** have the right to sail their *proper courses* when rounding or passing *marks*, and outside boats must *keep clear* of them. Rounding this way allows boats to make a smooth turn and will get them into the most tactically desirable position (clear air, ability to give bad air to boats behind, ability to tack, etc.) as they begin the beat, most of which will also help them to *finish* as soon as possible (see definition *Proper Course*).

Now let's take a look at the situation where the outside boat is the right-of-way boat:

When the outside boat has the right-of-way, rule 18.2(a) (Overlapped – Basic Rule) requires the outside boat to give the inside boat *room* to round or pass the *mark* or *obstruction*.

Clearly this requirement conflicts with rule 10 (On Opposite Tacks) and rule 11 (On the Same Tack, Overlapped) in Section A, and therefore it takes precedence for as long as rule 18.2(a) applies. In other words, when a *starboard-tack* (S) and a *port-tack* boat (P), or a *leeward* (L) and a *windward* boat (W), are rounding a *mark* with P or W on the inside, S or L has a "temporary requirement" to give P or W *room* until the boats have passed the *mark*; at that point S and L will get their full rights back under rules 10 or 11.

Note that rule 18.2(a) does not shift the right of way from the *leeward*/outside boat to the *windward*/inside boat. Approaching the *mark* or *obstruction*, W must keep clear of L under rule 11. When they are "about to round or pass" the *mark* or *obstruction*, L becomes required to provide W *room* under rule 18.2(a) **only if W needs the *room*.** ISAF Case 70 reads, "In this incident rule 11 did not cease to apply; it continued to obligate W to keep clear of L unless she was prevented from doing so by L's failure to give her sufficient room. Although rule 18 applied, because the boats were 'about to round or pass' the mark, and rule 18.2(a) gave W the right to the room she needed to round or pass it, the fact was that she already had this room before and at the time of contact. The boats were within the two-length zone, but this did not give W any additional rights. She therefore broke rule 11 by failing to keep clear of L."

"When inside boats do need 'room' and are entitled to have it, how much 'room' can they have?"

Room is defined as *"the space a boat needs in the existing conditions while manoeuvring promptly in a seamanlike way."* (See the preamble to rule 18 and the discussion of definition *Room*, including the excerpt from ISAF Case 21 that gives the definitive interpretation of *room*.) Therefore, if the inside boat is a give-way boat, she must confine her rounding to only the *room* the outside boat is required to give her under rule 18.2(a).

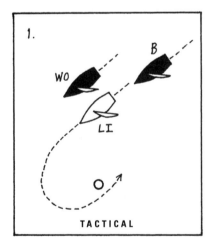
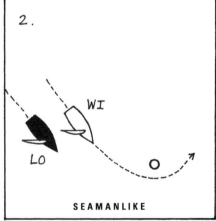

When overlapped boats are rounding a mark, the inside boat will either have the right or way or not; when not overlapped, the boat clear ahead will have the right of way. When the inside or clear ahead boat has the right of way, the other boat is required to "keep clear" during the passing maneuver; therefore the inside or clear ahead boat can make a "tactical rounding" (swing wide-cut close). When the inside boat does not have the right of way, the outside boat is required to give only "room," i.e. only the space the inside boat needs to make a "seamanlike rounding" (approximately equal distance on either side of the mark).

In essence, *room* is the space needed to sail between the *mark* and the outside boat in a safe and seamanlike way (often called a "seamanlike rounding"). Clearly, the rougher the conditions or the more difficult the boat handling requirements are, the more space a boat will need. *Room* does not include all the space the inside boat might like to take to make a tactically desirable "swing wide-cut close" type rounding, though in actual practice most outside boats are a little more forgiving. It is for this reason that the courses inside boats are permitted to sail around a *mark* differ depending on whether they are a right-of-way boat or a give-way boat.

Note the preamble to rule 18 that reads, "*In rule 18, **room** is **room** for an inside boat to round or pass between an outside boat and a **mark** or **obstruction**, including room to tack or gybe when either is a normal part of the manoeuvre.*" Therefore, an outside boat must be sure to leave enough space for the inside boat's stern to swing as they tack or gybe around the *mark*.

 "Does that mean that if I'm a windward / inside boat coming into the windward mark, I can tack with no regard for the outside boat?"

No; it's a bit trickier than that, because rule 18 ceases to apply altogether when boats are on opposite *tacks* (rule 18.1(b), When This Rule Applies). Consider two *overlapped port-tack* boats approaching a *windward* mark to be left to port. The inside *windward* boat (W) begins to tack to round the *mark*. The *leeward* boat (L) must leave *room* for the *windward* boat's stern to swing. But

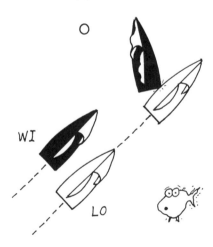

LO must give WI room at the mark under rule 18.2(a), which includes room to tack when tacking is a normal part of the rounding maneuver. However, the moment WI passes head to wind, she and LO are on opposite tacks and rule 18 shuts off. At that point rule 13 requires WI to keep clear of LO while tacking; and rule 14 always requires both boats to avoid contact. If the boats touch the moment after WI passes head to wind, both boats could be penalized: LO for not providing enough space a moment sooner when the boats were on the same tack; and WI for failing to keep clear of, and hitting, a right of way boat.

the moment W passes head to wind, she is on *starboard tack*. Because W and L are now on opposite *tacks*, rule 18 turns off and the boats are governed by the Section A rules. Under rule 13 (While Tacking), until W is down to a close-hauled course, she must *keep clear* of L. If W's stern touches L's side a second after W passes head to wind, it is fairly clear that W did not have *room* to tack a second before when she was head to wind and therefore still under rule 18. Therefore L breaks rule 18.2(a). But, at the moment of contact, rule 18 did not apply and therefore W breaks rule 13. And she will most likely not be exonerated under rule 64.1(b) (Penalties and Exoneration) as it will be difficult for W to satisfy the protest committee that she was compelled to hit L by L's breach of rule 18.2(a); W could have most likely slowed her turn in order to have avoided contact. The bottom line in this situation is that L should be sure to give W enough space to tack without hitting her; and W should be careful not to hit L while she is tacking.

Note a boat is not entitled to more space than usual just because her crew is short-handed or inexperienced. US SAILING Appeal 77 addresses this head on by saying, "Neither the experience of IW's crew nor their number is relevant in determining 'room'… the interpretation of 'seamanlike way' must be based on the boat-handling that can reasonably be expected from a crew with average experience and of appropriate number for the boat."

Also note that when a give-way boat sails farther from the *mark* than allowed under *room*, the rules of Section C no longer apply to her and she is

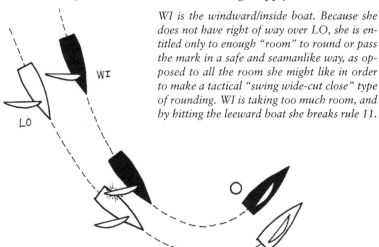

WI *is the windward/inside boat. Because she does not have right of way over LO, she is entitled only to enough "room" to round or pass the mark in a safe and seamanlike way, as opposed to all the room she might like in order to make a tactical "swing wide-cut close" type of rounding. WI is taking too much room, and by hitting the leeward boat she breaks rule 11.*

subject to the rules in Sections A and B. For instance, when a *windward/*inside boat is slow in coming up to close-hauled around a *mark* and contact occurs between her and a *leeward/*outside boat, and it is found that she took more *room* than was needed to round the *mark*, the Section A and B rules apply and WI breaks rule 11 (On the Same Tack, Overlapped). (See US SAILING Appeal 20.)

"Is it true that a boat with right of way can change course to round a mark as quickly as she wants, with no regard to boats overlapped with her (other than not causing damage to them)?"

Essentially yes! Rule 18.2(d) (Changing Course to Round or Pass) gives right-of-way boats this right (with a couple of exceptions discussed below).

Rule 18.2(d) – Changing Course to Round or Pass

When rule 18 applies between two boats and the right-of-way boat is changing course to round or pass a *mark*, rule 16 does not apply between her and the other boat.

Rule 18.2(d) provides the only exception to rule 16 (Changing Course). This is a common sense exception. If you have the right of way at a *mark*, you should be able to sail your course around that *mark* without concern for the boats required to *keep clear* of you. And those boats should be able to easily anticipate the course you are going to sail around the *mark*.

Remember that you are a "right-of-way" boat when another boat is required to "*keep clear*" of you (preamble to Part 2, Section A – When Boats Meet, Right of Way). That is one reason rules 18.2(a), (b) and (c) (Giving Room; Keeping Clear) use the term *keep clear*. It sets up the exception to rule 16 (Changing Course) in rule 18.2(d).

Remember also that rule 14 (Avoiding Contact) always applies, so even right-of-way boats rounding *marks* must be careful to avoid any contact, and particularly any contact that causes damage.

Note that the exception to rule 16 (Changing Course) in rule 18.2(d) only applies when rule 18 (Rounding and Passing Marks and Obstructions) applies. For instance, when boats are approaching a starting *mark* surrounded by water (like a race committee boat) to *start*, rule 18 does **not** apply (rule

18.1(a), When This Rule Applies). Therefore rule 16 does apply and right-of-way boats must give *keep clear* boats *room* to *keep clear* **anytime** they change course. The same applies at a windward *mark* when a *starboard-tack* boat (S) is bearing away around the *mark* and a *port-tack* boat (P) is approaching the *mark*. Because the boats are on opposite *tacks* and the *proper course* for P is to tack, rule 18 does not apply (18.1(b), When This Rule Applies), and therefore rule 16 does apply to S; i.e. S must be careful as she changes course near P (see discussion of rule 16).

Finally, note that this exception to rule 16 (Changing Course) only applies at *marks*; i.e. it does not apply at *obstructions*.

Let's look at some examples of this rule 16 (Changing Course) exception in action:

- A and B, two *port-tack* boats not *overlapped*, are approaching a leeward *mark* to be left to port. A reaches the *two-length zone* clear ahead of B. As A swings wide to make a "tactical" (swing wide-cut close) rounding, B puts her bow in between A and the *mark*. As A changes course to round the *mark*, B yells that A must give her *room* to *keep clear* under rule 16 (Changing Course) and that B can't *keep clear* of A due to the proximity of the *mark* on her port side.

  B is wrong. Rule 18 applies (because the boats are about to round or pass the *mark* on the same required side) and A is the right-of-way boat under both rule 18.2(c) (Not Overlapped at the Zone) and rule 11 (On the Same Tack, Overlapped). Therefore, rule 16 (Changing Course) does not apply to A, and she is free to change course without the need to give B *room* to *keep clear* of her.

- L and W, two *overlapped starboard-tack* boats, are approaching a gybe *mark* to be left to port. They enter the *two-length zone overlapped*. L then bears away sharply to gybe around the *mark* and her transom hits W's leeward side with no damage. Again, rule 16 (Changing Course) is "turned off" in this situation by rule 18.2(d). W has broken rule 18.2(a) (Overlapped – Basic Rule) and rule 11 (On the Same Tack, Overlapped), and rule 16 (Changing Course) does not apply to L. Note that L has broken rule 14 (Avoiding Contact), but she cannot be penalized under rule 14 unless the contact causes damage (see discussion of rule 14).

- PL and SW, two opposite *tack* close-hauled boats, are approaching a windward *mark* to be left to port. PL safely lee-bows SW (i.e. tacks to leeward of SW) outside the *two-length zone*. As the boats enter the *two-length zone* PL realizes she will not make the *mark* without luffing up to head to wind. When near the *mark*, PL luffs sharply and collides with SW, no damage. As PL was "changing course to round or pass a mark," rule 16 (Changing Course) did not apply to her, and SW breaks rule 18.2(a) and rule 11 as above.

In the same scenario, SW does keep clear of PL's luff, but as PL begins to pass the *mark* she bears away sharply to round the *mark* and her transom swings up and hits the leeward side of SW, no damage. Same answer as above. SW must *keep clear* (as well as give *room*), PL is rounding the *mark*, and therefore rule 16 does not apply.

 "What happens when I've obtained my inside overlap before reaching the two-length zone, but once inside the zone the outside boat breaks the overlap?"

You are still entitled to your rights as inside boat under rule 18.2(b).

Rule 18.2(b) – Overlapped at the Zone

If boats were *overlapped* before either of them reached the *two-length zone*, and the *overlap* is broken after one of them has reached it, the boat that was on the outside shall continue to give the other boat *room*. If the outside boat becomes *clear astern* or *overlapped* inside the other boat, she is not entitled to *room* and shall *keep clear*.

Rule 18.2(b) is clear. As long as you've obtained your inside *overlap* before either boat reached the *two-length zone*, your rights under rule 18.2(a) are "locked in" until the rule no longer applies.

 "What happens when boats on the outside that are keeping clear of overlapped boats on the inside never get to the two-length zone until after they've turned and begun heading for the mark; now can a boat that was well clear astern suddenly claim room?"

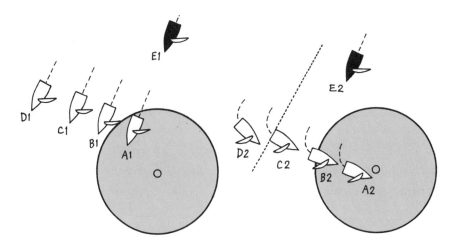

A, B, C and D are in a bunch at a mark. D is keeping clear of the three boats inside her, and as a result is outside the two-length zone. E is well astern. In position 2, the four boats gybe and line up to pass the mark one behind the other. The position of A and B make it obvious that C and D are outside the two-length zone. Because E is overlapped on their inside and is the right of way boat, C and D must both keep clear of her and

Yes! ISAF Case 59 clarifies this very common situation at crowded marks:

"QUESTION: Five boats are approaching a leeward mark dead before the wind. Four of them are overlapped in line with A nearest the mark. The fifth boat, E, is clear astern of A, B, C and D when A and B reach the two-length zone. When the four front boats come abreast of the mark and turn to round it, the change of bearing of C and D, relative to E, results in E becoming overlapped inside them while each of them is outside the two-length zone. E rounds the mark behind A and B but inside C and D, both of which are able to give room to E. Is E entitled to room under rule 18.2(a) from C and D?

"ANSWER: Since E is astern of A and B when they reach the two-length zone, she is required by Rule 18.2(c) to keep clear of them. Between E and the two outside boats, however, a different relationship develops. C and D, in order to leave room for the two inside boats with their booms fully extended, must approach the mark on courses that bring them abreast of it outside the two-length zone. When C and D change course towards the mark, E obtains an inside overlap while they are outside the two-length zone. Therefore, E is entitled to room under rule 18.2 (a), which C and D are able to give."

"I understand now about the significance of the 'two-length zone;' but how do I know where the 'two-length zone' actually is on the water?"

Well, at first it's difficult, and then after you've raced more and more it becomes easier to judge. Let's say you race a 30-foot boat. Two boat-lengths is 60 feet. That's the length of a bowling lane, or about the distance from the pitcher's mound to home plate on a baseball diamond. Doing 6 knots (about 10 feet per second) you'll cover two boat-lengths in 6 seconds. Measure it out and mark it with two orange poles or something at your club so everyone will learn to "guesstimate" it better.

"Okay, but what if two boats simply can't agree on whether an overlap was obtained or broken before reaching the two-length zone?"

Competitors and protest committees should try their hardest to remember and determine the facts. However, realizing that there will be disputes, the rule writers built in some "guidance" to help resolve such disputes. Rule 18.2(e) (Overlap Rights) reads, *"If there is reasonable doubt that a boat obtained or broke an overlap in time, it shall be presumed that she did not."*

In other words, if you come up from behind and claim that you got the inside *overlap* before the outside boat reached the *two-length zone*, but the outside boat disagrees saying that you were still *clear astern* when she arrived at the *two-length zone* and that you subsequently obtained the *overlap*, rule 18.2(e) states that if there is "reasonable doubt," it shall be presumed by the sailors that the *overlap* was not obtained in time. Similarly, if it goes to a protest hearing and the protest committee has "reasonable doubt," they shall presume that the *overlap* was not obtained in time. In other words, in a *protest* you will have to satisfy the protest committee that there is no doubt that you obtained the *overlap* in time.

By the same token, if you have an *overlap* on an outside boat at say five and then four boat-lengths away, she will be required to give you *room* under rule 18.2(a) unless she pulls *clear ahead* before reaching the *two-length zone*. If she claims to have "broken" the *overlap* just before she reached the *two-length zone*, but you disagree saying that you were still *overlapped* when she reached the *two-length zone*, then it is her who must satisfy the protest committee that there is no doubt that the *overlap* was broken in time.

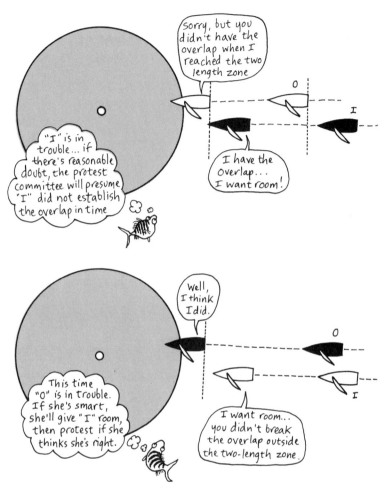

Satisfying the protest committee is generally very tough to do as it is usually one word against the other. Hails to each other regarding the *overlap* situation as the boats near the *two-length zone* are very helpful to the point that they are almost expected by good protest committees. Also, witnesses can be very useful, particularly independent witnesses who were positioned exactly at the *two-length zone* and in a position to determine *overlaps*.

"Does the inside boat have to call for room?"

No. When you are on the inside while rounding or passing a *mark* or *obstruction*, you are not required to call for *room*. ISAF Case 41 reads, "QUESTION 2: Does BW have to claim room to pass to leeward of A, or would BL risk disqualification by not automatically giving room? ANSWER 2: BW is not required to hail for room, although that is a prudent thing to do to avoid misunderstandings. Rule 18.2(a) requires BL to give room to BW when they both pass to leeward of the obstruction." In US SAILING Appeal 7, SL and SW were passing astern of another *starboard-tacker* that had been *clear ahead*. In this case SW didn't know SL was there or that she was even entitled to *room* at the *obstruction*. She bore off inadvertently and hit SL. The Appeals Committee stated, "The fact that [SW] was unaware of [SL's] presence in no way changed [SL's] requirement under the rules or justified her in not giving [SW] room to clear the obstruction." Clearly, outside boats must be aware at all times to be sure they give each inside boat enough *room* or they *keep clear* when required to.

 "What should I do in the situation where I'm entitled to room but when I'm about a boat-length away from the mark it becomes obvious that the outside boat isn't leaving me enough space to fit between her and the mark?"

At the moment it becomes clear that the outside boat is not going to give you *room*, rule 14 (Avoiding Contact) requires you to avoid hitting her if reasonably possible. This may result in you not being able to round or pass the *mark* on that approach. Though the outside boat's rule breach caused you to sail on the wrong side of the *mark* on that approach, it hasn't prevented you from ultimately rounding the *mark* correctly as required by rule 28.1 (Sailing the Course), i.e. she didn't compel you to break rule 28.1; therefore you are not entitled to exoneration under rule 64.1(b) (Penalties and Exoneration). You must circle around and try again. You should certainly win your *protest* against the outside boat, but there is nothing the protest committee can do to compensate you for the distance/places lost while making a second try to round or pass the *mark*.

Of course, if you do choose to hit the outside boat and force your way in between the outside boat and the *mark*, you can be penalized under rule 14 (Avoiding Contact) only if the contact causes damage. Remember, that if you hit the *mark* you have broken rule 31.1 (Touching a Mark). But you can be exonerated under rule 64.1(b) (Penalties and Exoneration) if the protest committee finds that the outside boat compelled you to touch the *mark* by failing to give you enough *room*.

"How long does the force of rule 18 last?"

Rule 18.1 – When This Rule Applies

Rule 18 applies when boats are about to round or pass a *mark* they are required to leave on the same side, or an *obstruction* on the same side, until they have passed it.

The last phrase clarifies when the requirements in rule 18 cease to apply. Notice the word "they." In other words, the requirements in rule 18 continue to apply until the latter of a pair or group of boats subject to rule 18 passes the *mark*. In my opinion, once a boat leaves the *mark* or *obstruction* astern she has "passed" it; i.e. once she is no longer "overlapping" it she has "passed" it.

Remember that the primary purpose of rule 18 is to allow boats to round or pass a *mark* or *obstruction* without the inside boats getting wedged in between the outside boats and the *mark* or *obstruction*, or getting forced onto the wrong side of the *mark*.

As discussed above, sometimes these outside boats are going to otherwise have the right of way. The "force" of rule 18 requires them to give only enough *room* for the inside boat to round or pass the *mark* or *obstruction*. The moment the inside boat has completed her passing maneuver, the purpose of rule 18 has been served and the "force" shuts off. At that moment the outside/right-of-way boat gets her full rights back, and the inside/give-way boat must *keep clear*.

For example, let's say that two *overlapped* boats on *port tack* are rounding the leeward *mark* onto a beat. The lee*ward*/outside boat (LO) is allowing just enough *room* for the *windward*/inside boat (WI) to round the *mark*, but LO is trying to keep her bow just ahead of WI. As WI comes up to close-hauled and her transom just passes the *mark*, LO luffs at a medium rate. WI responds by luffing and tacking onto *starboard-tack*. She *keeps clear* of LO and does not hit the *mark* or tack too close to any boat about to pass the *mark*. No foul. LO gave WI just enough *room* to round the *mark*, and when

LO asserted her rights as a *leeward* boat, WI was able to *keep clear* without hitting the *mark*. LO also gave her *room* to *keep clear* under rule 16 (Changing Course) which applied because rule 18 no longer applied once both boats had passed the *mark*.

Note that the circumstances will weigh heavily in determining exactly when the outside boat can assert her rights. If there are a lot of boats near the *mark* such that WI could not tack without fouling them under rule 15 (Acquiring Right of Way), LO will have to be careful to allow WI the *room* needed to *keep clear* without tacking. If there is current or strong wind or waves, LO will again have to wait until WI can *keep clear* without risk of losing speed and being pushed back into the *mark*.

Another example is when two close-hauled *port-tackers* are ducking a *starboard-tacker*. The *leeward*/outside boat can "luff" the *windward*/inside boat the moment WI's transom has passed S, assuming that WI can respond to the luff without hitting the *obstruction* (S).

The same principle arises when two *overlapped starboard-tackers* are rounding a windward mark to go onto a run, with O just to windward of I. As I is bearing away around the *mark*, O must *keep clear*, **even if I gybes.** When O's transom leaves the mark astern, the boats are now fully subject to the rules in Sections A and B, and I must then be careful if she wants to gybe. (See ISAF Case 25 and 62 and US SAILING Appeal 3.)

 "What if a boat sails into the two-length zone and then back out; when they re-enter, do they retain their original rights or is it a whole new ball game?"

It's a whole new ball game. Whenever a boat sails beyond the point where they are "about to round or pass" the *mark* or *obstruction* (and remember, that could be farther than two lengths away), whether intentionally or accidentally, rule 18 ceases to apply. Rule 18.1 says, *"Rule 18 applies **when** (emphasis added) boats are about to round or pass a mark..."* When boats are **not** "about to round or pass it," rule 18 does not apply. When boats get close enough again to be considered "about to round or pass it," they are required to give *room* or otherwise *keep clear* of any boat *overlapped* on their inside.

WHEN THE BOATS ARE NOT OVERLAPPED

"Okay, I've got it so far; now how about when the boats are not overlapped when they get to the two-length zone?"

Rule 18.2(b) covers the situation where the boats are not *overlapped* when the boat *clear ahead* reaches the *two-length* zone.

Rule 18.2(c) – Not Overlapped at the Zone

If a boat is *clear ahead* at the time she reaches the *two-length zone*, the boat *clear astern* shall thereafter *keep clear*. If the boat *clear astern* becomes *overlapped* outside the other boat she shall also give the inside boat *room*. If the boat *clear astern* becomes *overlapped* inside the other boat she is not entitled to *room*. If the boat that was *clear ahead* passes head to wind, rule 18.2(c) no longer applies.

Remember that rule 18 applies until the latter of a pair or group of boats subject to rule 18 passes the *mark*. So if you are *clear astern* when the boat *clear ahead* of you arrives at the *two-length zone*, then you must *keep clear* of that boat until **you** have passed the *mark* or *obstruction*, provided the boat *clear ahead* doesn't pass head to wind; or put another way, provided the boat *clear ahead* stays on the same *tack* or gybes.

In my opinion, a boat has "passed" a *mark* when her transom leaves it astern. So, once you have left the *mark* astern, the "force" of rule 18 shuts off and the boats are subject to the rules in Sections A and B. At that point a boat ahead must be careful if she then chooses to gybe. An example is when two

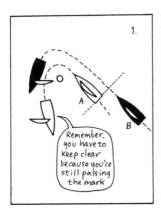

In both situations 1 and 2, rule 18.2 requires the black boat to keep clear of the white boat, including when the white boat gybes, until the black boat has passed the mark.

boats are rounding a windward *mark* onto a run. As long as the boat behind (B) remains "overlapped" with the *mark*, she must *keep clear* of the boat ahead (A). This will permit A to make an immediate gybe around the *mark* if she so chooses. (See ISAF Case 62.)

Another example is when two boats on opposite *tacks* are approaching the leeward *mark*, with S astern of P. S hails, "Starboard tack, get out of my way!" If P is not yet "about to round or pass the mark," she is not yet within the "force-field" of rule 18, and the rules of Section A apply. In this case S has the right-of-way under rule 10 (On Opposite Tacks). However, if P **is** "about to round or pass the mark," then rule 18 applies, meaning that the terms *clear ahead* and *clear astern* now apply to boats on opposite *tacks*. Therefore, when P reaches the *two-length zone clear ahead*, she becomes the right-of-way boat because rule 18.2(c) requires S to *keep clear* of her during her rounding or passing maneuver.

ISAF Case 30 discusses an interesting case where a line of boats were running downwind on *starboard tack* as close to the shore as possible to get out of the current. The leading boat (P) gybed to *port tack* but was still sailing as close to the shore as possible. The boat immediately astern (S), still on starboard, then came up and hit the *port tack* boat. The Appeals Committee stated that rule 18.2(c) applies throughout this incident and it requires B to *keep clear* of A whether or not A gybes.

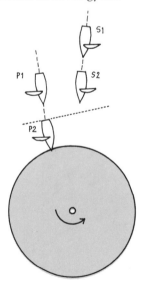

Before reaching the two-length zone, S has right of way over P under rule 10. However, the moment P reaches the two-length zone clear ahead of S, rule 18.2(c) requires S to keep clear of P until both boats have passed the mark.

Note that rule 18.2(c) also has a "lock-in" provision ("...shall thereafter *keep clear*") similar to that in rule 18.2(b). Therefore, if you are *clear ahead* when you reach the *two-length zone*, the boat(s) *clear astern* of you must *keep clear* of you even if they *overlap* you later during your rounding or passing maneuver.

"What if the boat ahead wants to tack around the mark or obstruction?"

She must be very careful! A boat that was *clear ahead* when she reaches the *two-length zone* that tacks around a *mark* gets no protection from rule 18.2(c) what-so-ever. Rule 18.2(c) says, "*If the boat that was **clear ahead** passes head to wind, rule 18.2(c) no longer applies.*" In other words, the moment the boat ahead passes head to wind, rule 18.2(c) instantly shuts off, and the boat is subject to the rules in Sections A and B thereafter, beginning with rule 13 (While Tacking).

Notice also that the boat *clear astern* can sail above close-hauled to make it more difficult for the boat *clear ahead* to tack.

Let's say you (A) and another boat (B) are sailing close-hauled on *port tack* into the windward *mark* to be left to port, not *overlapped*. You thought you were allowed to just tack around the *mark*. After you had passed head to wind but before you were close-hauled, B had to bear away to miss your transom. You have fouled by breaking rule 13 (While Tacking). Notice, though,

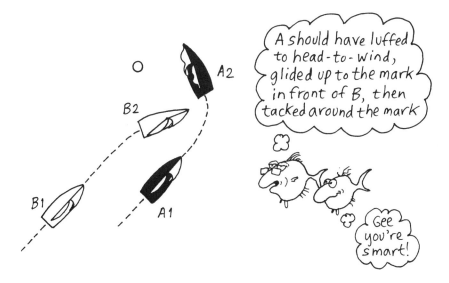

A should have luffed to head-to-wind, glided up to the mark in front of B, then tacked around the mark

Gee you're smart!

that you can luff up to head to wind just prior to tacking around the *mark*, which will make it difficult for a boat close astern to prevent you from tacking. Tactically speaking for a moment, in this situation your best move is to luff to head to wind, glide up to the *mark*, then tack around making it difficult for a boat close astern to prevent you from tacking. (See US SAILING Appeal 28.)

ISAF Case 81 discusses the situation where two boats, A and B, close reach on *starboard tack* into a windward *mark* to be left to starboard. A enters the *two-length zone clear ahead* and to leeward of B, then proceeds to tack to *port tack* in order to round the *mark*. B (still on *starboard tack*), collides with A (now on *port tack*), causing no damage. The Appeals Committee said, "Rule 18 applies when two boats on the same tack are about to round or pass a mark, whether or not they are on a beat. Therefore, rule 18.2(c) applied, beginning when A entered the two-length zone clear ahead of B on the same tack. Rule 18.2(c) requires a boat clear astern to keep clear of a boat clear ahead until they have passed the mark except, if the boat clear ahead tacks, rule 18.2(c) ceases to apply when she passes head to wind at which time she becomes subject to rule 13. After she is on a close-hauled port-tack course, she is subject to rule 10."

"Now I understand when I can and cannot be entitled to 'room,' but what if an outside boat leaves enough space between her and the mark; is it a foul to sneak in there?"

Absolutely not, as long as you don't hit the *mark* or the outside boat or force the outside boat to change course to avoid hitting you. US SAILING Appeal 5 is clear: "When a boat voluntarily or unintentionally makes room available to another boat that, under the rules, has no right to that room and makes no claim to it, that other boat may take advantage, at her own risk, of the room so given. In that case, she breaks no rule."

"Is it legal to force someone onto the wrong side of a mark once you are in the two-length zone?"

No! However, a leeward boat that is not "limited" (i.e. that has the right to sail above her *proper course*) can still hold a *windward* boat to windward of the rhumb line, and in fact can "carry" that *windward* boat right on past the *mark*, provided the boats never get so close to the *mark* that rule 18 begins to apply. Clearly, when L gets to the *two-length zone*, rule 18 applies; and it can begin to apply at a farther distance depending on the circumstances. Once rule 18 begins to apply, L must begin to allow for W to have *room* at the *mark*.

WHEN ONE OF TWO OPPOSITE TACK BOATS TACKS WITHIN TWO LENGTHS OF THE MARK

Rule 18.3 – Tacking

If two boats were approaching a *mark* on opposite *tacks* and one of them completes a *tack* in the *two-length zone* when the other is fetching the *mark*, rule 18.2 does not apply. The boat that tacked

(a) shall not cause the other boat to sail above close-hauled to avoid her or prevent the other boat from passing the *mark*, and

(b) shall give *room* if the other boat becomes *overlapped* inside her, in which case rule 15 does not apply.

The concept in this rule is to improve the racing by trying to minimize the frustrating and sometimes dangerous congestion that can occur at crowded windward *mark* roundings, especially when the *mark* is to be left to port. Problems are often caused by *port-tack* boats approaching on or near the port layline and trying to squeeze their boats in between the *starboard-tack* boats on the starboard layline and the *mark*. Too often, these *port-tackers* don't even get to their close-hauled courses before shooting back up to try to make it around the *mark*, or they get hung up on the *mark* itself, or worse: they fall back onto *port tack* directly in front of the approaching *starboard-tackers*! Too many otherwise excellent close races have been ruined by these actions; and with the popular trend toward shorter courses and more races, the rule writers have taken this proactive step to improve the game.

In a nutshell, the rule works like this (we'll get into the technicalities below):

A boat that completes a tack within the *two-length zone* in front of another boat that is "fetching the *mark*" must do it in a place that allows the other boat to pass the *mark* with no interference, and without ever having to sail above close-hauled to avoid hitting the boat that tacked.

If the boat that tacks causes the other boat to sail above close-hauled to keep from hitting her or prevents the other boat from being able to pass the *mark*, the boat that tacked has broken rule 18.3(a).

If the other boat gets an inside *overlap* on the boat that tacked at any time during her rounding, the boat that tacked must give her *room* to round or pass the *mark* (rule 18.3(b)). Furthermore, presumably the inside boat will also be a *leeward* boat with right of way. Therefore the boat that tacked will also have to *keep clear* of the inside boat under rule 11 (On the Same Tack, Overlapped). Note also that the inside boat does not initially need to give the boat that tacked *room* to *keep clear* under rule 15 (Acquiring Right of Way), and the inside boat can change course to round or pass the *mark* without concern for rule 16 (Changing Course) (see rule 18.2(d), Changing Course to Round or Pass). In other words, the boat that tacked becomes more or less a "sitting duck" for the *leeward*/inside boat.

 "Okay, I'm ready to have you lead me through this rule!"

Well, first the two boats must be approaching a *mark* on opposite *tacks*, as they would be at a windward *mark*. Remember that rule 18 doesn't apply at all yet (rule 18.1(b), When This Rule Applies).

Next, one of the boats must be "fetching" the *mark*. "Fetching" means the boat can pass the *mark* without sailing past head to wind to do so.

Finally, if the tacking boat "completes her tack" (i.e. arrives on a close-hauled course) within the *two-length zone*, rule 18.3 applies. Note that she could have started her tack, and even passed head to wind, outside the *two-length zone*. That is immaterial. In order for rule 18.3 **not** to apply, a boat must complete her tack (i.e. be down to a close-hauled course) **before** she enters the *two-length zone*.

It can be argued that it is difficult to know exactly where the *two-length zone* is, but that is the case when applying the *two-length zone* in any *mark* or *obstruction* rounding or passing situation. Sailors approaching port-hand windward *marks* on *port tack* will be well advised to be conservative when the *mark* area is congested and to tack clearly outside the *two-length zone*.

In interpreting and applying rule 18.3(a), it can be viewed as one obligation on the boat that tacks not to do either of two things; i.e. she breaks rule 18.3(a) if either:

1) she causes the other boat to sail above close-hauled to avoid hitting her, or

2) she prevents the other boat from passing the *mark*.

In my opinion, "causes" means "is the primary and reasonable reason for;" "avoid" means "avoid contact with;" and "prevents" means "physically prevent," as opposed to prevent as a result of disturbing the air and water, etc.

Let me make a brief comment on interpreting words used in rules. When there is some latitude in the interpretation of the word, it is my opinion that one should use the meaning that most reasonably fits the intent and meaning of the rule in order to avoid a strained interpretation that results in an undesirable result for the sport. Interpreting the word "causes" is a good example. One can argue that, in the situation where P tacks just ahead of S such that S needs to either sail above close-hauled or bear away to avoid hitting P, S can't claim that she was "caused" to sail above close-hauled because she could have borne away. This argument would conclude that S is only "caused" to sail above close-hauled when she has no other option by which to avoid hitting P.

In my opinion, this is not a reasonable interpretation of "causes." Clearly, a boat astern has many options other than to sail above close-hauled. She can bear away even if that means she can't make the *mark*, back her sails and stop (in a dinghy) or even drag her feet in the water to slow the boat down. I do not think these are reasonable expectations for racing sailors. If my house burns down and I choose to re-build it, I can accurately say that my house burning down "caused" me to re-build it, although I had other options (buy a new home with my own money, live in a tent, etc.). The event of my house burning down clearly was the primary reason I needed to re-build it, and it was a reasonable reason for doing so. Therefore it is accurate to say I was "caus-ed" to re-build it.

The reason for this discussion is that interpreting the word "causes" is central to the interpretation and application of rule 18.3(a). I interpret rule 18.3(a) to say that P "causes" S to sail above close-hauled when either that is the only way S can avoid hitting her, or if bearing off in that situation would not be reasonable. Certainly, bearing off into a position where S is then prevented from passing the mark is unreasonable to me. However, if S can clearly bear off and pass the *mark*, then I would say she was not "caused" to sail above close-hauled.

"I thought that if a boat tacked in front of me inside the two-length zone and caused me to change course at all, she broke rule 18.3(a)."

No! She breaks rule 18.3(a) only if she causes you to sail above a close-hauled course. If you are overstood, for instance, and avoid her by luffing up to a close-hauled course, she has not broken rule 18.3(a).

"Okay, but if a boat tacks in front of me inside the two-length zone, I can just bear off and overlap her to leeward and she has to keep clear of me, right?"

Yes, and it's even better for you than that. Not only does she have to *keep clear* of you, she has to give you *room* to round or pass the *mark* as well; and you are not limited by either rule 15 (Acquiring Right of Way) or rule 16 (Chang-ing Course). The reason is that rule 18.3(b) states that rule 15 does not apply, and rule 18.2(d) (Changing Course to Round or Pass) states that rule 16 does not apply. Therefore, whenever a boat *clear astern* obtains a *leeward*/inside *overlap* at any point in the rounding or passing maneuver of the boat that tacked, the boat that tacked must immediately *keep clear* of her and give her *room*, and the inside *overlapping* boat does not need to give the boat that tacked any *room* to *keep clear* of her what-so-ever.

The only word of caution to the boat clear astern (B) is that if contact occurs almost immediately after the *overlap* occurs, it can be argued that the moment **before** the *overlap* occurred, contact was imminent such that the boat *clear ahead* (A) could be said to have had a "need to take avoiding action" at that time (despite the fact that there was little action that could have been taken to avoid the contact). In this case, it could be found that B broke rule 12 (On the Same Tack, Not Overlapped) immediately prior to the *overlap* occurring. Therefore, B should be careful as she first becomes *overlapped* to *leeward* of A.

Let's look at some scenarios that will involve rule 18.3.

P approaches S at a port-hand windward *mark*, and completes a tack within the *two-length zone* just to *leeward* of S who is fetching the *mark*:

First of all, if S is caused to change her course **at all** to avoid P while P is still on *port tack*, or during the time that P is past head to wind but not yet close-

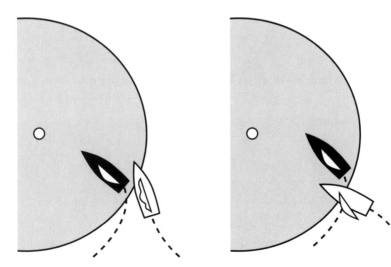

When a boat completes a tack within the two-length zone and a boat that is fetching the mark approaches her, she breaks rule 18.3(a) if she causes that boat to sail above close-hauled to avoid hitting her or prevents that boat from passing the mark.

hauled, then P has broken either rule 10 (On Opposite Tacks) or rule 13 (While Tacking).

Let's say that P gets to close-hauled without requiring any change of course by S, and the boats are now one hull length from the *mark*. As P (now the *leeward*/inside boat) approaches the *mark*, she realizes she won't make the *mark* unless she luffs above close-hauled. She does so, thereby clearing the *mark*, but as a result of her luff, S is caused to sail above close-hauled to avoid hitting her. P has broken rule 18.3(a). Note that even though she's an inside/right-of-way boat, P is not entitled to rights under rule 18.2 (Giving Room; Keeping Clear) because rule 18.3 specifically states so. The same would be true if S had to sail above close-hauled to avoid P's transom as she bore off around the *mark*.

Had S been able to pass the *mark* without needing to sail above close-hauled to avoid P, then P would not have broken rule 18.3(a), and S would simply be required to *keep clear* under rule 11 (On the Same Tack, Overlapped).

At a port-hand windward *mark*, P completes a tack within the *two-length zone* directly ahead of S who is fetching the *mark*; once P is close-hauled, S must change course either up or down to avoid colliding with her:

First of all, once P gets to a close-hauled course *clear ahead* of S, S is required to *keep clear* of her under rule 12 (On the Same Tack, Not Overlapped). If, despite her best efforts to avoid P beginning the moment P is close-hauled, S is unable to do so and she hits P on the transom, P has "tacked too close" and broken rule 15 (Acquiring Right of Way). If S does have *room* to *keep clear* of P but hits P on the transom anyway, then S breaks rule 12 as well as rule 14 (Avoiding Contact).

It could happen that when P gets to a close-hauled course, S can avoid hitting P but is faced with the choice of *overlapping* P *to leeward* and probably not being able to pass the *mark* or sailing above close-hauled. If S chooses to sail above close-hauled, then P has broken rule 18.3(a) by causing S to sail above close-hauled to avoid her, because it isn't reasonable to expect S to bear away and not make the *mark*. And if S chooses to *overlap* P to leeward, but once there finds that she can't pass the *mark* due to P's physical presence, even when she luffs up to head to wind, P has "prevented" S from passing the *mark* thereby breaking rule 18.3(a). (Note that S is not allowed to sail past

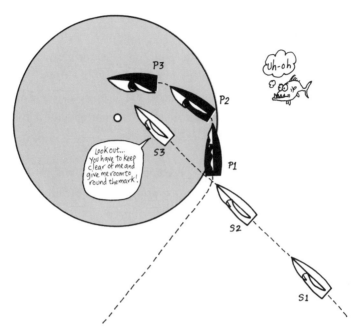

Because P completed her tack within the two-length zone, and S is fetching the mark, P must keep clear of S at any time S gets an inside overlap until both boats have passed the mark; and rule 15 does not apply, meaning that S does not need to give P room to keep clear of her. Furthermore, P must give S room to round or pass the mark; and rule 16 does not apply, meaning that S can change course in either direction necessary to round or pass the mark without needing to give P room to keep clear.

head to wind as she would be tacking onto *port tack* and required to give-way first under rule 13 (While Tacking) and then under rule 10 (On Opposite Tacks.).

Note that in congested roundings S may have boats to windward of her making it impossible to sail above close-hauled. In this case her only option may be to *overlap* P to *leeward*; and if S then can't make the *mark*, P has broken rule 18.3(a).

Now if P tacks far enough to windward of the layline such that S can clearly *overlap* P to *leeward* and pass the *mark*, then P has not caused S to sail above close-hauled to avoid her because it would be reasonable to expect S to bear away and pass the *mark*. However, if S chooses to sail above close-hauled and protest, it will be the **protest committee** who decides whether S would have been "prevented" from passing the *mark* had she chosen to *overlap* P to *leeward* (and my guess is, they will give S the benefit of the doubt). So P's will want to be very conservative with where they choose to tack in the *two-length zone* near opposite *tack* boats!

Finally, if S is fetching the *mark* and P tacks sufficiently far ahead of her such that S is not required to take any action to avoid hitting P after the tack, but then S fails to make the *mark* due to the disturbed air and water caused by P, in my opinion P has not "prevented" S from passing the *mark* due to her physical presence, and therefore has not broken rule 18.3(a).

At a port-hand windward *mark*, P completes a tack within the *two-length zone* and one length later, as P is preparing to bear off around the *mark*, S sails in to *leeward* telling P to *keep clear* of her:

Once P completes her tack within the *two-length zone*, then for the duration of her rounding or passing maneuver a *clear astern* boat (S) is allowed to obtain a *leeward*/inside overlap on P and P must *keep clear* of her! To make life even tougher on P, rule 18.3(b) "shuts off" rule 15 (Acquiring Right of Way) and rule 18.2(d) (Changing Course to Round or Pass) "shuts off" rule 16 (Changing Course), such that when S does obtain the *leeward* inside overlap, S does not have to give P any *room* to *keep clear* what-so-ever, even if S luffs up to make it around the *mark*!

As an example, P tacks within the *two-length zone* clear ahead of S. One length later, S chooses to *overlap* P to *leeward*. If the moment S sticks her bow in to *leeward* of P she hits P, then she probably wasn't *keeping clear* of P while rule 12 (On the Same Tack, Not Overlapped) applied to her immediately before she became *overlapped* with P. But, on the other hand, the moment S sticks her bow in to *leeward* of P, P must *keep clear* under rule 11 (On the Same Tack, Overlapped) and must give S *room* under rule 18.3(b). If S makes contact with P (other than immediate contact), or if S is unable to round or pass the *mark* because she would hit P, then P has not given *room* nor *kept clear* and has broken rules 11 and 18.3(b). If P can stay out of S's way such that S has no need to take action to avoid P and is not prevented from rounding or passing the *mark*, then P has not broken rule 18.3(b).

Note however that when S becomes *overlapped* to *leeward* of P from *clear astern*, S is "limited" under rule 17.1 (On the Same Tack; Proper Course) to sailing no higher than her *proper course*. Therefore S must bear away to follow her *proper course* around the windward *mark*.

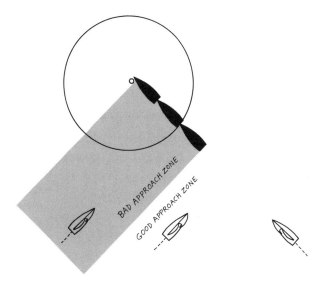

"It sounds like this rule eliminates the port-tack layline and a port-tacker's tactic of lee-bowing a starboard tacker right at the mark!"

I don't think the rule dramatically changes the way the top of the beat is sailed. If you are doing well in the race, the windward *mark* rounding won't be that congested, and you will probably approach it as close to the layline as you want. If you are farther down in the pack (out of the top ten, let's say), coming in right on the *port-tack* layline isn't a great look anyway. For at least some of the time, you are sailing more slowly in the disturbed air and water of the boats going down the reach, or trying to pick your way through the *starboard-tack* boats as they turn and go down the run. So for tactical reasons, as well as because of rule 18.3, you will want to approach a port-hand windward *mark* at least three lengths below the *port-tack* layline.

To me, the most significant effect of this rule is on the decision the *port-tacker* makes on whether to duck the nearby *starboard-tackers* and tack safely up to windward of them or to lee-bow them (i.e. tack just to *leeward* of them) and hope to make the *mark* from there. My personal experience (and I've been there myself!) is that too often sailors choose the (dare I say) "greedier" choice, and end up not only not making the *mark*, but causing a real mess for others at the *mark*. I think the net effect of rule 18.3 is that fewer *port-tackers* tack right at the *mark* in crowds, which is a welcome situation for all.

WHEN AN INSIDE RIGHT-OF-WAY BOAT NEEDS TO GYBE TO SAIL HER PROPER COURSE AROUND A MARK

Rule 18.4 – Gybing

When an inside *overlapped* right-of-way boat must gybe at a *mark* or *obstruction* to sail her *proper course*, until she gybes she shall sail no farther from the *mark* or *obstruction* than needed to sail that course.

First of all, rule 18.4 puts a "limit" on inside right-of-way boats, i.e. *leeward* boats and *starboard-tack* boats. Essentially, that "limit" is that whenever their *proper course* is to gybe at a *mark*, they must do so. Actually, the instruction in the rule is that up until she actually gybes, the right-of-way boat "shall sail no farther from the *mark* or *obstruction* than needed to sail [her *proper course*]." This means that not only does she have to gybe when it is her *proper course* to do so, but she can't luff (turn) away from the *mark* or *obstruction* prior to gybing if that takes her farther from it than necessary to sail her *proper course*. This applies even when the outside/*windward* boat initially obtained the *overlap* to *windward* such that L would otherwise have the right to sail above her *proper course*. (See ISAF Case 75.)

Note that rule 18.4 has a clear "shut off" time built in. The rule no longer applies once the inside boat gybes (i.e. the boom crosses the centerline). After that, the inside boat is not limited by rule 18.4, but she will most likely be a *windward* boat and therefore only entitled to *room* (i.e. only the space needed to pass safely between the outside boat and the *mark*) under rule 18.2(a) (Giving Room; Keeping Clear).

The situation will commonly arise at gybe *marks* when the *leeward*/inside boat will be required to gybe around the *mark*, and at leeward *marks* to be left to port when the *starboard tack*/inside boat will be required to gybe in order to round the *mark*. Notice that a boat's *proper course* is the course she thinks will get her to the finish line as quickly as possible. Therefore she can certainly make a "tactical" (swing wide-cut close) rounding.

Note that rule 18.4 applies any time boats are *overlapped*. Therefore, if the boats are not *overlapped* when the boat ahead enters the *two-length zone*, but the boat astern obtains an outside *overlap* later, rule 18.4 applies.

Note also that rule 18.4 applies only when the inside right-of-way boat **must** gybe to sail her *proper course*. Therefore, at a windward *mark* going

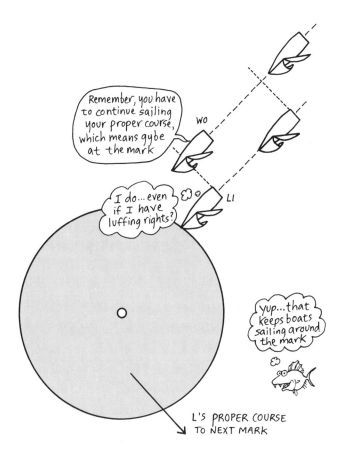

L'S PROPER COURSE TO NEXT MARK

onto a run, when either tack can be a *proper course* (i.e. she'll be on a *proper course* whether she stays on the same tack or gybes), the inside right-of-way boat needs to gybe only if she decides it is her *proper course* to do so. The same applies at a gybe *mark* going onto a very broad reach where it may be faster for a boat to delay its gybe.

Finally note that the Team Racing Rules (Appendix D) delete rule 18.4 entirely (rule D1.1(b), Team Racing Rules, Changes to the Racing Rules). This will enable team racers to continue setting "mark traps" whereby they enter the *two-length zone clear ahead* and then stop their boats. "Enemy boats" astern must *keep clear* of them. They can't *overlap* them on the inside because of rule 18.2(c); and if they *overlap* the boat ahead on the outside, the boat ahead can luff or otherwise sail them past the *mark*, meanwhile letting team-mates round the *mark* on the inside.

WHEN PASSING A CONTINUING OBSTRUCTION

Rule 18.5 – Passing a Continuing Obstruction

While boats are passing a continuing *obstruction*, rules 18.2(b) and 18.2(c) do not apply. A boat *clear astern* that obtains an inside *overlap* is entitled to *room* to pass between the other boat and the *obstruction* only if at the moment the *overlap* begins there is *room* to do so. If there is not, she is not entitled to *room* and shall *keep clear*.

First of all, we need to discuss what a "continuing *obstruction*" is. It is an *obstruction* that a boat "continues" to sail next to, as opposed to one that is passed in a matter of seconds. For instance, a breakwater that a boat is sailing along is a "continuing *obstruction*," whereas a small spectator boat that gets sailed by in a few seconds is not a "continuing *obstruction*." When a *windward* boat is sailing parallel to a *leeward* boat for a few boat-lengths, the *leeward* boat, as a right-of-way boat, is an *obstruction* (see definition *Obstruction*), and a "continuing" one, as the two boats are sailing side by side for several lengths. However, when a *port-tacker* converges with a *starboard-tacker* upwind, S is not a "continuing *obstruction*" as P won't be sailing near her for more than a few seconds. Rule 18.5 modifies rule 18.2 (Giving Room; Keeping Clear) to clarify when the rights and obligations of the inside and outside boats begin and end.

ISAF Case 29 reads in part, "rule 18.5 makes an exception to rule 18.2(c), stating that 'A boat clear astern that obtains an inside overlap is entitled to

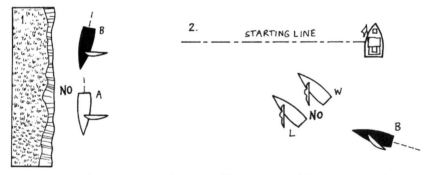

In situation 1, there is not room for B to sail between A and the shoreline without hitting one or the other. Therefore, if she did establish an overlap between them, she would not be entitled to room under rule 18.2(a) and she would be required to keep clear of A under rule 18.5. The same principle applies in situation 2.

room to pass between the other boat and the obstruction only if at the moment the overlap begins there is room to do so.' L was an obstruction to W, as she was to M as well, because they both were required to keep clear of her. Was she also a continuing obstruction? Once W overtook L, the two boats sailed overlapped at least six hull lengths towards the finishing line. That was easily long enough to qualify L as a continuing obstruction."

ISAF Case 33 interprets the situation where boats are sailing by the very end of a long breakwater protruding from shore as follows, "…the two boats, still overlapped, are outside the two-length zone of an obstruction, the end of the breakwater. PL, the outside boat, is required by rule 18.2(a) to give PW, inside, room to pass the obstruction. While the breakwater is a continuous structure from the shore to its outer end, it does not qualify as a continuing obstruction, since the boats are concerned only with the very end."

"So when can a boat come up from clear astern and obtain an inside overlap and be entitled to room at a continuing obstruction?"

The answer is: A boat *clear astern* (B) can obtain an inside *overlap* on the boat *clear ahead* (A) only when, **at the moment the overlap is obtained**, there is enough *room* for B to pass completely between A and the *obstruction* without touching either. In other words, imagine that the moment the *overlap* on A is made, you could "freeze" the motion of A and the *obstruction*. If there is enough physical space for B to sail through between them in a seamanlike way without touching either, then the *overlap* is legal and A must give B *room* for as long as they are *overlapped* and B needs the *room* to keep from touching the *obstruction*; i.e. hitting the wall, running aground, hitting the right-of-way boat, etc. If B loses the *overlap* on A, then A ceases to be required to give *room* until B obtains another legal *overlap* and again needs *room*. (See US SAILING Appeal 47.)

One sensitive situation occurs when A is sailing as close as she dares to shore but it's not obvious how close a boat of her class can really go without running aground. Boat B comes up and wants to obtain an inside *overlap*. The question becomes, "How do you determine if there is *room* for her to pass inside of A?" The essence of *room* is whether, under the conditions existing, the inside boat can safely sail between the outside boat and the *obstruction*. If B decides to risk it and obtain the *overlap*, US SAILING Appeal 47 says, "If the inside boat, upon obtaining an inside overlap, immediately runs aground, she has demonstrated that there was not room for her at the time she obtained the overlap. After she has sailed inside for a while, however, any question of the failure of the outside boat to give sufficient room must be answered by the facts found by the protest committee."

"If I do obtain an overlap when there isn't room to sail between the outside boat and the continuing obstruction, have I broken rule 18.5?"

No. You don't break rule 18.5 merely because you obtained an *overlap*. However, you are required to *keep clear* of the outside boat under rule 18.5. If the outside boat has to take action to avoid you, you have broken rule 18.5.

TWO EXCEPTIONS

"I notice there seem to be two exceptions to rule 18 listed as rules 18.1(a) and (b); could you go over those please?"

You bet. There are two very narrow situations when boats are rounding or passing *marks* and *obstructions* in which rule 18 does not apply at all. They are listed as rules 18.1(a) and 18.1(b).

Rule 18.1(a)

Rule 18...does not apply at a starting *mark* surrounded by navigable water or at its anchor line from the time the boats are approaching them to *start* until they have passed them...

Essentially, rule 18.1(a) "shuts off" the "buoy/*obstruction* room" rules at the starting *marks*. The reason is that it would lead to chaotic starts if *windward*/inside boats were entitled to *room* to pass between the committee boat and *leeward*/outside boats at the start (it's often chaotic enough without them having that right!).

To accurately apply this rule, be sure you understand that an object large enough to satisfy the definition *Obstruction* is always an *obstruction*, even when it is used as a *mark*; i.e. it does not cease being one when it becomes the other. Therefore a race committee boat used as one end of the starting line is **both** a starting mark and an *obstruction* at the same time.

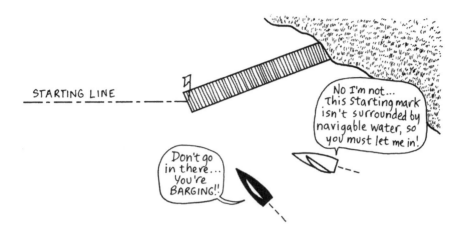

Now, having said that rule 18.1(a) "shuts off" rule 18 (Rounding and Passing Marks and Obstructions), there are in fact two narrow situations when, for reasons of safety, the rules do entitle a *windward*/inside boat to room at a starting *mark* under rule 18.2(a) (Giving Room; Keeping Clear) from a *leeward*/outside boat. Let's look at those first.

1) At a starting *mark* not surrounded by navigable water

Though this situation is not common, it will arise when one end of the starting line is the end of a dock or breakwater, or is a bell buoy that marks some shallow rocks or sandbars. Rule 18 always applies at starting *marks* not surrounded by navigable water, i.e. enough water so that the inside boat can sail around the *mark* without running aground or hitting a dock or other object. Therefore, an inside boat is entitled to *room* at such a *mark* under rule 18.2(a) from any outside boat provided she was *overlapped* with the outside boat before the boats reached the *two-length zone* or, if the starting *mark* is a continuing *obstruction*, then when there was *room* at the time of the *overlap* to pass between the outside boat and the *obstruction* (rules 18.2(a), Giving Room; Keeping Clear and 18.5, Passing a Continuing Obstruction).

2) At a starting *mark* when the boats are not approaching it to *start*

If the boats are **not** approaching the starting *mark* to *start*, an inside boat is entitled to *room* at any starting *mark* from any outside boat provided she was *overlapped* with the outside boat before the boats reached the *two-length*

zone. Notice that this applies whether the starting *mark* is a buoy or large boat (*obstruction*). This is for safety purposes as boats are sailing past the *marks* well before *starting*.

So, if say at three minutes before the starting signal you were sailing along to *leeward* of W and were about to sail to *leeward* of the race committee boat, and for whatever reason W wanted to pass to *leeward* of it also, you would have to give her *room* to do so under rule 18.2(a) (Giving Room; Keeping Clear), provided she had her inside *overlap* before either of you reached the *two-length zone.* Now to play this out, because the *mark* doesn't have a "required" side yet (rule 28.2, Sailing the Course), you two can pass it on either 19 On the Same Tack, Overlapped), provided you make no sudden, fast course changes (rule 16, Changing Course); therefore, you can choose to luff and pass to *windward* of the committee boat. If, however, you choose to pass to *leeward* of the committee boat and fail to provide enough *room* for W to do likewise if she wishes to, you have broken rule 18.2(a).

Note that when you break a rule before the starting signal, you can make your 720 Turns Penalty immediately; i.e. you do not have to wait until your starting signal to do so (rule 44.1, Penalties for Breaking Rules of Part 2). If W happens to hit the *mark* (i.e. break rule 31.1, Touching a Mark) because you didn't give her enough *room*, she can ask the protest committee, normally by protesting you, to exonerate her under rule 64.1(b) (Penalties and Exoneration).

"When is a boat considered to be 'approaching a starting mark to start?'"

Though this question has never been discussed in an appeal, I would develop my opinion as follows. What is the purpose of the rule? Rule 18.1(a) is preventing the situation where *windward*/inside boats can reach in and demand *room* at the starting *mark* from *leeward*/outside boats that are trying to *start* there. And "when approaching the starting *mark* to *start*" is establishing the period of time during which these *windward*/inside boats know that they are not entitled to any *room*. Before LO is "approaching the starting *mark* to *start*," WI is entitled to *room* at the *mark*; and the rules are consistently clear in providing predictable and specific times when a boat's rights change. To me, this is no exception. When LO is clearly on her final approach toward the line with the intention of *starting*, i.e. crossing the line after the gun, it will be obvious to WI and she will know to *keep clear*. Furthermore, a boat that is "approaching the starting *mark* to *start*" and is close enough to the starting *mark* to shut out a *windward* boat, will clearly be *starting* in close proximity distance-wise to the starting *mark*.

Therefore, in my opinion, a boat that in 15 knots of breeze goes reaching full-speed by the committee boat with one-and-a-half minutes to go before the starting signal, and ends up starting halfway down the starting line, was in no way "approaching the starting *mark* to *start*" at the moment she went by the starting *mark*. But a boat that is passing the starting *mark* with ten seconds to go certainly is on her final approach to *start* very near to the starting *mark*. In addition, I feel that a boat that in light air sits nearly wayless behind the race committee boat may be approaching the line to *start* at one minute to go, and it will be more obvious and predictable that she plans to *start* near the *mark*, and the *windward*/inside boats can see this and *keep clear* accordingly.

This is a distinction that in general has caused very few problems, and in general has been very liberally interpreted in the *leeward*/outside boat's favor. But until it is officially interpreted, the safe move on LO's part would be to allow WI *room* up to one minute before the starting signal; and the safe move for WI would be not to try to force *room* with much less than two minutes to go. Both boats have the option to protest, and the protest committee can then decide whether LO was "approaching the starting *mark* to *start*" in the particular circumstances.

There are no other times that rule 18 applies at a starting *mark*; therefore, at all other times, boats are subject to the rules in Sections A and B. For a complete explanation of how these rules work when *starting* near starting *marks*, see "The Section A and B Rules in Action" section at the end of Chapter 7.

Rule 18.1(b)

Rule 18... does not apply between boats on opposite *tacks*, either on a beat to *windward* or when the *proper course* for one or both of them to round or pass the *mark* or *obstruction* is to tack.

 "Does rule 18.1(b) mean that 'buoy room' doesn't apply at the windward mark?"

No; rule 18.1(b) means that if two boats are coming into a windward *mark* on **opposite** *tacks*, rule 18 (Rounding and Passing Marks and Obstructions) doesn't apply. But if the boats are coming into the windward *mark* on the **same** *tack*, then rule 18 applies just like at any other *mark*.

Though the phrase "a beat to windward" has never been interpreted by an appeal, my opinion is that a boat is on a "beat to windward" if her *proper course* to the *mark* is to sail close-hauled. However, the second phrase in rule 18.1(b) takes the pressure off deciding whether boats are on a beat to windward. Anytime one or both of two boats on opposite *tacks* will have to tack at a *mark* or *obstruction* in order to continue sailing their *proper course*, rule 18.1(b) "shuts off" rule 18.2(a) (Giving Room; Keeping Clear).

Picture a windward *mark* to be left to port. It would be chaos if suddenly a *port-tack* boat could come in and call for *room* from a *starboard-tack* boat while still on *port tack*. While the boats are on opposite *tacks*, rule 10 (*port/starboard*) applies; and if the *port-tack* boat (PI) wants to tack to *leeward* of the *starboard-tack* boat (SO), rules 13 (changing tacks) and 15 (acquiring right of way) apply. Once the *port-tack* boat has borne away to a close-hauled course without breaking rule 13 or 15, she is on the same *tack* as SO and is the *leeward* boat.

If she completes her tack outside the *two-length zone* (i.e. gets down to a close-hauled course outside the *two-length zone*), then she is "doubly protected" to sail around the *mark*. PI, as the *leeward* boat, is the right-of-way boat under rule 11 (On the Same Tack, Overlapped); and because she did not obtain her *overlap* from *clear astern*, she is free to sail where she pleases, i.e. she's not "limited" under rule 17.1 (On the Same Tack; Proper Course). Therefore she can luff head to wind if she pleases, which she may need to do anyways to sail her *proper course* around the *mark*. Secondly, PI, as the inside boat, is entitled to *room* from SO; and because PI is also the right-of-way boat, SO is required to *keep clear* of her as well (rule 18.2(a), Giving Room; Keeping Clear).

If she has completed her tack within the *two-length zone*, she is subject to rule 18.3 (Rounding and Passing Marks and Obstructions, Tacking).

Notice that the exception in rule 18.1(b) applies only at a *mark* that one or both of the opposite-*tack* boats needs to **tack** around. The reasoning is that at all the other *marks*, even though the boats may be on opposite *tacks*, they are going in the same direction, or at least generally converging at much smaller angles. Therefore, at leeward *marks*, inside/*port-tack* boats are entitled to *room* under rule 18.2(a) from outside/*starboard-tack* boats.

The same exception applies when passing an *obstruction*. When two boats on a beat to windward are on opposite *tacks*, the inside boat cannot ask for *room* to pass an *obstruction*. Therefore, if in a narrow harbor you are sailing close-hauled on *port tack* as close to the shore or a dock as you can get, you cannot call for *room* from a converging close-hauled *starboard-tack* boat. Rule 10 (On Opposite Tacks) applies and you must slow down or bear off and take their stern. (See ISAF Cases 9 and 43.)

We've discussed thoroughly how rule 18 applies slightly differently at a windward *mark* and at a starting *mark*. These are its only two exceptions. The rules for "buoy room" are exactly the same at every other *mark* on the course, including the finishing *marks*.

"Cool; does this mean that I now know everything there is to know about the rules at marks and obstructions?"

Almost!

RULE 19 – ROOM TO TACK AT AN OBSTRUCTION

Rule 19.1

When safety requires a close-hauled boat to make a substantial course change to avoid an *obstruction* and she intends to tack, but cannot tack and avoid another boat on the same *tack*, she shall hail for *room* to do so. Before tacking she shall give the hailed boat time to respond...

This is the rule that is used when calling for "sea-room" at a shore, breakwater or dock; however, it is also commonly used when two *port-tack* boats are sailing side-by-side up a beat and are converging with a *starboard-tacker*. The purpose of the rule is to permit a close-hauled boat caught between another boat on the same *tack* and an *obstruction* to avoid the *obstruction* without loss of distance when a substantial change of course is required to clear it.

Notice that rule 19.1 does not apply to boats on opposite *tacks*. ISAF Case 43 describes a situation where a *port-tack* boat (P) is sailing close-hauled as close to shore as possible. A *port-tack* boat to leeward tacks to *starboard tack* onto a collision course with P. S hails "Starboard" and P hails for "sea-room." In ISAF Case 43, the Appeals Committee said, "P is subject to rule 10 and must keep clear. S establishes right of way over P when she tacks onto starboard, but must observe rules 13 and 15. S meets rule 13's requirement by not tacking so close that P has to take avoiding action before S reaches her close-hauled course, and she meets rule 15's requirements by initially leaving P room to keep clear when S gains right of way. Rule 18.1(b) makes rule 18 in-

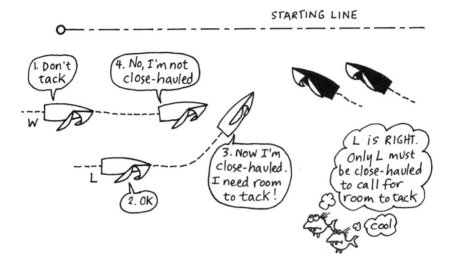

applicable." Therefore, P is not entitled to hail for *room* since rule 19.1 applies to two boats on the "same" *tack* approaching an *obstruction*. So, in this situation P must slow down or bear away and pass astern of S.

When all the conditions in rule 19.1 are met, a *leeward* boat or one *clear ahead* will be able to call for "*room* to tack at the *obstruction*" when nearby *windward* boats are otherwise preventing her from tacking.

Here is how rule 19.1 works:

1) Two boats must be on the **same** *tack* and approaching an *obstruction*, and the *leeward* boat (L) or the boat *clear ahead* (A) must be sailing **close-hauled**.

2) Rule 19.1 is intended for the use of L or A when she is about to hit, or be hit by, an *obstruction*, e.g. a sandbar, a dock, a fishing boat, a *starboard-tack* boat or the like. When there is any doubt as to whether L or A actually is in imminent danger of colliding with an *obstruction*, I would always expect the protest committee to give L or A the benefit of the doubt, and I would encourage sailors on the water to do the same.

3) Rule 19.1 can be used only when L or A must make a "**substantial change of course**" to avoid the *obstruction*. Here, the change is simply that needed not to hit the *obstruction*. In this case, as my general guideline, a course change of less than 10 degrees is not very "substantial." That's

only 3 feet, 6 inches, in a 20-foot boat. Therefore, in a 20-foot boat, if you can bear away and miss an *obstruction* that you would otherwise hit only 3 feet from its edge, you are not entitled to use rule 19.1; but if you need to tack to avoid the last 3 feet, then that's "substantial."

US SAILING Appeal 15 reads, "If [L] had approached the police launch sufficiently close to its leeward end so that, with only a slight change of course when one of her hull lengths from it, she could have safely passed to leeward of it, she should have done so. This was not the case here. As is clear in the diagram, L's course brought her close to the windward end of the police launch. She had to either tack to pass it to windward or bear away substantially to pass it to leeward. Inasmuch as she was required to change course substantially to clear the obstruction whichever side she passed it, she had a right under rule 19.1 to hail W for room to tack." (See also ISAF Case 11.) Notice that even when an obstruction is surrounded by open water, L or A can use rule 19.1 (See US SAILING Appeal 15.)

4) When there is a *windward* boat (W) or a boat *clear astern* (B) that is very close by, L or A can hail for "room to tack" to avoid the *obstruction* only when she can't tack and avoid a collision with W or B. If the course of L or A is sufficiently to *leeward* of W's or B's course such that, after tacking onto *port tack* she has *room* to bear away and pass astern, she is required to do so, since she then is able to tack and avoid the other boat. This means that if L or A can tack and immediately bear away sharply and miss W or B, she must do so and cannot use rule 19.1. (See ISAF Case 35.)

5) When L or A is approaching an *obstruction*, and safety requires her to make a substantial course change to avoid the *obstruction*, and when L or A intends to tack but cannot tack and avoid a collision with W or B, she **shall hail** W or B for "room to tack."

Notice four things about the hail:

a) L or A is **required** to hail; i.e. the hail is mandatory! If a boat does not hail, she cannot claim that she intended to tack. Therefore, if a boat does not hail, rule 19.1 does not apply.

b) L or A's hail must be **adequate**, which implies that it must be loud enough for W or B to hear it above the wind and noise of the boats, and it must be absolutely clear as to what the hail means. I personally try to turn my head toward the other boat, use their helmsman's name if I know it, and say to the effect, "I have a dock or a *starboard-tacker* coming up; I need *room* to tack."

ISAF Case 54 reads, "… the failure of a hailed boat to hear an adequate hail does not relieve her of her obligations under rule 19… Where a leeward boat… receives no response after her hail, a second and more vigorous hail is required to constitute proper notice of her intention to tack… rule 19.1 provides that after hailing the hailing boat shall give the other boat time to respond. The purpose of that is to provide time for the specific response called for under rules 19.1(a) and (b) (to tack or reply 'You tack'). In either case, the hailing boat must tack after the appropriate response from the hailed boat. Therefore, the leeward boat must not sail into a position, before hailing, where she cannot allow sufficient time for a response."

c) After hailing, L or A must give the hailed boat **time to respond**; i.e. she cannot hail and tack simultaneously. US SAILING Appeal 45 reads, "Since PL hailed and tacked simultaneously, she also broke rule 19.1." This is intended to require L or A to keep a good lookout so she is not "surprised" by an *obstruction*.

d) She must adequately hail **in time** for W or B to respond so that both boats can clear the *obstruction*. This will obviously require more time if W or B will have to subsequently hail a boat or boats to *windward* of them. Also, US SAILING Appeal 45 reads, "[The finding] that PW should have been aware of the presence of S and should have been prepared to respond is unwarranted." Therefore W or B does not have to anticipate that L or A might be approaching an *obstruction*. If L or A does not adequately hail in time and subsequently runs aground or fouls a *starboard-tack boat*, she cannot blame W or B. (See ISAF Case 54.)

"I thought that when two port-tack boats were approaching a starboard-tacker, it was whoever hailed first that got to tell the other what to do."

No. The applicable phrase in rule 19.1 is, "and she intends to tack." So when L or A will have to make a substantial change of course to bear away and pass astern of an *obstruction*, it is **her choice** whether to duck or tack. When two *port-tack* boats (PW and PL) are approaching a *starboard-tack* boat (S), US SAILING Appeal 24 says, "PW obtained an inside overlap on PL when the two boats were more than two lengths from the obstruction. However, this fact alone did not give PW right to room under rule 18.2(a) because at that point the two boats were not necessarily about to pass the obstruction on the same side. Therefore, PL was under no obligation to give PW room to pass astern of the obstruction if in fact PL desired to tack." If PL chooses to pass astern of S and PW wants to pass astern of S also, then ISAF Case 11 reminds PL that, as an outside boat passing an obstruction, "Under rule 18.2(a) PW was entitled to room to pass between PL and the stern of S." But if PL chooses to tack, PW must comply even when she'd rather duck. This is reinforced by the last sentence in rule 19.2, "When rule 19.1 applies, rule 18 does not."

When L or A adequately hails, rule 19.1 tells W or B how to respond.

Rule 19.1 (continued)

The hailed boat shall either

(a) **tack as soon as possible, in which case the hailing boat shall also tack as soon as possible, or**

(b) **immediately reply 'You tack', in which case the hailing boat shall tack as soon as possible and the hailed boat shall give *room*, and rules 10 and 13 do not apply.**

So when L or A adequately hails, W or B has only two choices for a response: either tack as soon as possible or **immediately** reply "You tack." W or B does not have the option of disputing L or A's judgment about her need to hail. When W or B feels L or A's hail is not proper (e.g. she is not really near an *obstruction* or she will not have to make a substantial course change to go around an *obstruction*) she nevertheless must respond. She can then protest claiming she was improperly forced to take avoiding action under rule 19.1.

Notice that if you choose to reply "You tack," you must make that hail **immediately**, i.e. without delay. Note also that you must use those exact two words in your hail.

In situation 1, L *breaks rule 19.1(a) by delaying her tack to starboard. After W tacks in response to L's hail, L must tack as soon as possible.*

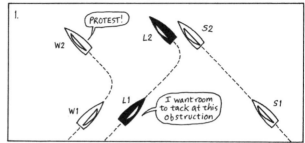

In situation 2, L *breaks rule 19.1(b) by not tacking as soon as possible after W replies, "You tack."*

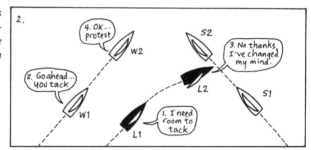

However, if you choose to respond by tacking, you need only do that "as soon as possible." The reason is that often it will not be possible for W or B to respond by tacking immediately after hearing a hail. Examples would include: (a) when there are several boats to *windward* of W or B which need to be hailed; (b) when coming in on *port tack* to a windward *mark* where the boats already going down the first reach are so close that tacking is impossible or (c) when some object in the water such as a log or *mark* momentarily restricts her ability to respond. When it is not possible for W or B to respond by tacking immediately, it is good seamanship for them to inform L or A.

Notice also that it makes no difference whether the hailed boat (W or B) can clear the *obstruction* herself (unless it is also a *mark*; see rule 19.2). If the hailing boat (L or A) cannot clear it without tacking or bearing away sharply, she is entitled to hail and to get a response, regardless of whether the hailed boat can clear the *obstruction*.

Now let's say that you are L and have hailed W for *room* to tack because of a converging *starboard-tacker*. Upon hearing your hail, W tacks. You must begin your tack as soon as you can without hitting W. In other words, you must put your helm down within a couple of seconds after W puts hers down. You break rule 19.1(a) if you continue another couple of boat-lengths before tacking.

If W responds to your hail with the reply "You tack," again you must put your helm down and tack as soon as it is possible, which normally will be immediately. If you don't, you break rule 19.1(b). Once W hails "You tack" she assumes all the obligation to give you *room* to tack and clear her; so if you hear her reply and immediately put your helm down and hit her, she is wrong. And if you decide to stop your tack or otherwise change course before completing your tack in order to avoid her, she is wrong as well. Notice that while you are tacking and clearing her, rules 10 (On Opposite Tacks) and 13 (While Tacking) don't apply. Clearly, once you have tacked and cleared her, you are subject to those rules again.

 "Could you discuss the situation where two port-tackers (PW and PL) are sailing close-hauled side by side on a converging course with a starboard-tacker (S). PL hails PW for 'room to tack,' gets no response, and ultimately S must change course to avoid hitting PL. Who should be penalized?"

The answer will depend on the protest committee's judgment as to whether PL hailed adequately and gave the hailed boat enough time to respond.

ISAF Case 3 states, "Having hailed three times, PL was entitled to expect that PW would respond and give her room to tack. She was not obliged to anticipate PW's failure to comply with rule 19.1 or to bear away below the obstruction S. PL is exonerated as the innocent victim of another boat's breach of a rule, under the provisions of rule 64.1(b)."

US SAILING Appeal 19 is another good example of how PL fulfilled her obligation to adequately hail, but then was forced to foul S by PW's failure to respond. "FACTS: [PW and PL] were close-hauled on port tack. S, which was to leeward and ahead of both PW and PL, tacked to starboard. S completed her tack in compliance with rule 15 (Acquiring Right of Way). Twice, PL hailed PW to tack, so that she also could tack and avoid S. By the time it was clear that PW would not respond, it was too late for PL to make any alternative maneuver without interfering with the oncoming S. PL called to S that she could not respond, whereupon S tacked back to port to avoid a collision.

"DECISION: Inasmuch as PL would have had to make a substantial course change to pass astern of S, even if she had borne away instantly when S tacked to starboard, she had the right to hail PW as she did. However, by the time it was clear that PW would not respond, it was too late for PL to clear S by bearing away. PW was properly disqualified for breaking rule 19.1... Since PL was compelled to break a rule as a consequence of PW's breaking 19.1, PL is exonerated under rule 64.1(b)."

However, there will be times when L or A simply waits too long before hailing. Though deleted for other reasons, an old US SAILING Appeal contained an excellent summation of this situation. "The situation developed slowly with rights and obligations established at some distance from the point of convergence. In fact PL acknowledged recognizing the problem a minute before S hailed her. Had she taken timely action then, either by hailing PW for *room* to tack under rule 19.1 or by bearing away and passing astern of S, she could have avoided S. Under the circumstances, the failure of her late reliance on rule 19.1 does not entitle her to exoneration as an innocent victim, her principal obligation having been to keep clear of S under rule 10."

The key to all this is that L or A must keep a good lookout and begin hailing in time for W or B to hear and understand the hail and then respond. If L or A waits until the last second to hail, and then immediately fouls S, she cannot blame W or B. But if after two clear hails W or B does not respond, L or A must make a reasonable effort to *keep clear* of S. If she cannot *keep clear* she should be exonerated under rule 64.1(b), and W or B should be penalized for breaking rule 19.1. If, however, L or A did have enough time and space to *keep clear* of S after getting no response from W or B but failed to make an effort to use it, she should also be penalized under rule 10 (On Opposite Tacks).

This situation commonly occurs at the windward *mark*. Note that when PW and PL are within the *two-length zone*, PW is entitled to "buoy *room*" from PL under rule 18.2(a) (Giving Room; Keeping Clear). However, the *room* will not be given until the boats reach the *mark*. If PL wants to tack to avoid a converging S, she can hail PW for "*room* to tack," and as long as it is possible for PW to respond, PW must do so. (See US SAILING Appeal 2.)

"What about when the obstruction is also a mark; can I still call for room to tack?"

Good question. The answer is in rule 19.2.

Rule 19.2

Rule 19.1 does not apply at a starting *mark* surrounded by navigable water or at its anchor line from the time boats are approaching them to *start* until they have passed them or at a *mark* that the hailed boat can fetch. When rule 19.1 applies, rule 18 does not.

Notice that at an *obstruction* that is also a **starting** *mark*, including the *mark*'s anchor line, a boat, once she is approaching it to *start*, cannot call for "*room* to tack." (For a full discussion on the phrase "approaching a starting *mark* to *start*," see the discussion of rule 18.1(a), Rounding and Passing Marks and Obstructions, When This Rule Applies, on page 193.) This situation usually develops when there is a race committee boat anchored as the port or "leeward" end of the starting line. A *leeward* boat is truly in "coffin corner" if she sails into a position where she can neither tack without fouling the *windward* boat nor bear away and pass astern of the race committee boat.

But if any other *mark* is a boat or other object large enough to qualify as an *obstruction*, then L or A is allowed to call for "*room* to tack" unless W or B can "fetch" it (i.e. pass the *mark* without passing head to wind). Note that this exception applies only at *obstructions* that are also *marks*.

Let's say you are approaching a *mark/obstruction* and cannot pass it on its required side without tacking, and that you want to tack but can't without colliding with the boat just to *windward* of you (W). First you must hail W for "*room* to tack" under rule 19.1. If W cannot "fetch" it herself, then she must respond under rule 19.1(a) or (b), i.e. tack or reply "You tack." But if she can "fetch" it, she does **not** have to respond at all (though it is good seamanship for her to do so). In this case you are going to have to gybe or bear away and tack around to try it again. Of course, if after not giving *room* to tack she does not "fetch" it on that tack due to a miscalculation or a wind shift, etc., she breaks rule 19.1 by not responding to your hail.

 "What happens when I'm the leeward hailing boat and by the time I learn that the windward hailed boat is fetching the mark/obstruction, it's too late for me to bear away without hitting the mark/obstruction?"

Well, it's not a pretty picture! You should begin hailing soon enough so that, if W doesn't respond, you still have the option to bear away before it's too

late. However, if you do get stuck, a quick hail to W will usually be enough to encourage her to give you *room* to clear the *mark/obstruction*, realizing that you would then do your "720" Turns Penalty.

It's also possible in this situation that a boat might calculate that she will actually lose fewer places by forcing the *windward* boat to give her *room* to pass the *mark* and then doing a "720," rather than gybing around and making a second run at the *mark*, particularly at a crowded windward *mark*. This doesn't work, however. Rule 44.1 (Penalties for Breaking Rules of Part 2) reads, "However, if she... gained a significant advantage in the race or series by her breach she shall retire."

Finally, notice the last sentence of rule 19.2. This clarifies that when L and W are about to pass an *obstruction* and all the conditions in rule 19.1 are met, including the fact that L intends to tack, rule 19.1 takes precedence over rule 18 (Rounding and Passing Marks and Obstructions) by stating that rule 18 doesn't apply. Therefore W, which may prefer to pass on the other side of the *obstruction*, is nevertheless governed by L's choice of action. Also notice that when L intends to tack, rule 19.1 requires her to hail for *room* to do so. Therefore, as far as W is concerned, rule 19.1 begins to apply the moment L hails for "*room* to tack."

"Now do I know everything there is to know about room at marks and obstructions?"

Yes!

TWO-LENGTH ZONE

As boats appr
mark or obstruc
"force" of rule
exists inside th
zone; and whe
are moving fast
exists at a gre
distance from
or obstructi

9

Part 2, Section D
When Boats Meet –
Other Rules

SECTION D contains rules that apply in special situations that arise on the race course (rules 20-22). Again, these rules contain times when a right-of-way boat may find herself with a **temporary requirement** to *keep clear* of, or otherwise avoid, a give-way boat. An example is if you are on *port tack* shortly after the start and a *starboard-tack* boat is sailing back to the line because she was over early, rule 20 (Starting Line Errors; Penalty Turns; Moving Astern) requires her to *keep clear* of you because you have *started* correctly, even though she is on *starboard tack* and you are on *port tack*. In this case you become the right-of-way boat and she the give-way boat for as long as the rule requires her to *keep clear*. Another example is that all boats are required to avoid a boat that is capsized, whether holding right of way over her or not (rule 21, Capsized, Anchored or Aground; Rescuing).

PREAMBLE TO SECTION D

When rule 20 or 21 applies between two boats, Section A rules do not.

This preamble clarifies that whenever rule 20 (Starting Errors; Penalty Turns; Moving Astern) or rule 21 (Capsized, Anchored or Aground; Rescuing) applies, it takes precedence over the basic right-of-way rules in Section A. Note, however, that the rules of Section B still apply, which most significantly means that rule 16 (Changing Course) applies to a boat given the right of way in rule 20.

Rule 20 – Starting Errors; Penalty Turns; Moving Astern

A boat sailing towards the pre-start side of the starting line or its extensions after her starting signal to comply with rule 29.1 or 30.1 shall *keep clear* of a boat not doing so until she is completely on the pre-start side. A boat making a penalty turn shall *keep clear* of one that is not. A boat moving astern by backing a sail shall *keep clear* of one that is not.

Rule 20 is actually three rules in one. Let's take them one at a time.

1) *A boat sailing towards the pre-start side of the starting line or its extensions after her starting signal to comply with rule 29.1 or 30.1 shall* ***keep clear*** *of a boat not doing so until she is completely on the pre-start side.*

Rule 29.1 (On the Course Side at the Start) reads, "*When at a boat's starting signal any part of her hull, crew or equipment is on the course side of the starting line, she shall sail completely to the pre-start side of the line before* ***starting.***" If you aren't completely behind the starting line at the starting signal, you are considered to be "on the course side" of the line (OCS). However, even when you and everyone else knows you are OCS, you keep all your right of way until you are sailing back **toward** the pre-start side of the starting line or its extensions, i.e. are converging with it. This means that you continue to have rights even while slowing down or luffing in order to get clear enough to turn back. When it is obvious that you are sailing back toward the starting line, you must then *keep clear* of all boats that have *started* properly or are on the pre-start side of the starting line.

Once you are completely on the pre-start side of the starting line or its extensions, you are instantly subject to the Section A rules again; however, remember that if you acquire the right of way over another boat, you have to initially give her *room* to *keep clear* of you under rule 15 (Acquiring Right of Way).

Notice that when the "one minute rule" (rule 30.1, Round-an-End Rule) is in effect, the requirement to *keep clear* in rule 20 only applies when you are sailing toward either end of the starting line to comply with rule 30.1 **after** your starting signal. Before your starting signal you have your normal right of way, even when you are over the line and obviously sailing towards an end to comply with rule 30.1.

Between two or more OCS boats sailing toward the pre-start side of the line, the Section A rules apply in the usual way.

"I realize that if another boat fouls me and forces me over the starting line just before the gun I'm OCS, but do I have to go back and restart?"

I'm afraid you do. Rule 29.1 (On the Course Side at the Start) requires that, when you are OCS, you sail completely to the pre-start side of the line before *starting*. If you don't, then you haven't *started* the race and have broken rule 29.1. You can only be exonerated from breaking a *rule* when another boat "compels" you to break a *rule* (rule 64.1(b), Penalties and Exoneration). In your case, the other boat may have forced you over the line, and you certainly should win your *protest* against her, but she hasn't prevented you from returning to the pre-start side and *starting*. Therefore no exoneration is available. This is similar to the situation when an outside boat wrongfully fails to give you enough *room* at a *mark* and forces you on the wrong side of it. Though you were clearly fouled, you still must round the *mark* on the correct side.

These are two examples of situations where you can be right under the rules but have your finishing place seriously hurt by a give-way boat with no way for a protest committee to compensate you. At these times I'm reminded of the old saying, "He had the right of way as he sped along; but he's just as dead as though he were wrong!"

2) A boat making a penalty turn shall keep clear of one that is not.

This rule talks to boats that are either doing a 360-degree Turns Penalty for touching a *mark* under rule 31.2 (Touching a Mark) or a 720-degree Turns Penalty for possibly breaking a rule of Part 2 under rule 44.2 (720-degree "Turns" Penalty). It clearly tells them that, while they are making their penalty turns, they have to *keep clear* of other boats, which makes sense.

Notice that when you hit a *mark* or possibly break a rule of Part 2, you still have all your rights as long as you continue sailing the course and while you are sailing well clear of the other boats preparatory to doing your penalty turn(s). But the moment it is obvious to other boats that you are clearly beginning to make a penalty turn, you must then *keep clear* of other boats in the race. You get your rights back when you have completed your last turn;

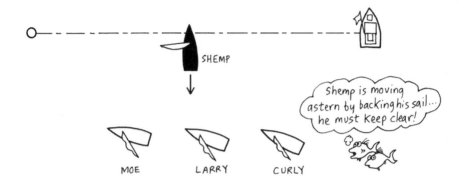

but remember that if you acquire the right of way over another boat, you must initially give her *room* to *keep clear* of you under rule 15 (Acquiring Right of Way).

Note that if you touch a starting *mark* or possibly break a rule of Part 2 before the starting signal, you can make your penalty turn(s) immediately, as opposed to waiting for the starting signal before doing them. And when two boats are making a penalty turn, the Section A rules apply in the usual way, as does rule 22.2 (Interfering with Another Boat).

3) A boat moving astern by backing a sail shall **keep clear** of one that is not.

This covers the situation where a boat actually backs its sail (i.e. holds the sail against the wind) and thereby causes the boat to move backward through the water. When a boat does this, she must *keep clear* of any other boat that is not doing likewise. Furthermore, she must remember that when she begins sailing backward, her action gives the right of way to boats astern; therefore they do not have to give her any *room* to *keep clear* of them under rule 15 (Acquiring Right of Way) because they acquired the right of way by the action of the boat moving astern.

Note that if a boat begins to move backward due to the backing of her sail, she continues to be subject to this rule for as long as she is moving astern, even if she lets her boom come amidships. However, if a boat simply begins to move backward because she has lost her headway, rule 20 does not apply to her.

However, the rule is somewhat different for boardsailors. Rule B2.1 (Sailboard Racing Rules, Part 2 – When Boats Meet) reads, "*A sailboard moving astern shall **keep clear** of other sailboards and boats.*" Therefore, **anytime** a sailboard is moving backward, regardless of the reason, she must *keep clear* of other sailboards and boats.

Rule 21 – Capsized, Anchored or Aground; Rescuing

If possible, a boat shall avoid a boat that is capsized or has not regained control after capsizing, is anchored or aground, or is trying to help a person or vessel in danger. A boat is capsized when her masthead is in the water.

SPECIAL SAILBOARD DEFINITIONS AND RULES

Rule B1 – Definitions:

Capsized   A sailboard is *capsized* when her sail or the competitor's body is in the water.

Recovering   A sailboard is *recovering* from the time her sail or, when water-starting, the competitor's body is out of the water until she has steerage way.

Rule B2.2 – Add to Section D:

Rule 23 – Sail Out of the Water When Starting

When approaching the starting line to *start*, a sailboard shall have her sail out of the water and in a normal position, except when accidentally *capsized*.

Rule 24 – Recovering

A sailboard recovering shall avoid a sailboard or boat under way.

Rule 21 is a common sense rule of safety, and as such it complements rule 1 (Safety). These two rules place the safety of sailors and their boats well above the importance of any race they may be in. The rationale for rule 21 is clear: if a boat is anchored, aground or capsized it cannot very well "move" to get out of another boat's way, and it may be in peril; and if one boat is in the act of rescuing another boat or person, no other boat should hinder the rescue in any way.

Note that rule 21 requires you to "avoid" the boats described in the rule. In my opinion, this means not only avoid contact but keep away from them as well. However, the rule's opening phrase ("If possible...") clarifies that if for whatever reasonable reason it is not possible for you to avoid them, you should not be penalized. This further emphasizes the safety principle in that if you are attempting to assist a boat that otherwise has right-of-way over you, you should not be penalized.

Also note that the definition *Obstruction* states that boats which others must "avoid" under rule 21 are considered *"obstructions."* This is a further safety aspect requiring outside boats to give inside boats *room* to avoid these boats in distress under rule 18 (Rounding and Passing Marks and Obstructions).

Finally, note that a sailboard is "capsized" when any part of its sail is in the water; but for sailboats, it is the location of the masthead that determines when the boat is "capsized." Given that it is possible to "capsize" a boat without the very top of the mast ever touching the water, I interpret "masthead" to include the top few feet of the mast. Note also that rule 21 offers protection to a sailboat while she is regaining control after capsizing, whereas a sailboard must avoid other sailboards and boats once her sail or the competitor's body is lifted from the water.

Rule 22 – Interfering with Another Boat

Rule 22 states two situations in which a boat cannot interfere with other boats.

Rule 22.1

If reasonably possible, a boat not *racing* shall not interfere with a boat that is *racing*.

Rule 22.1 makes it clear that before you begin *racing* and once you are no longer *racing*, you cannot interfere with boats that are *racing*. "Interfere" means that you have adversely affected a boat's forward progress or maneuverability. The principle of the rule is that a boat that is not *racing* should not adversely affect a boat that is *racing*.

Note that **any** "interference" will potentially break this rule. Particularly after *finishing*, boats need to be very careful where they sail so that their windshadow and physical presence do not hurt boats still *racing*. However, the rule's opening phrase ("If reasonably possible...") means that boats do not need to go to unreasonable measures to avoid interfering. If they are careful, they should have no problems.

Rule 22.2

A boat shall not deliberately interfere with a boat making penalty turns to delay her.

Rule 22.2 is intended to provide some protection to boats while they exonerate themselves. Notice there is no reference to a boat's *proper course* in the rule. Simply put, a boat can never intentionally interfere with another boat with the intent to delay her doing her turns, even if she can "justify" it by claiming she was sailing her *proper course*.

White got clear of other boats, then immediately did her circle, so she's exonerated for touching the mark.

10

Part 3 and Part 4
Conduct of a Race and Other Requirements When Racing

Part 3 contains the rules that govern the conduct of a race (rules 25-36). Part 4 contains other rules that govern us while we are *racing* (rules 40-54). Most of the rules are straightforward and simple to understand. I'll focus on the four for which an explanation might be helpful: rule 31 (Touching a Mark), rule 42 (Propulsion), rule 44 (Penalties for Breaking Rules of Part 2) and rule 50 (Setting and Sheeting Sails).

RULE 31 – TOUCHING A MARK

Rule 31.1

While *racing*, a boat shall not touch a starting *mark* before *starting*, a *mark* that begins, bounds or ends the leg of the course on which she is sailing, or a finishing *mark* after *finishing*.

Rule 31.2

A boat that has broken rule 31.1 may, after getting well clear of other boats as soon as possible, take a penalty by promptly making one complete 360° turn including one tack and one gybe. When a boat takes the penalty after touching a finishing *mark*, she shall sail completely to the course side of the line before *finishing*. However, if a boat has gained a significant advantage in the race or series by touching the *mark* she shall retire.

Prior to the 1969-73 rules, if you touched a *mark* and it was your fault, you had to drop out of the race. In the 1968 Olympics in Mexico, the late Carl Van Duyne, sailing the Finn for the United States, saw the leech of his main touch the windward *mark* as he rounded it in first place. Despite the claims of the race officer at the *mark* who insisted that Carl did not touch the *mark*, Carl withdrew from the race. From this example and others, the rule writers saw the obvious over-severity of this penalty for the infraction, and changed the rule to permit sailors to take a penalty when they accidentally touch a *mark*.

Notice that the rule applies only while you are *racing*, which is the time from your preparatory signal until you have finished and cleared the finishing line and finishing *marks*. Also, if the starting line is set to leeward of the leeward *mark* on the first leg or the finishing line is set to windward of the windward *mark* on the last leg, that leeward or windward *mark* does not begin, bound or end that first or last leg so there is no penalty for touching it. Otherwise, when you touch a starting or finishing *mark*, or any *mark* that begins, bounds or ends a leg on which you are sailing, you have broken rule 31.1.

When you've broken rule 31.1 and want to take a penalty, here's how the penalty works. You must first get well clear of other boats **as soon as possible** after touching the *mark* (not half-way down the leg!). Then, once clear you must **promptly** (i.e. without delay) make a 360-degree turn including one tack and one gybe. While you are making your turn, you have to *keep clear* of other boats under rule 20 (Starting Errors; Penalty Turns; Moving Astern). Once you have completed your turn, you have completed your penalty and the rules of Section A apply to you again. Remember, if you acquire right of way over another boat after your turn, you have to initially give them *room* to *keep clear* under rule 15 (Acquiring Right of Way).

 "If I hit one of the starting marks after the preparatory signal but well before the starting signal, when can I make my penalty turn?"

As soon as possible! The rule does not require you to wait until the starting signal. The rationale is that the penalty should fit the crime. Touching the *mark* three minutes before your start probably has little effect on anyone's race; likewise your penalty turn will be of little adverse consequence to you. However, touching it ten seconds from the start means that you are probably somewhere you shouldn't be and are likely adversely affecting the start for

others; by the same token, making a penalty turn while others are *starting* will be of more negative consequence to you.

"What do I do if I accidentally hit the finishing mark after I've finished but before I've cleared the mark?"

If you touch a finishing *mark* before you have cleared the finishing line and *marks* (i.e. while you are still *racing*), you can make your penalty turn anywhere, but you then have to cross the finishing line again from the course side of the line. The second time you cross will be your finishing place or time.

Notice the last sentence in rule 31.2, *"However, if a boat has gained a significant advantage in the race or series by touching the mark she shall retire."* This is clearly intended to deter boats from sailing into situations where they calculate that they can hit the *mark*, do a quick 360-degree turn and still come out well ahead of where they would be had they not done so. One example is at a crowded windward *mark* with a long line of *starboard-tackers*, where there is not enough space for a *port-tacker* (P) to tack in to *leeward* of the *starboard-tackers* and make it around the *mark* without either fouling the *starboard-tackers* or hitting the *mark*. P could probably come out ahead by hitting the *mark* and doing a quick "360" as opposed to ducking the line of *starboard-tackers*, but this wouldn't be fair; hence the rule against it in 31.2.

"What happens when I'm forced to touch a mark by another boat that was required to keep clear of me or give me room?"

Whenever you touch a *mark*, you have three options:

1) If you think it was your own fault that you touched the *mark*, you can get clear of other boats and take your penalty as described in rule 31.2; or

2) If you believe another boat wrongfully compelled you to hit the *mark*, you can choose to not take a penalty. But you must protest the other boat (by hailing the word "Protest" and, if required, flying your flag at the first reasonable opportunity). If the other boat acknowledges breaking a rule of Part 2 and takes a voluntary penalty ("720" or Scoring Penalty, etc. under rule 44, Penalties for Breaking Rules of Part 2) or retires from the race, the protest committee should exonerate you from breaking rule 31.1 under rule 64.1(b) (Penalties and Exoneration), provided they decide that it was that breach that caused you to touch the *mark*. Otherwise, you must hope the protest committee decides that in fact it was the other boat's Part 2 rule breach that compelled you to touch the *mark*, in which case they will disqualify the other boat and exonerate you under rule 64.1(b). If they don't, you will be disqualified for breaking rule 31.1.

3) If you believe another boat wrongfully compelled you to hit the *mark*, you can do a 360-degree turn, i.e. take the penalty in rule 31.2 as insurance, and protest the other boat. If the protest committee decides the other boat broke a *rule*, she will be disqualified. If the protest committee decides she didn't break a *rule*, you will not be disqualified for breaking rule 31.1 because you already took a penalty for that.

"Does it count if just my head brushes against the mark?"

Absolutely yes. In fact, if you have a late spinnaker take-down and your spinnaker sheet trails behind the boat and rubs against the *mark* after you're already around and a boat-length away from it, you still have to take your penalty. ISAF Case 77 sums it up, "A boat touches a *mark* within the meaning of rule 31 when any part of her hull, crew or equipment comes in contact with the mark. The fact that her equipment touches the mark because she has maneuvering or sail-handling difficulties does not excuse her breach of the rule."

"If I get the mark's anchor line caught on my centerboard but quickly raise my board and clear the line before I touch the mark, have I hit the mark? What happens when I'm not so quick and the mark is dragged in and touches my boat?"

Remember that the anchor line of a *mark* is **not** part of the *mark* (see the definition *Mark*). So on a race committee boat with a high bow, where 15 feet of anchor line may be above the water, the *mark* begins at the bow of the boat. The same is true when a *mark's* anchor line is partially or wholly submerged. In both cases, there is no penalty for touching the line. However, if touching its anchor line causes the *mark* to be drawn against your boat, you have touched the *mark* and must do a 360-degree turn penalty or protest. US SAILING Appeal 10 reads, "If, however, fouling its anchor line causes the mark to be drawn against the boat, the boat has broken rule 31."

"What if I foul another boat and hit a mark in the same incident?"

Good question. Rule 44.4(a) (Penalties for Breaking Rules of Part 2, Limits on Penalties) says, *"When a boat intends to take a penalty as provided in rule 44.1 and in the same incident has touched a **mark**, she need not take the penalty provided in rule 31.2."* Therefore, when a 720-degree Turns Penalty or a Scoring Penalty under rule 44 is available, and you choose to accept that penalty, you do not have to also do a 360-degree turn penalty for hitting the *mark*.

SPECIAL SAILBOARD RULE

(Rule B3, Conduct of a Race)

Rule 31 is changed to: 'A competitor shall not hold on to a starting *mark*.' Notice that, other than the prohibition against holding onto the starting *mark*, there is no rule 31 for boardsailing. This means that when sailboard racing, it is legal to touch the *marks*! Just remember that you still must leave them on the correct side (rule 28.1, Sailing the Course).

RULE 42 – PROPULSION

Rule 42.1 – Basic Rule

Except when permitted in rule 42.3 or rule 45, a boat shall compete by using only the wind and water to increase, maintain or decrease her speed. Her

crew may adjust the trim of sails and hull, and perform other acts of seamanship, but shall not otherwise move their bodies to propel the boat.

Rule 42 is the "pumping, rocking, ooching, sculling" rule. The rule specifically tells sailors how they can, and cannot, propel their boats in a sailboat race. The principle behind rule 42 is simple: the rule writers (and most sailors themselves) want people to race their sailboats by sailing them (i.e. using the natural wind) as opposed to by propelling or slowing them in other ways. If you are a bit too early for a start, it is more of a sport if you have to slow down using your sails and rudder than if you could just stick your arms in the water and backpaddle; just as it's more challenging and fun to try to ride the waves on a windy reach as opposed to handing all the sheets to Igor and telling him to "pump" nonstop to the leeward *mark*.

Compliance with this rule continues to be a major problem facing the sport. In my opinion, the rule clearly states what is permitted and what is prohibited. After an explanation of the rule, I will discuss the more central issue of competitor self-control and self-policing.

Rule 42.1 clearly states the basic premise: "*A boat shall compete by using only the wind and water to increase, maintain or decrease her speed. Her crew may adjust the trim of sails and hull, and perform other acts of seamanship, but shall not otherwise move their bodies to propel the boat.*" This is the way sailboats are to be raced; i.e. they can be powered only by the natural action of the wind and water. The last phrase in the rule serves to prohibit any crew action that **in and of itself** propels the boat (paddling is an obvious example), and serves to prohibit any newly discovered kinetic technique not listed in rule 42.2. Note that the term "crew" refers to **all sailors on board**, including the helmsman.

Notice that it is just as illegal to slow yourself down ("decrease speed") unnaturally as it is to propel yourself. So if you're early for a start or trapped on the outside of a crowd at a *mark*, you can't stick your leg in the water to slow down. Likewise, if you luff a boat before the start and hit them, you can't hang on to them to slow yourself down so you're not early. However, there are legal ways to slow yourself down using the natural action of the wind and water. One is to physically hold the boom out so the wind pushes against the sail; another is to turn the rudder hard over against the flow of the water provided it is not done repeatedly back and forth (see discussion of "sculling" in rule 42.2(d)). (See US SAILING Appeal 25.)

Note also that a boat can be penalized for breaking rule 42 only while she is *racing* (see preamble to Part 4). ISAF Case 69 says, "During the period in which the boat was racing she was using wind and water as sources of power as required by rule 42.1. Her motion resulted from momentum created by engine power that propelled her before she began racing. Nothing in the rule requires that a boat be in any particular state of motion or non-motion when she begins racing." Likewise, in light air and adverse current, a boat can just get its bow across the finish line (thereby *finishing*), drift backward, and, when clear of the finishing line and finishing *marks* (i.e., no longer *racing*), turn on her engine and power out of the course area.

There are some common sense exceptions built into rule 42 for safety reasons.

Rule 42.3(c) Any means of propulsion may be used to help a person or another vessel in danger.

Rule 42.3(d) To get clear after grounding or colliding with another boat or object, a boat may use force applied by the crew of either boat and any equipment other than a propulsion engine.

These reinforce the overriding safety principle that you should get to a boat or person's rescue as fast as you can using any means available, including paddling, rocking, or an engine when you have one. Obviously, this is not intended to be misused as a deceitful way to advance along the race course. ISAF Case 20 and the discussion of rule 1.1 (Safety, Helping Those in Danger) are clear as to the responsibility all racing sailors have, and when and how a boat that renders assistance should be compensated.

Also, when you go aground or hit another boat, you may use whatever means of force is necessary to clear yourself, except that you can't use your engine to propel yourself. Note that you can use the power from your engine to run a winch or windlass, etc. if necessary.

"Can I anchor?"

Yes. Rule 45 (Hauling Out; Making Fast; Anchoring) states, "*[A boat] may anchor or the crew may stand on the bottom.*" Rule 42.1 specifically permits

the actions described in rule 45. Generally boats anchor either as a safety measure or to decrease the speed at which they are moving away from their desti-
nation (as in adverse current). Note that a means of anchoring is the crew
standing on the bottom. Of course if that crew starts walking the boat around,
rule 42 is broken.

ISAF Case 5 says, "Recovering an anchor, whether it was lowered or thrown
forward, so as to gather way over the ground breaks rule 42.1." The point is
clear: anchoring should be a means of keeping you where you are, and not a
means of advancing yourself along the race course. Clearly, if you throw your
anchor forward and then recover the anchor, you will be "pulling yourself"
forward past where you were when you threw out the anchor. Therefore,
when *racing*, the anchor must be **dropped straight** down. Likewise, when you
pull the anchor back up, you can't generate momentum that will cause the
boat to move **past** the point where the anchor was on the ground, i.e. where
it was dropped.

*"Now what about the actions listed in rule 42.2; are they always prohibit-
ed, or only when they are actually capable of propelling the boat?"*

Rule 42.2 lists five specific types of actions which are **always** prohibited, regardless of whether they are capable of propelling the boat or not. This makes
it easier for sailors to know what they can't do, and for judges to administer
the rule on the water and in protest hearings.

The five are the major "offenses" and are listed in order of perceived fre-
quency of use (or abuse!).

Rule 42.2 - Prohibited Actions

Without limiting the application of rule 42.1, these actions are prohibited:

(a) **pumping: repeated fanning of any sail either by trimming and releasing
the sail or by vertical or athwartships body movement;**

(b) **rocking: repeated rolling of the boat, induced either by body movement
or adjustment of the sails or centreboard, that does not facilitate steering;**

(c) **ooching: sudden forward body movement, stopped abruptly;**

(d) **sculling: repeated movement of the helm not necessary for steering;**

(e) repeated tacks or gybes unrelated to changes in the wind or to tactical considerations.

Let me reemphasize: if you do any of these above-listed actions, you have broken rule 42.2. It does not matter whether the action actually propelled the boat, or even if it was capable of propelling the boat! Therefore, it applies to boats of all sizes. Note that class rules and sailing instructions can change rule 42, including some of the prohibitions in rule 42.2 (see rule 86, Rule Changes).

To understand these descriptions, notice the use of the word "repeated" throughout, indicating that for the actions to be illegal they must continue nonstop for an extended period of time or for more than just one movement. "Ooching" is the only action that involves a singular movement.

(a) **Pumping:** for a sail to be "pumped," it must be trimmed and then released. When a sail is pumped "repeatedly" in short succession, it will look like the sail is being "fanned." This is illegal. This can be done using the sheets, or by using body motions. Bouncing up and down on the rail is an example of "vertical" movement; and crossing the boat quickly from side to side is "athwartships" movement. In a small boat with a flexible mast, bouncing can "pump" the top of the sail. Likewise, movement side to side will commonly cause the angle of heel to change, which in turn can act to "pump" the sail. These means of "pumping" are also illegal. Rule 42.3(b) allows limited "pumping" in certain conditions.

This rule is not designed to inhibit good sailing techniques. On a puffy windy day, the mainsail can be played in and out constantly to keep the boat flat, provided it doesn't become a "fanning" action. Similarly, downwind, the spinnaker sheet can be constantly played in response to changes in apparent wind.

(b) **Rocking:** Your boat is "rocking" when it is rolling back and forth. You may be intentionally doing it with your body, or you may have simply encouraged it by pulling your centerboard up, letting your boom way out, and then starting the action like a pendulum. It doesn't matter whether your body is moving. If your boat is rhythmically rolling back and forth, it's "rocking," and that is illegal at all times. Obviously, waves themselves will cause the boat to toss about. You do not have to run all over the boat counteracting every wave action. If you've ever watched a fleet of boats on a broad reach or run, you know that they all are being tossed in a similar way. If one boat is being intentionally "rocked," she will stand out instantly as being different from the others.

Notice that the rule permits "rolling" the boat to facilitate steering. For instance, going down a wavy reach it is legal to heel the boat to leeward to head up over a wave, then heel it to windward to steer down the backside, etc. Notice also that on a run most boats sail faster when heeled to windward, and the crew can position their weight to do this, provided the boat doesn't start "rocking" back and forth as a result.

(c) **Ooching:** "Ooching" is a "sudden forward body movement, stopped abruptly." The key to "ooching" is that it is forward motion, it is sudden, and it is stopped abruptly. Even just one "ooch" is illegal. Pushing or pulling on the mast or shrouds (forward hand movements), slamming forward on the front of the cockpit, mast shrouds or forestay, and subtle abrupt forward motions with the rear or feet are all examples of "ooching" and are illegal at all times.

(d) **Sculling:** "Sculling" is "repeated movement of the helm not necessary for steering." Notice there is no reference to "forceful" or to "crossing the centerline." Simply put, you cannot "wiggle" your tiller unless you are attempting to steer the boat.

There are two common situations in which repeated movement of the helm is often required to help steer a boat. One is when you are trying to bear off on a broad reach in heavy air when about to broach and forcefully moving the helm back and forth can help prevent the rudder from "stalling," thereby increasing steerageway; and the second is in very light winds in order just to turn the boat.

e) **Repeated tacks or gybes unrelated to changes in the wind or to tactical considerations:** You cannot repeatedly tack or gybe back and forth in quick succession unless you can justify your maneuvers based on changes in the wind (windshifts, etc.) or tactical considerations (covering another boat, etc.). Notice, you can tack or gybe for any reason you want; you just can't do it "repeatedly" without the specific reasons listed in this rule.

"Are there any exceptions to the prohibitions in rule 42.2?"

Yes. They are in rule 42.3, Exceptions

42.3 – Exceptions

(a) A boat's crew may move their bodies to exaggerate the rolling that facilitates steering the boat through a tack or a gybe, provided that, just after the tack or gybe is completed, the boat's speed is not greater than it would have been in the absence of the tack or gybe.

(b) Except on a beat to windward, when surfing (rapidly accelerating down the leeward side of a wave) or planing is possible, the boat's crew may pull the sheet and the guy controlling any sail in order to initiate surfing or planing, but only once for each wave or gust of wind.

"So it is legal to roll-tack?"

Absolutely yes. Rule 42.3(a) specifically permits you to exaggerate the rolling provided it helps you steer the boat onto the new *tack*, and provided you don't come out of your tack going faster than just before you began it. Therefore, you can begin with a heel to *leeward* to begin the boat heading up. Then, as the boat is at or near head to wind, you can roll the boat hard to the new *leeward* side to help "pivot" the boat onto its new close-hauled course. Finally, you can bring the boat upright as it gets to its close-hauled course.

The most important thing is that once the boat is brought up from its roll, the mast cannot make a major dip to *leeward* and back up again. This second "pump," which serves to accelerate the boat rather than steer it, is illegal.

"Does rule 42.3(b) permit one pump of each sail per wave?"

Yes. Rule 42.3(b) permits "pumping," but only to initiate surfing or planing. The rule permits one "pump" for each sail (main, spinnaker and jib if desired, though pumping the jib is generally slow). However, if the "pump" on the main gets the boat surfing, a subsequent "pump" on the spinnaker sheet would not be legal. If the main and spinnaker were "pumped" simultaneously, there would be no problem.

Notice that you must be just ready to launch down the leeward face of the wave. You can't "pump" up the windward side of the wave claiming it will get you over the top and down the leeward side faster. A "planing" boat will be lifted partly out of the water by its own bow wave, and its stern wave will disappear. Visually it will look like the boat is skimming across the surface of the water. The phrase "except on a beat to windward" prohibits you from "pumping" upwind at all for any reason.

Notice also that you can only "pump" using the sheet or guy controlling the sail. You cannot therefore "pump" using the vang or a special "pumping" line.

 "Is it true I can never ooch?"

That's right. Rule 42.3 makes no exception for ooching.

 "Why is rule 42.3(b) so restrictive, and can the rule ever be made more permissive?"

The rule writers have taken this step to reduce the strength factor required to race sailboats successfully, and to ensure that the sport remains a sailing contest. Notice that the class rules or sailing instructions can make this rule more permissive by modifying it with a specific reference to it (rule 86, Rule Changes). Therefore a class can permit more than one pump per wave or ooching, etc. This is an issue all the members of each class should thoroughly discuss.

 "I heard that a protest committee can throw me out under rule 42 without a hearing, and that a DSQ under rule 42 can't be used as a 'throwout' race; is this true?"

Rule 67 (Rule 42 and Hearing Requirement) states, *"When so stated in the sailing instructions, the protest committee may penalize without a hearing a boat that has broken rule 42, provided that a member of the committee or its designated observer has seen the incident, and a disqualification under this rule shall not be excluded from the boat's series score. A boat so penalized shall be informed by notification in the race results."* Notice that the protest committee can only disqualify you without a hearing **if** the sailing instructions give them that permission. Also, if you are disqualified without a hearing and feel you did not break rule 42, you can request redress under rule 62.1(a)

(Redress) which entitles you to a hearing under rule 63.1 (Hearings, Requirement for a Hearing).

Furthermore, rule 67 prevents a boat from "dropping" a DSQ under rule 42!

"What about this new "three strikes and you're out" system the judge can use on the water?"

In fact, the system is not "new." It has been used successfully at the international level, including the Olympics and ISAF class World Championships for several years now. The system has been revised enough to the point where ISAF feels it is useful to the sport to include it in *The Racing Rules of Sailing*. It is contained in Appendix N, Immediate Penalties for Breaking Rule 42. Note that it is in effect **only** if the sailing instructions state that it is.

APPENDIX N – IMMEDIATE PENALTIES FOR BREAKING RULE 42

This appendix applies only if the sailing instructions so state.

N1 PROTESTS

A member of the protest committee or its designated observer who sees a boat breaking rule 42 may protest her by, as soon as reasonably possible, making a sound signal, pointing a yellow flag at her and hailing her sail number, even if she is no longer *racing*. A boat so protested is not subject to another *protest* under rule 42 for the same incident.

N2 PENALTIES

N2.1 First Protest

When a boat is first protested under rule N1 she may acknowledge her breach by taking a 720° Turns Penalty under rule 44.2. If she fails to do so she shall be disqualified without a hearing.

N2.2 Second Protest

When a boat is protested a second time during the series she may acknowledge her breach by immediately retiring from the race. If she fails to do so she shall be disqualified without a hearing and her score shall not be excluded.

N2.3   Third Protest

When a boat is protested a third time during the series she may acknowledge her breach by immediately retiring from the race and from all other races in the series. If she fails to do so she shall be disqualified without a hearing from all races in the series, with no score excluded, and the protest committee shall consider calling a hearing under rule 69.1(a).

N3   POSTPONEMENT, GENERAL RECALL OR ABANDONMENT

If a boat has been protested under rule N1 and the race committee signals a *postponement*, general recall or *abandonment*, the penalty from her first or second *protest* is cancelled, but the *protest* is counted to determine the number of times she has been protested during the series.

"Now I understand what rule 42 allows and doesn't allow; but what do I do when another competitor starts to rock or pump by me?"

Most active racers believe that the rule itself is clear enough and is not the cause of the problem. The real problem is the enforcement of the rule. There are several extreme positions, and there have been many creative attempts made at resolving this issue. Some say the enforcement should be left completely up to judges around the course; i.e. flood the course with referees. Others argue that it is impractical to put that many judges on the course; and that because competitors will never police themselves, the rule itself should be abolished altogether and the race committees given the authority to proclaim before a race that either "anything" or "nothing" goes.

Fortunately, the majority of us believe that the racing is best when the sailors themselves have the responsibility to sail within the **rules**. We have seen too many regattas with either too few judges or poorly qualified ones. More to the point, we like the concept of competitor-enforced **rules** which makes our sport unique from almost all others.

But it takes only a few people in each fleet to ruin it for the rest. If some decide that doing well in the race by cheating is okay, and they start pumping and sculling off the starting line and rocking downwind, it puts the other sailors in a very awkward position. Either they can join in, or warn and then protest the other boat, or do nothing. To join in, they have to admit that the problem is not worth their effort to fight it. To do nothing is frustrating because those sailors will feel that not only are they being left behind, but that nothing is being done to enforce the rule.

I strongly recommend these three steps: 1) first warning the other boat; 2) then get the attention of some other boats nearby with the hopes that they'll say something too; and 3) then protest if the illegal actions continue. You are not being the "bad guy" for simply doing what you'd do if a *port-tacker* hit you when you were on *starboard-tack*. It is destructive to the racing when people feel they can get away with cheating; and they will continue to only get worse if no one calls them on it.

In the hearing the protest committee should (a) find out exactly what the wind and wave conditions were; (b) discuss what the sailing characteristics of the boat are from their shared experiences, competitors' testimony and expert witnesses when useful; and (c) determine what the exact actions of the protestee were. Witnesses are useful to everyone and are desired. Remember, it is permissible for members of the protest committee to also be the protestor, but they must be sure to give their entire testimony with evidence while all the *parties* to the hearing are present and able to ask questions and otherwise respond. (See rule 60, Right to Protest and Request Redress; rule 63.3, Right to be Present; and rule 63.6, Taking Evidence and Finding Facts.)

The bottom line to the rule 42 issue is that everyone who races should make the effort to understand exactly what the rule does and does not allow, and then sail within the rule's limits. The rule is not that complex to understand, and my guess is that most sailors who have studied it have a good sense of what is right and wrong. Where it breaks down is when sailors intentionally ignore the rule for their own personal gain. All fleets of sailors should talk about this issue.

SPECIAL SAILBOARD RULE RELATING TO RULE 42

Rule B4.1 – Part 4-Other Requirements When Racing

Rule 42 is changed to: 'A sailboard shall be propelled only by the action of the wind on the sail, by the action of the water on the hull and by the unassisted actions of the competitor.'

For sailboard racing, the rule writers have removed any prohibition on how the sailors use their bodies to propel their sailboards. This is a "black and white" step that removes any need to worry about what is "natural sailing motion" and what is "illegal kinetics."

Remember that rule B3 (Part 3-Conduct of a Race) does not permit sailboard sailors to hold onto starting *marks*.

Rule 44 – PENALTIES FOR BREAKING RULES OF PART 2

Rule 44.1 – Taking a Penalty

A boat that may have broken a rule of Part 2 while *racing* may take a penalty at the time of the incident. Her penalty shall be a 720° Turns Penalty unless the sailing instructions specify the use of the Scoring Penalty or some other penalty. However, if she caused serious damage or gained a significant advantage in the race or series by her breach she shall retire.

Rule 44.1 states that if you think you may have broken a rule of Part 2 while *racing*, you can **always** take a voluntary penalty at the time of the incident. This is sensible. Mistakes happen, and there should be a consequence for breaking a rule; but forcing sailors to retire and sail in for a minor infraction is not in balance with the great effort, time and expense that goes into participating in a race.

Rule 44.1 states that the voluntary penalty is the "720" (described below) unless the sailing instructions specify the use of some other penalty. Another common penalty is the Scoring Penalty, often known as the "percentage penalty." This is clearly described in rule 44.3 (Scoring Penalty) and won't be described in this book.

Note that even a right-of-way boat can need to take a penalty. If a right-of-way boat fails to avoid contact with another boat when it was reasonably possible for her to do so, she breaks rule 14 (Avoiding Contact). If damage results from the contact, she is liable to being penalized and can do a "720" to absolve herself.

Notice, however, that if any boat causes "serious damage" or gains a "significant advantage" in the race or series by her breach, **she must retire**; i.e. she cannot absolve herself by taking a voluntary penalty. This is a clear reminder to all competitors, whether holding the right of way or not, to be careful and sportsmanlike.

"Before going on, could you discuss the term 'serious damage'?"

Sure. Understand, however, that this is one of those terms that is impossible to define. I will discuss what, in my opinion, are the important considerations based on the rule, the appeals, the dictionary and my interpretation.

The dictionary offers the following definitions:

"serious": having significant or dangerous possible consequences, not trifling or inconsequential.

"damage": harm or injury impairing the value or usefulness of something, or the health or normal function of a person.

The three primary considerations are:

1) what was the extent of the damage; i.e. how much damage or injury was done, did the damage or injury require immediate repair or medical attention to prevent further damage or injury, what was the cost of the repair or medical attention, and what affect did the damage or injury have on the boat in future races.

2) was it feasible or prudent for the boat to continue in the race; and

3) did the damage markedly affect the boat's speed, performance or maneuverability; i.e. did the damage significantly worsen her finishing place in the race?

Certainly, if the damage causes the boat to discontinue the race, it is "serious," including when the "damage" is an injury to a person on board. If the boat can safely continue in the race and loses no finishing places as a direct result of the damage, and the nature and cost of any necessary repair isn't too high, the damage is not "serious." (Note that it is most impossible to put a price tag on "serious;" that will have to be decided by the protest committee after considering all the relevant factors.)

If the damage is a deep scratch that penetrates the fiberglass, thereby requiring immediate repair after the race so that further damage doesn't result or so that the future speed, performance or maneuverability of the boat isn't affected, that damage would begin to fall into the "serious" category. If the extent of the repair were such that it could be handled that evening by the sailors involved with a minimum of hassle and expense, I would be inclined to rule it not "serious." But if the repair required more professional work and became a more costly and time-consuming affair, I would be more inclined to rule it "serious." If, however, the damage is a 12-inch surface scratch in the gelcoat, which does not affect the overall speed, performance or maneuverability of the boat, I would not be as inclined to rule it "serious."

If the damage is a broken boom near the finish and the boat loses no places but cannot repair or replace the boom before the second race of that day, I'd consider the damage to be "serious;" but if the damage was to something that could normally be repaired or replaced on the water, such as a bent guyhook, the damage would not be "serious."

 "Thanks! Now how do I take a "720" turns penalty?"

Rule 44.2 – 720° Turns Penalty

After getting well clear of other boats as soon after the incident as possible, a boat takes a 720° Turns Penalty by promptly making two complete 360° turns (720°) in the same direction, including two tacks and two gybes. When a boat takes the penalty at or near the finishing line, she shall sail completely to the course side of the line before *finishing*.

When you want to do a "720," you must first get well clear of other boats **as soon as possible** after the incident (not half-way down the leg!). Remember that while you are getting clear you still have all your Section A rights; i.e. your penalty does not begin until you clearly begin making your turns (rule 20, Starting Errors; Penalty Turns; Moving Astern).

Once you are clear, you must **promptly** (i.e. without delay) make two complete 360-degree turns in the same direction, including one tack and one gybe. Notice that you have to do one turn immediately after the other, though it is generally acceptable to build enough speed after the first circle to be able to sail efficiently through the second one. While you are making your turns, you have to *keep clear* of other boats (rule 20).

Once you have completed your turns, you have completed your penalty and the rules of Section A apply to you again. Remember, if you acquire right of way over another boat after your second turn, you have to initially give them *room* to *keep clear* under rule 15 (Acquiring Right of Way).

Note that if you break a rule before the starting signal, you can do your "720" immediately; i.e. you don't have to wait until after the starting signal. As in touching a *mark*, the rationale is that the penalty should fit the crime. Breaking a rule three minutes before your start probably has little effect on anyone's race; likewise your "720" will be of little adverse consequence to you. However, breaking a rule ten seconds from the start means that you are probably somewhere you shouldn't be and are likely adversely affecting the start for others; by the same token, doing a "720" while others are *starting* will be of more negative consequence to you.

If you break a *rule* near the finishing line, you can do your "720" anywhere, but you then have to cross the finishing line again from the course side of the line. The second time you cross will be your finishing place or time.

Rule 44.4 – Limits on Penalties

(a) **When a boat intends to take a penalty as provided in rule 44.1 and in the same incident has touched a *mark*, she need not take the penalty provided in rule 31.2.**

(b) **A boat that takes a penalty shall not be penalized further with respect to the same incident unless she failed to retire when rule 44.1 required her to do so.**

These limits are very straightforward. In rule 44.4(a), the rule writers are being compassionate saying, "You know you got yourself in trouble; do your two circles for fouling the other boat but there's no need to do a third circle!"

Rule 44.4(b) states that a boat can only be penalized once per incident, regardless of how many *rules* she may have broken in that incident. Therefore, when a give-way boat breaks rule 10 (On Opposite Tacks) and fails to avoid a collision, thereby breaking rule 14 (Avoiding Contact), she need only do one "720." US SAILING Appeal 65 discusses the question of when two occurrences are considered one or two incidents, saying in essence that the test is whether the second occurrence was the inevitable result of the first.

"If I'm not sure who's right, can I do a '720' and still protest the other boat, or am I admitting guilt by doing my '720'?"

Excellent question. You can definitely protest the other boat and your "720" is not an admission of guilt. Rule 44.1 carefully says, "A boat that **may** (emphasis added) have broken a rule…may take a penalty." Furthermore, the US SAILING prescription to rule 68 (Damages) says, "*A boat that retires from a race or accepts a penalty does not, by that action alone, admit liability for damages.*" Let's say you do a "720" and protest and that the other boat did neither. If the protest committee finds that the other boat was wrong in your incident, she will be disqualified. If the protest committee decides that you actually were wrong, you can't be further penalized because you already took a voluntary penalty (rule 44.4(b)). Therefore, you can view your "720" as "insurance" against further penalty in an incident where you're not 100% certain how the protest committee will decide it.

RULE 50 – SETTING AND SHEETING SAILS

Rule 50.1 – Changing Sails

When headsails or spinnakers are being changed, a replacing sail may be fully set and trimmed before the replaced sail is lowered. However, only one mainsail and, except when changing, only one spinnaker shall be carried set at a time.

Rule 50.2 – Spinnaker Poles, Whisker Poles

Only one spinnaker pole or whisker pole shall be used at a time except when gybing. When in use, it shall be attached to the foremost mast.

Rule 50.3 – Use of Outriggers

(a) No sail shall be sheeted over or through an outrigger, except as permitted in rule 50.3(b). An outrigger is any fitting or other device so placed that it could exert outward pressure on a sheet or sail at a point from which, with the boat upright, a vertical line would fall outside the hull or deck planking. For the purpose of this rule, bulwarks, rails and rubbing strakes are not part of the hull or deck planking and the following are not outriggers: a bowsprit used to secure the tack of a working sail, a bumkin used to sheet the boom of a working sail, or a boom of a boomed headsail that requires no adjustment when tacking.

(b) (1) Any sail may be sheeted to or led above a boom that is regularly used for a working sail and is permanently attached to the mast from which the head of the working sail is set.

    (2) A headsail may be sheeted or attached at its clew to a spinnaker pole or whisker pole, provided that a spinnaker is not set.

50.4 – Headsails

The difference between a headsail and a spinnaker is that the mid-girth of a headsail, measured from the mid-points of its luff and leech, does not exceed 50% of the length of its foot, and no other intermediate girth exceeds a percentage similarly proportional to its distance from the head of the sail. A sail tacked down behind the foremost mast is not a headsail.

Note that this rule does not require that a spinnaker pole be used at all when flying a spinnaker! The only pole requirements are in rule 50.2. In other words, you can only use one pole at a time; and when it is "in use," i.e. projecting the spinnaker or headsail outboard, it must be attached to the mast.

    With no requirement to use a pole, boats are free to do "gybe-sets" and "floater-drops." In both of these maneuvers, the spinnaker is set and drawing with no pole attached. In other words, a boat can legally gybe around the windward *mark*, set her spinnaker, fill it, and sail on down the leg with no pole. And likewise, when coming into a leeward *mark*, a boat can legally remove her pole and sail for as long as she chooses before lowering her spinnaker. However, when the pole is down, note that rule 49.2 (Crew Position) forbids competitors from leaning their torsos out over the lifelines "except briefly to perform a necessary task."

"So can a crew member lean out over a boat's lifelines to hold the spinnaker guy after the pole has been removed?"

Yes, but only "briefly." US SAILING Appeal 72 reads, "Without a spinnaker pole, a spinnaker is less efficient and more unstable. As a boat prepares to round a leeward *mark*, removing the pole is one of the first necessary steps. From that time until the spinnaker is lowered, holding the guy by hand is a less effective but nonetheless useful means of controlling the spinnaker, which remains a "necessary task" even without the pole. The interval of time is normally a brief one, since generally there is no advantage in flying a spinnaker without a pole."

Also note that there is no requirement that the tack of the spinnaker be in "close proximity" to the outboard end of the spinnaker pole. The rationale is that it is generally faster to have the tack close to the outboard end, such that why penalize a boat if she chooses not to do so.

Note that rule 86.1(c) (Rule Changes) permits class rules to change this rule.

 "I see a lot of boats flying asymmetrical spinnakers from bowsprits; I assume this is legal?"

Yes. Rule 50.3(a) specifically states, *"For the purpose of this rule... the following are not outriggers: a bowsprit used to secure the tack of a working sail..."* Rule 50.3 is not broken provided that the bowsprit is used to attach the tack (the windward corner) of the spinnaker or as a lead for a line attached to the tack. Rule 50.3 prohibits "sheeting" a spinnaker with an outrigger; e.g. controlling the clew (the leeward corner) with a sheet led through a bowsprit, because a bowsprit is an outrigger.

11

Part 5
Protests, Redress, Hearings, Misconduct and Appeals

PART 5 contains all the rules governing who can protest, how to protest, how to ask for redress, how and when a protest hearing should be run, what penalties can be applied and how to appeal (rules 60-71). It is divided into four sections: Section A, Protests and Redress; Section B, Hearings and Decisions; Section C, Gross Misconduct; and Section D, Appeals. I will focus on the Section A rules governing protests by boats.

Remember that a *protest* is defined as *"An allegation made under rule 61.2 by a boat, a race committee or a protest committee that a boat has broken a rule"* (see definition *Protest*). A *protest*, therefore, is merely a means of bringing a *rules* issue to a hearing after the race where the sailors involved and the members of the protest committee can review the incident and decide how the *rules* apply.

Our sport is premised on competitors doing just that when there is an incident in which neither boat acknowledges being in the wrong. *Protests* that are the result of honest differences of opinions on the *rules* or observations of the incident should never have a negative taint to them.

Competitor enforcement of the *rules* is the tradition of our sport, and when the *rules* are not followed, or their application is in question, we owe it to our fellow competitors, for the quality and fairness of the racing, to protest.

SECTION A – PROTESTS and REDRESS

Rule 60 – RIGHT TO PROTEST AND REQUEST REDRESS

Rule 60.1

A boat may

(a) **protest another boat, but not for an alleged breach of a rule of Part 2 unless she was involved in or saw the incident; or**

(b) **request redress.**

Any boat that thinks another boat may have broken a *rule* can protest. This can occur during a race, or before or after a race; and it can involve a boat in the same race or one in a different race. Note, however, that the use of the word "may" in rule 60.1 clarifies that it is a boat's choice as to whether or not she protests. A boat cannot be penalized for choosing not to protest.

If you want to protest another boat for breaking a rule of Part 2 (When Boats Meet), you must have been directly involved in the incident or have seen it happen yourself. A *protest* involving a Part 2 rule cannot be initiated by you when you learn about the incident from a "report" by a competitor from another boat in the race, or some other *interested party*.

 "What is a 'third-party protest,' and are they allowed?"

If you witness an incident in which you are not involved, and in which you think that at least one of the boats has broken a rule of Part 2, you can protest. It doesn't matter if they have contact or not. In this case you are the "third party." The protest committee will simply call a hearing based on your *protest*, find the facts about what happened in the incident, and penalize any boat that broke a *rule*.

Rule 61 – PROTEST REQUIREMENTS

Rule 61.1 – Informing the Protestee

(a) **A boat intending to protest shall always inform the other boat at the first reasonable opportunity. When her *protest* concerns an incident in the racing area that she is involved in or sees, she shall hail 'Protest' and conspicuously display a red flag at the first reasonable opportunity for each.**

However, boats of hull length less than 6 metres need not display the flag, and if the other boat is beyond hailing distance the protesting boat need not hail but shall inform the other boat at the first reasonable opportunity. A boat required to display a flag shall do so until she is no longer *racing*.

When you are involved in or see an incident in the racing area and you want to protest, you have to:

1) hail the word "Protest" at the first reasonable opportunity (unless the other boat wouldn't be able to hear your hail in which case you have to tell the other boat at the first reasonable chance you have that you intend to protest them); and

2) if you are sailing a boat whose hull is 6 meters (19.68 feet) or longer, conspicuously display a red flag at the first reasonable opportunity.

Notice that rule 61.1(a) says you "shall" do these things. "Shall" means it is mandatory. If you do not correctly do these two things, your *protest* will not be valid and no hearing on the incident should occur. Rule 63.5 (Validity of the Protest or Request for Redress) states clearly, "*At the beginning of the hearing the protest committee shall decide whether all requirements for the **protest** or request for redress have been met, after first taking any evidence it considers necessary. If all requirements have been met, the **protest** or request is valid and the hearing shall be continued. If not, it shall be closed.*"

THE HAIL

Note that you must use the actual word "Protest." Telling another boat to "do your '720'!" does not satisfy this rule. The purpose of the requirement is to be sure that the other boat clearly knows you intend to protest her. As with other mandatory hails in the *rules*, the hail should be loud and clear, and it should be unambiguous as to which boat is being protested. When there could be confusion, I strongly suggest including in the hail the boat's number or name, or the person's name if you know it.

The hail must be made at the first reasonable opportunity after you become aware of the incident. Though some may exist, it is very difficult to imagine a situation in which the first reasonable opportunity to say the word "Protest" isn't **immediately** after the incident. Remember that you can always decide not to go through with a *protest*, including for the reason that you just aren't sure who it was that fouled you. But if you don't say the word "Protest" at the time of the incident, you lose the opportunity to protest that incident. Therefore, it is always prudent to simply say "Protest" immediately. (See US SAILING Appeal 61.)

Note that the rule anticipates that there may be an instance where the boat you intend to protest is so far away at the time of the incident that there is no way the sailor(s) on that boat could possibly hear a hail. This would depend of course on factors such as the distance between the boats, the amount of wind, and the relationship of the boats to the wind (sound travels farther downwind than upwind). In this case, the rule simply requires you to tell the other boat at the first reasonable chance you have that you intend to protest them. I expect that this exception will typically apply to "third-party" *protests*; i.e. situations where the protestor is not directly involved in the incident but, for instance, sees a boat hit another boat or cut a *mark*.

If you intend to protest based on an incident that either occurred in the racing area without you being aware of it, or did not occur in the racing area, you do not need to say the word "Protest," but you do need to inform the other boat of your intent to protest as soon as is reasonably possible after becoming aware of the incident. The purpose of this rule is to be sure that boats intending to protest make every prompt and reasonable effort to go tell the other boat that a *protest* will be lodged, so that all the boats involved can be prepared and present for the hearing.

 "So is it correct that if I am racing a dinghy I don't need to fly a protest flag to protest; and if that's correct, won't sailors try to get out of protests by saying that they didn't know they were being protested?"

It is correct that if you are racing on a boat less than 19.5 feet long (6 meters or 19.68 feet to be exact), you do not have to fly a protest flag to protest (unless of course the sailing instructions change rule 61.1(a)). The length refers to the hull length, i.e. from the bow to the stern, and does not include protrusions such as bowsprits, rudders, etc. This will encompass most dinghies, sailboards, catamarans and even some small keel boats.

My opinion is that with no flag requirement, more *protests* will be heard than fewer. Many *protests* get bogged down, and many get disallowed, on the issue of whether the flag was flown quickly enough, leaving the actual *rules* issue unresolved. Not having to endure this frustrating situation should be a welcome relief to competitors and protest committees. Furthermore, often a dinghy was forced to sail a little more slowly while one of its sailors put up the flag, which was both unfair and a reason that often dinghy sailors chose not to protest.

In an incident, the boats are typically near each other such that a quick and audible hail of the word "Protest" should clearly inform the other boat that it is being protested. In college racing, where thousands of races a year have been run successfully for over forty years with no protest flag requirement, when protestors say they hailed "Protest," the protest committees take them at their word unless the protestees can satisfy the protest committees otherwise. This puts an end to the nefarious claims that the protestor did not hail. But sailors who say they hailed "Protest" when they know full well that they did not, do themselves and the sport a great disservice, and typically that lack of integrity catches up with them.

THE FLAG

Now, in the event you are required to fly a flag to protest, let's look at the flag requirements (rule 61.1(a), Informing the Protestee). When you are aware of an incident as it occurs in the racing area and want to protest because of it, you must conspicuously display a red flag at the first reasonable opportunity. Again, the purpose of the requirement is to provide a visual signal to the other boat that you intend to protest her. The Appeals are loud and clear throughout that if you are required to fly a flag and do not, then the protest committee cannot accept your *protest*. Notice that even if the incident involves a breach of a class rule or sailing instructions, etc., you must display your flag. (See rule 63.5, Validity of the Protest or Request for Redress, ISAF Case 39 and US SAILING Appeal 67.)

On the other hand, if you intend to protest because of an incident that either occurred in the racing area without you being aware of it, or did not occur in the racing area, you do not need to display a flag. Remember that you do need to inform the competitor that you intend to protest at the first reasonable opportunity after becoming aware of the incident.

"Just how quickly do I need to get my flag up?"

Rule 61.1(a) requires that it be displayed "at the first reasonable opportunity." My best advice is that the "first reasonable opportunity" is normally **immediately** after the incident. Remember that the purpose of the rule is to provide a visual signal to the other boat, and to any other boats in the incident or vicinity, that you intend to protest because of **that** incident. Any delay at all only raises the likelihood that the boat being protested won't be aware of that fact, or that it won't be clear for which incident your flag is being displayed.

The timeliness of the flag issue is the cause of some acrimony in our sport, generally arising when a boat's protest is refused because the protest committee decides that her flag was not displayed soon enough after the incident. Often it is suggested that the flag requirement is less important when the other boat is fully aware of the protesting boat's intent to protest, e.g. after a collision and an immediate hail of "Protest." I agree that it is frustrating when a *protest* is refused on a technicality rather than resolving the *rules* issue contained in the *protest*. But the *rules* are carefully worded to provide safe and fair racing, and that would be undermined if protest and appeals committees were permitted to overlook the requirements in *rules* when they decide that the "intent" of the *rule* was satisfied.

With a little attention and preparation, each boat can prepare a flag that can be easily displayed (Velcro is wonderful), and find a reasonable and convenient place to store their flag during a race so that members of the crew know where it is and so it can be displayed very quickly after an incident with a minimum of hassle (when all else fails put it in your windsuit pocket or on your backstay). You may never use it, but if you do and you put it up immediately after an incident, you will not have your *protest* refused for that reason.

As for examples of when it might be reasonable to delay the display of the flag for a brief time, in my opinion it would be reasonable to delay the display of the flag after a big collision until just after you and your crew finish checking to be sure things were okay; or when setting the spinnaker, when all hands were no longer involved putting it up. However, if after the collision or during the spinnaker set, at least one crew member is not doing anything, it is reasonable to expect that he or she can display the flag. Delaying because the flag is in the ditty bag, which is up in the bow under the anchor, is not reasonable to me. (See US SAILING Appeal 67.)

"Can I just fly anything red and call it a protest flag?"

Absolutely not. ISAF Case 72 reads, "QUESTION: What is the test of whether an object is a flag within the meaning of rule 61.1(a)? ANSWER: In the context of rule 61.1(a), a flag is used as a signal to communicate the message 'I intend to protest'. Only if the object used as a flag communicates that message, with little or no possibility of causing confusion on the part of those on competing boats, will the object qualify as a flag. A flag must be seen primarily to be a flag." The bottom line is that whatever you display must be RED, and it must be obvious that it's a flag, and not a telltale, baseball-type cap or piece of clothing.

"Does the flag have to be flown on the starboard shroud?"

No. The flag must simply be "conspicuously displayed." There is no requirement in the rule that the flag need be put anywhere in particular. The test of "conspicuous" is whether the flag is initially highly visible to the protested boat. In many cases the starboard side of the boat may be the worst (least conspicuous) place to display it. Notice also, that the flag can be displayed simply by holding it up and waving it at the other boat, which you can do as you head for the location where you will attach it.

Note also that "conspicuous" applies not only to the location of the display but to the actual size of the flag. In US SAILING Appeal 66, the Appeals Committee decided that a two-inch by eight-inch flag on a 40-foot boat was not of sufficient size or of suitable proportions to be "conspicuously displayed."

Also notice that you must keep your flag displayed until you are no longer *racing*, i.e. until you have finished and cleared the finishing line and *marks* or retired. If your flag blows off your shroud while you are still *racing*, **you can't protest.** My advice is to devise a good system and carry a spare. If your incident occurs so close to the finishing line that the first reasonable opportunity to display the flag doesn't occur until after you are no longer *racing*, I'd say you still need to display your flag because the incident occurred "in the racing area;" and that it would be prudent, though not required, to ensure that the race committee sees that you have displayed your flag.

Rule 61.2 - Protest Contents

A *protest* shall be in writing and identify

(a) the protestor and protestee;

(b) the incident, including where and when it occurred;

(c) any *rule* the protestor believes was broken; and

(d) the name of the protestor's representative.

Provided the written *protest* identifies the incident, other details may be corrected before or during the hearing.

Rule 61.2 clearly lists the details about the *protest*. Notice that the *protest* must be **in writing**. Also notice that the only detail that cannot be corrected once the time limit for lodging *protests* is past is an omission of a description of the incident itself. Therefore, be sure you clearly identify the incident, including where and when it occurred (ISAF Case 80).

Rule 61.3 – Protest Time Limit

A *protest* by a boat, or by the race committee or protest committee about an incident the committee observes in the racing area, shall be delivered to the race office no later than the time limit stated in the sailing instructions. If none is stated, the time limit is two hours after the last boat in the race *finishes*. Other race committee or protest committee *protests* shall be delivered to the race office within two hours after the committee receives the relevant information. The protest committee shall extend the time if there is good reason to do so.

Notice that the first place to look for the time limit for lodging a *protest* is the sailing instructions. If the sailing instructions are silent, then the default time limit in rule 61.3 is "two hours after the last boat in the race *finishes*."

Also notice that the protest committee must extend the time limit if there is a good reason to do so. This may be useful to you if you have made every reasonable effort to deliver your *protest* in time but were unable to do so for good reason.

THE
RACING RULES
OF SAILING

2001-2004

Including US SAILING Prescriptions

15 Maritime Drive   Post Office Box 1260   Portsmouth, RI 02871

www.ussailing.org

A Note from US SAILING's President

Sailing is a wonderful sport. Sailors of all ages and abilities compete with each other and enjoy themselves. There are very few other sports where national and international champions often vary in age from their teens to their 50's or even 60's.

Our sport, like golf and a few others, is different in another way as well. We rely on the competitors themselves to know and follow the rules of our game. In the typical sport where many people compete at the same time, the prevailing attitude is often "it's OK so long as I don't get caught." That attitude does not work in sailing. We rely on the sailors themselves to decide when they have broken a rule and voluntarily take a penalty. A basic principle of the rules is that "Competitors in the sport of sailing are governed by a body of *rules* that they are expected to follow and enforce. A fundamental principle of sportsmanship is that when competitors break a *rule* they will promptly take a penalty or retire." This basic principle is often described as "Corinthian," but no matter what words you use to describe the concept, it is central to how our sport operates.

We as competitors need to abide by this basic principle for the good of our sport. I urge you to study the rulebook and learn the rules, particularly the rules of Part 2. When you break a rule (as we all do from time to time) take your penalty. The 720° Turns Penalty was introduced some years ago specifically so that competitors could take a penalty and still either win the race or finish well enough in a single race to win the regatta. Remember, if in finishing first you have lost your self-respect or the respect of your competitors then you have lost more than you have won.

Fair winds and good sailing!

Dave Rosekrans, President

© 2001 International Sailing Federation
Reprinted by permission of the International Sailing Federation
Foreword and Prescriptions © 2001
By United States Sailing Association, all rights reserved
ISBN 1-882502-87-6

Contents

Foreword

This 2001–2004 edition of *The Racing Rules of Sailing* refines the rules introduced in 1997 and makes a number of other modifications, mainly to clarify wording. Marginal markings in Parts 1 to 7, Definitions and Appendix J indicate significant changes made to the rules in effect during 2000.

Among the most important changes are: a revised rule 18 - *Rounding and Passing Marks and Obstructions*, a new starting system in rule 26, elimination in rule 61.1(a) of the red flag requirement for protests by boats under six meters in length, and significant changes in the Advertising Code, which now appears in Appendix 1.

In addition to the ISAF rules, this rule book contains rules adopted by US SAILING for events held in the United States. These added rules, called 'prescriptions', appear in *bold italics*. If competitors take this rule book to a regatta in another country, they need only study the prescriptions in that country's rule book.

Many rule changes result from comments or proposals from competitors and race officials. The US SAILING Racing Rules Committee welcomes suggestions for improving the racing rules. Please send your comments and suggestions to US SAILING Racing Rules Committee, 15 Maritime Drive, Post Office Box 1260, Portsmouth, RI 02871-6015, fax them to (401) 683-0840, or e-mail them to rules@ussailing.org. More information about the rules and the Racing Rules Committee is available on the US SAILING website (*www.ussailing.org/rules*).

Rob Overton, Outgoing Chairman
Dick Rose, Incoming Chairman
US SAILING Racing Rules Committee

Introduction

The Racing Rules of Sailing includes two main sections. The first, Parts 1-7, contains rules that affect all competitors. The second section contains appendices that provide details of rules, rules that apply to particular kinds of racing, and rules that affect only a small number of competitors or officials.

Revision The racing rules are revised and published every four years by the International Sailing Federation (ISAF), the international authority for the sport. This edition becomes effective on 1 April 2001. With the exception of Appendices 1, 2 and 3, changes to the racing rules are permitted under ISAF Regulations 11.2 and 11.3. No changes are contemplated before 2005, but any changes determined to be urgent before then will be announced through national authorities and posted on the ISAF website (www.sailing.org).

ISAF Codes New Appendices 1, 2 and 3 contain the ISAF Advertising Code, the ISAF Eligibility Code and the ISAF Anti-Doping Code, which replace former Appendices G, K and L. These codes are ISAF regulations and are also racing rules. For more information see the preamble to Appendices, Section II.

Terminology A term used in the sense stated in the Definitions is printed in italics or, in preambles, in bold italics (for example, *racing* and ***racing***). Other words and terms are used in the sense ordinarily understood in nautical or general use. 'Race committee' includes any person or committee performing a race committee function. 'Class rules' includes rules of handicapping and rating systems.

Appendices When the rules of an appendix apply, they take precedence over any conflicting rules in Parts 1-7. Each appendix is identified by a letter or a number. A reference to a rule in a lettered appendix will contain the letter of the appendix and the rule number (for example, 'rule A1'). There is no Appendix I. A reference to Appendix 1, 2 or 3 will contain the number of the appendix and the regulation number; for example, 'Appendix 1, Regulation 20.1'.

Changes to the Rules The prescriptions of a national authority, class rules or the sailing instructions may change a racing rule only as permitted by rule 86.

US SAILING prescriptions are printed in bold italics except Appendices F, P and Q. There is no Appendix O.

Basic Principle

Sportsmanship and the Rules

Competitors in the sport of sailing are governed by a body of *rules* that they are expected to follow and enforce. A fundamental principle of sportsmanship is that when competitors break a *rule* they will promptly take a penalty or retire.

Equal Opportunity

As the national authority for the sport of sailing in the United States of America, the United States Sailing Association is committed to providing an equal opportunity to all sailors to participate in the sport of sailing.

Part 1 – Fundamental Rules

1   SAFETY

1.1   Helping Those in Danger

A boat or competitor shall give all possible help to any person or vessel in danger.

1.2   Life-Saving Equipment and Personal Buoyancy

A boat shall carry adequate life-saving equipment for all persons on board, including one item ready for immediate use, unless her class rules make some other provision. Each competitor is individually responsible for wearing personal buoyancy adequate for the conditions.

2   FAIR SAILING

A boat and her owner shall compete in compliance with recognized principles of sportsmanship and fair play. A boat may be penalized under this rule only if it is clearly established that these principles have been violated. A disqualification under this rule shall not be excluded from the boat's series score.

3   ACCEPTANCE OF THE RULES

By participating in a race conducted under these racing rules, each competitor and boat owner agrees

(a)   to be governed by the *rules*;

(b)   to accept the penalties imposed and other action taken under the *rules,* subject to the appeal and review procedures provided in them, as the final determination of any matter arising under the *rules*; and

(c)   with respect to such determination, not to resort to any court or other tribunal not provided by the *rules*.

4   DECISION TO RACE

The responsibility for a boat's decision to participate in a race or to continue *racing* is hers alone.

5   DRUGS

A competitor shall neither take a substance nor use a method banned by the Olympic Movement Anti-Doping Code or the World Anti-Doping Agency and shall comply with Appendix 3 (ISAF Regulation 19, ISAF Anti-Doping Code). An alleged or actual breach of this rule shall be dealt with under Regulation 19. It shall not be grounds for a *protest* and rule 63.1 does not apply.

Part 2 – When Boats Meet

The rules of Part 2 apply between boats that are sailing in or near the racing area and intend to **race***, are* **racing***, or have been* **racing***. However, a boat not* **racing** *shall not be penalized for breaking one of these rules, except rule 22.1. The International Regulations for Preventing Collisions at Sea or government right-of-way rules apply between a boat sailing under these rules and a vessel that is not, and they replace these rules if the sailing instructions so state.*

Section A – Right of Way

A boat has right of way when another boat is required to **keep clear** *of her. However, some rules in Sections B, C and D limit the actions of a right-of-way boat.*

10   ON OPPOSITE TACKS

When boats are on opposite *tacks,* a *port-tack* boat shall *keep clear* of a *starboard-tack* boat.

11   ON THE SAME TACK, OVERLAPPED

When boats are on the same *tack* and *overlapped,* a *windward* boat shall *keep clear* of a *leeward* boat.

12   ON THE SAME TACK, NOT OVERLAPPED

When boats are on the same *tack* and not *overlapped,* a boat *clear astern* shall *keep clear* of a boat *clear ahead.*

13   WHILE TACKING

After a boat passes head to wind, she shall *keep clear* of other boats until she is on a close-hauled course. During that time rules 10, 11 and 12 do not apply. If two boats are subject to this rule at the same time, the one on the other's port side shall *keep clear.*

Section B — General Limitations

14   AVOIDING CONTACT

A boat shall avoid contact with another boat if reasonably possible. However, a right-of-way boat or one entitled to *room*

(a)   need not act to avoid contact until it is clear that the other boat is not *keeping clear* or giving *room,* and

(b)   shall not be penalized under this rule unless there is contact that causes damage.

15   ACQUIRING RIGHT OF WAY

When a boat acquires right of way, she shall initially give the other boat *room* to *keep clear,* unless she acquires right of way because of the other boat's actions.

16   CHANGING COURSE

16.1   When a right-of-way boat changes course, she shall give the other boat *room* to *keep clear.*

16.2   In addition, when after the starting signal boats are about to cross or are crossing each other on opposite *tacks,* and the *port-tack* boat is *keeping clear* of the *starboard-tack* boat, the *starboard-tack* boat shall not change course if as a result the *port-tack* boat would immediately need to change course to continue *keeping clear.*

17   ON THE SAME TACK; PROPER COURSE

17.1   If a boat *clear astern* becomes *overlapped* within two of her hull lengths to *leeward* of a boat on the same *tack,* she shall not sail above her *proper course* while they remain *overlapped* within that distance, unless in doing so she promptly sails astern of the other boat. This rule does not apply if the *overlap* begins while the *windward* boat is required by rule 13 to *keep clear.*

17.2   Except on a beat to windward, while a boat is less than two of her hull lengths from a *leeward* boat or a boat *clear astern* steering a course to *leeward* of her, she shall not sail below her *proper course* unless she gybes.

Section C — At Marks and Obstructions

To the extent that a Section C rule conflicts with a rule in Section A or B, the Section C rule takes precedence.

18   ROUNDING AND PASSING MARKS AND OBSTRUCTIONS

In rule 18, **room** *is* **room** *for an inside boat to round or pass between an outside boat and a* **mark** *or* **obstruction,** *including* **room** *to tack or gybe when either is a normal part of the manoeuvre.*

18.1   When This Rule Applies

Rule 18 applies when boats are about to round or pass a *mark* they are required to leave on the same side, or an *obstruction* on the same side, until they have passed it. However, it does not apply

(a)   at a starting *mark* surrounded by navigable water or at its anchor line from the time the boats are approaching them to *start* until they have passed them, or

(b)   between boats on opposite *tacks,* either on a beat to windward or when the *proper course* for one or both of them to round or pass the *mark* or *obstruction* is to tack.

18.2   Giving Room; Keeping Clear

(a)   OVERLAPPED – BASIC RULE

When boats are *overlapped* the outside boat shall give the inside boat *room* to round or pass the *mark* or *obstruction,* and if the inside boat has right of way the outside boat shall also *keep clear.* Other parts of rule 18 contain exceptions to this rule.

(b)   OVERLAPPED AT THE ZONE

If boats were *overlapped* before either of them reached the *two-length zone* and the *overlap* is broken after one of them has reached it, the boat that was on the outside shall continue to give the other boat *room.* If the outside boat becomes *clear astern* or *overlapped* inside the other boat, she is not entitled to *room* and shall *keep clear.*

(c)   NOT OVERLAPPED AT THE ZONE

If a boat is *clear ahead* at the time she reaches the *two-length zone,* the boat *clear astern* shall thereafter *keep clear.* If the boat *clear astern* becomes *overlapped* outside the other boat she shall also give the inside boat *room.* If the boat *clear astern* becomes *overlapped* inside the other boat she is not entitled to *room.* If the boat that was *clear ahead* passes head to wind, rule 18.2(c) no longer applies.

(d)   CHANGING COURSE TO ROUND OR PASS

When rule 18 applies between two boats and the right-of-way boat is chang-

5, 6, 7

ing course to round or pass a *mark,* rule 16 does not apply between her and the other boat.

(e)   OVERLAP RIGHTS

If there is reasonable doubt that a boat obtained or broke an *overlap* in time, it shall be presumed that she did not. If the outside boat is unable to give *room* when an *overlap* begins, rules 18.2(a) and 18.2(b) do not apply.

18.3   Tacking at a Mark

If two boats were approaching a *mark* on opposite *tacks* and one of them completes a tack in the *two-length zone* when the other is fetching the *mark,* rule 18.2 does not apply. The boat that tacked

(a)   shall not cause the other boat to sail above close-hauled to avoid her or prevent the other boat from passing the *mark,* and

(b)   shall give *room* if the other boat becomes *overlapped* inside her, in which case rule 15 does not apply.

18.4   Gybing

When an inside *overlapped* right-of-way boat must gybe at a *mark* or *obstruction* to sail her *proper course,* until she gybes she shall sail no farther from the *mark* or *obstruction* than needed to sail that course.

18.5   Passing a Continuing Obstruction

While boats are passing a continuing *obstruction,* rules 18.2(b) and 18.2(c) do not apply. A boat *clear astern* that obtains an inside *overlap* is entitled to *room* to pass between the other boat and the *obstruction* only if at the moment the *overlap* begins there is *room* to do so. If there is not, she is not entitled to *room* and shall *keep clear.*

19   ROOM TO TACK AT AN OBSTRUCTION

19.1   When safety requires a close-hauled boat to make a substantial course change to avoid an *obstruction* and she intends to tack, but cannot tack and avoid another boat on the same *tack,* she shall hail for *room* to do so. Before tacking she shall give the hailed boat time to respond. The hailed boat shall either

(a)   tack as soon as possible, in which case the hailing boat shall also tack as soon as possible, or

(b)   immediately reply 'You tack', in which case the hailing boat shall tack as soon as possible and the hailed boat shall give *room,* and rules 10 and 13 do not apply.

19.2   Rule 19.1 does not apply at a starting *mark* surrounded by navigable water or at its anchor line from the time boats are approaching them to *start* until they have passed them or at a *mark* that the hailed boat can fetch. When rule 19.1 applies, rule 18 does not.

Section D – Other Rules

When rule 20 or 21 applies between two boats, Section A rules do not.

20   STARTING ERRORS; PENALTY TURNS; MOVING ASTERN

A boat sailing towards the pre-start side of the starting line or its extensions after her starting signal to comply with rule 29.1 or 30.1 shall *keep clear* of a boat not doing so until she is completely on the pre-start side. A boat making a penalty turn shall *keep clear* of one that is not. A boat moving astern by backing a sail shall *keep clear* of one that is not.

21   CAPSIZED, ANCHORED OR AGROUND; RESCUING

If possible, a boat shall avoid a boat that is capsized or has not regained control after capsizing, is anchored or aground, or is trying to help a person or vessel in danger. A boat is capsized when her masthead is in the water.

22   INTERFERING WITH ANOTHER BOAT

22.1   If reasonably possible, a boat not *racing* shall not interfere with a boat that is *racing.*

22.2   A boat shall not deliberately interfere with a boat making penalty turns to delay her.

Part 3 – Conduct of a Race

25   SAILING INSTRUCTIONS AND SIGNALS

Sailing instructions shall be made available to each boat before a race begins. The meanings of the visual and sound signals stated in Race Signals shall not be changed except under rule 86.1(b). The meanings of any other signals that may be used shall be stated in the sailing instructions.

26   STARTING RACES

Races shall be started by using the following signals. Times shall be taken from the visual signals; the absence of a sound signal shall be disregarded.

Signal	Flag and sound	Minutes before starting signal
Warning	Class flag; 1 sound	5^*
Preparatory	P, I, Z, Z with I, or black flag; 1 sound	4
One-minute	Preparatory flag removed; 1 long sound	1
Starting	Class flag removed; 1 sound	0

*or as stated in the sailing instructions

The warning signal for each succeeding class shall be made with or after the starting signal of the preceding class.

27   OTHER RACE COMMITTEE ACTIONS BEFORE THE STARTING SIGNAL

27.1   No later than the warning signal, the race committee shall signal or otherwise designate the course to be sailed if the sailing instructions have not stated the course, and it may replace one course signal with another, signal that a desig-nated short course will be used (display flag S with two sounds), and signal that wearing personal buoyancy is required (display flag Y with one sound).

27.2   No later than the preparatory signal, the race committee may move a starting *mark* and may apply rule 30.

27.3   Before the starting signal, the race committee may for any reason *postpone* (display flag AP, AP over H, or AP over A, with two sounds) or *abandon* the race (display flag N over H, or N over A, with three sounds).

28   SAILING THE COURSE

28.1   A boat shall *start,* leave each *mark* on the required side in the correct order, and *finish,* so that a string representing her wake after *starting* and until *finishing* would when drawn taut pass each *mark* on the required side and touch each rounding *mark*. After *finishing* she need not cross the finishing line completely. She may correct any errors to comply with this rule, provided she has not already *finished*.

28.2   A boat may leave on either side a *mark* that does not begin, bound or end the leg she is on. However, she shall leave a starting *mark* on the required side when she is approaching the starting line from its pre-start side to *start*.

29   STARTING; RECALLS

29.1   On the Course Side at the Start

When at a boat's starting signal any part of her hull, crew or equipment is on the course side of the starting line, she shall sail completely to the pre-start side of the line before *starting*.

29.2   Individual Recall

When at a boat's starting signal she must comply with rule 29.1 or 30.1, the race committee shall promptly display flag X with one sound. The flag shall be displayed until all such boats are completely on the pre-start side of the starting line or its extensions and have complied with rule 30.1 if it applies, but not later than four minutes after the starting signal or one minute before any later starting signal, whichever is earlier.

29.3   General Recall

When at the starting signal the race committee is unable to identify boats that are on the course side of the starting line or to which rule 30 applies, or there has been an error in the starting procedure, the race committee may signal a general recall (display the First Substitute with two sounds). The warning signal for a new start for the recalled class shall be made one minute after the First Substitute is removed (one sound), and the starts for any succeeding classes shall follow the new start.

30   STARTING PENALTIES

30.1   Round-an-End Rule

If flag I has been displayed before, with, or as a boat's preparatory signal, and any part of her hull, crew or equipment is on the course side of the starting line or its extensions during the minute before her starting signal, she shall sail to the pre-start side of the line around either end before *starting*.

30.2   20% Penalty Rule

If flag Z has been displayed before, with, or as a boat's preparatory signal, no part of her hull, crew or equipment shall be in the triangle formed by the ends of the starting line and the first *mark* during the minute before her starting signal. If a boat breaks this rule and is identified, she shall receive, without a hearing, a 20% scoring penalty calculated as stated in rule 44.3(c). She shall be penalized even if the race is restarted, resailed or rescheduled, but not if it is *postponed* or *abandoned* before the starting signal.

30.3   Black Flag Rule

If a black flag has been displayed before, with, or as a boat's preparatory signal, no part of her hull, crew or equipment shall be in the triangle formed by the ends of the starting line and the first *mark* during the minute before her starting signal. If a boat breaks this rule and is identified, she shall be disqualified without a hearing, even if the race is restarted, resailed or rescheduled, but not if it is *postponed* or *abandoned* before the starting signal. If a general recall is signalled or the race is *abandoned* after the starting signal, the race committee shall display her sail number, and if the race is restarted or resailed she shall not sail in it. If she does so, her disqualification shall not be excluded in calculating her series score.

31   TOUCHING A MARK

31.1 While *racing,* a boat shall not touch a starting *mark* before *starting,* a *mark* that begins, bounds or ends the leg of the course on which she is sailing, or a finishing *mark* after *finishing.*

31.2 A boat that has broken rule 31.1 may, after getting well clear of other boats as soon as possible, take a penalty by promptly making one complete 360° turn including one tack and one gybe. When a boat takes the penalty after touching a finishing *mark,* she shall sail completely to the course side of the line before *finishing.* However, if a boat has gained a significant advantage in the race or series by touching the *mark* she shall retire.

32   SHORTENING OR ABANDONING AFTER THE START

32.1 After the starting signal, the race committee may *abandon* the race (display flag N, N over H, or N over A, with three sounds) or shorten the course (display flag S with two sounds), as appropriate,

(a)   because of an error in the starting procedure,

(b)   because of foul weather,

(c)   because of insufficient wind making it unlikely that any boat will *finish* within the time limit,

(d)   because a *mark* is missing or out of position, or

(e)   for any other reason directly affecting the safety or fairness of the competition.

However, after one boat has sailed the course and *finished* within the time limit, if any, the race committee shall not *abandon* the race without considering the consequences for all boats in the race or series.

32.2 After the starting signal, the race committee may shorten the course (display flag S with two sounds) to enable further scheduled races to be sailed.

33   CHANGING THE POSITION OF THE NEXT MARK

At any rounding *mark* the race committee may signal a change of the direction of the next leg of the course by displaying flag C with repetitive sounds and the compass bearing of that leg before any boat begins it. The race committee may change the length of the next leg by displaying flag C with repetitive sounds and a '–' if the leg will be shortened or a '+' if the leg will be lengthened.

34   MARK MISSING; *RACE COMMITTEE ABSENT*

When a *mark* is missing or out of position, the race committee shall, if possible,

(a)   replace it in its correct position or

(b)   substitute one of similar appearance, or a buoy or vessel displaying flag M with repetitive sounds.

US SAILING prescribes that, in the absence of the race committee, a boat shall take her own finishing time and report it to the race committee as soon as possible. If there is no longer an established finishing line, it shall be a line extending from the required side of the finishing mark at right angles to the course from the last mark and of the shortest practicable length.

35 TIME LIMIT AND SCORES

If one boat sails the course as required by rule 28.1 and *finishes* within the time limit, if any, all boats that *finish* shall be scored according to their finishing places unless the race is *abandoned.* If no boat *finishes* within the time limit, the race committee shall *abandon* the race.

36 RACES TO BE RESTARTED OR RESAILED

If a race is restarted or resailed, a breach of a *rule,* other than rule 30.3, in the original race shall not prohibit a boat from competing or, except under rule 30.2, 30.3 or 69, cause her to be penalized.

Part 4 – Other Requirements When Racing

*Part 4 rules apply only to boats **racing**.*

40 PERSONAL BUOYANCY; *LIFE-SAVING EQUIPMENT*

When flag Y is displayed with one sound before or with the warning signal, competitors shall wear life-jackets or other adequate personal buoyancy. Wet suits and dry suits are not adequate personal buoyancy.

US SAILING prescribes that every boat shall carry life-saving equipment conforming to government regulations.

41 OUTSIDE HELP

A boat may receive outside help as provided for in rule 1. Otherwise, she shall not receive help except for an ill or injured crew member or, after a collision, from the crew of the other boat.

42 PROPULSION

42.1 Basic Rule

Except when permitted in rule 42.3 or 45, a boat shall compete by using only the wind and water to increase, maintain or decrease her speed. Her crew may adjust the trim of sails and hull, and perform other acts of seamanship, but shall not otherwise move their bodies to propel the boat.

42.2 Prohibited Actions

Without limiting the application of rule 42.1, these actions are prohibited:

(a) pumping: repeated fanning of any sail either by trimming and releasing the sail or by vertical or athwartships body movement;

(b) rocking: repeated rolling of the boat, induced either by body movement or adjustment of the sails or centreboard, that does not facilitate steering;

(c) ooching: sudden forward body movement, stopped abruptly;

(d) sculling: repeated movement of the helm not necessary for steering;

(e) repeated tacks or gybes unrelated to changes in the wind or to tactical considerations.

42.3 Exceptions

(a) A boat's crew may move their bodies to exaggerate the rolling that facilitates steering the boat through a tack or a gybe, provided that, just after the tack or gybe is completed, the boat's speed is not greater than it would have been in the absence of the tack or gybe.

(b) Except on a beat to windward, when surfing (rapidly accelerating down the leeward side of a wave) or planing is possible, the boat's crew may pull the sheet and the guy controlling any sail in order to initiate surfing or planing, but only once for each wave or gust of wind.

(c) Any means of propulsion may be used to help a person or another vessel in danger.

(d) To get clear after grounding or colliding with another boat or object, a boat may use force applied by the crew of either boat and any equipment other than a propulsion engine.

43   COMPETITOR CLOTHING AND EQUIPMENT

43.1 (a) Competitors shall not wear or carry clothing or equipment for the purpose of increasing their weight.

(b) Furthermore, a competitor's clothing and equipment shall not weigh more than 8 kilograms, excluding a hiking or trapeze harness and clothing (including footwear) worn only below the knee. Class rules or sailing instructions may specify a lower weight or a higher weight up to 10 kilograms. Class rules may include footwear and other clothing worn below the knee within that weight. A hiking or trapeze harness shall have positive buoyancy and shall not weigh more than 2 kilograms, except that class rules may specify a higher weight up to 4 kilograms. Weights shall be determined as required by Appendix H.

(c) When a measurer in charge of weighing clothing and equipment believes a competitor may have broken rule 43.1(a) or 43.1(b) he shall report the matter in writing to the race committee, which shall protest the boat of the competitor. |

43.2 Rule 43.1(b) does not apply to boats required to be equipped with lifelines.

44   PENALTIES FOR BREAKING RULES OF PART 2

44.1 Taking a Penalty

A boat that may have broken a rule of Part 2 while *racing* may take a penalty at the time of the incident. Her penalty shall be a 720° Turns Penalty unless the sailing instructions specify the use of the Scoring Penalty or some other penalty. However, if she caused serious damage or gained a significant advantage in the race or series by her breach she shall retire.

44.2 720° Turns Penalty

After getting well clear of other boats as soon after the incident as possible, a boat takes a 720° Turns Penalty by promptly making two complete 360° turns (720°) in the same direction, including two tacks and two gybes. When a boat takes the penalty at or near the finishing line, she shall sail completely to the course side of the line before *finishing.*

44.3 Scoring Penalty

(a) A boat takes a Scoring Penalty by displaying a yellow flag at the first reasonable opportunity after the incident, keeping it displayed until *finishing,* and calling the race committee's attention to it at the finishing line. At that time she shall also inform the race committee of the identity of the other boat involved in the incident. If this is impracticable, she shall do so at the first reasonable opportunity within the time limit for *protests.*

(b) If a boat displays a yellow flag, she shall also comply with the other parts of rule 44.3(a).

(c) The boat's penalty score shall be the score for the place worse than her actual finishing place by the number of places stated in the sailing instructions, except that she shall not be scored worse than Did Not Finish. When the sailing instructions do not state the number of places, the number shall be the whole number (rounding 0.5 upward) nearest to 20% of the number of boats entered. The scores of other boats shall not be changed; therefore, two boats may receive the same score.

44.4 Limits on Penalties

(a) When a boat intends to take a penalty as provided in rule 44.1 and in the same incident has touched a *mark,* she need not take the penalty provided in rule 31.2.

(b) A boat that takes a penalty shall not be penalized further with respect to the same incident unless she failed to retire when rule 44.1 required her to do so.

45 HAULING OUT; MAKING FAST; ANCHORING

A boat shall be afloat and off moorings at her preparatory signal. Thereafter, she shall not be hauled out or made fast except to bail out, reef sails or make repairs. She may anchor or the crew may stand on the bottom. She shall recover the anchor before continuing in the race unless she is unable to do so.

46 PERSON IN CHARGE

A boat shall have on board a person in charge designated by the member or organization that entered the boat. See rule 75.

47 LIMITATIONS ON EQUIPMENT AND CREW

47.1 A boat shall use only the equipment on board at her preparatory signal.

47.2 No person on board shall intentionally leave, except when ill or injured, or to help a person or vessel in danger, or to swim. A person leaving the boat by accident or to swim shall be back on board before the boat continues in the race.

48 FOG SIGNALS AND LIGHTS

When safety requires, a boat shall sound fog signals and show lights as required by the *International Regulations for Preventing Collisions at Sea* or applicable government rules.

US SAILING prescribes that the use of additional special purpose lights such as masthead, spreader and jib-luff lights shall not constitute a breach of this rule.

49 CREW POSITION

49.1 Competitors shall use no device designed to position their bodies outboard, other than hiking straps and stiffeners worn under the thighs.

49.2 When lifelines are required by the class rules or the sailing instructions they shall be taut, and competitors shall not position any part of their torsos outside them, except briefly to perform a necessary task. On boats equipped with upper and lower lifelines of wire, a competitor sitting on the deck facing outboard with his waist inside the lower lifeline may have the upper part of his body outside the upper lifeline.

50 SETTING AND SHEETING SAILS

50.1 Changing Sails

When headsails or spinnakers are being changed, a replacing sail may be fully set and trimmed before the replaced sail is lowered. However, only one mainsail and, except when changing, only one spinnaker shall be carried set at a time.

50.2 Spinnaker Poles, Whisker Poles

Only one spinnaker pole or whisker pole shall be used at a time except when gybing. When in use, it shall be attached to the foremost mast.

50.3 Use of Outriggers

(a) No sail shall be sheeted over or through an outrigger, except as permitted in rule 50.3(b). An outrigger is any fitting or other device so placed that it could exert outward pressure on a sheet or sail at a point from which, with the boat upright, a vertical line would fall outside the hull or deck planking. For the purpose of this rule, bulwarks, rails and rubbing strakes are not part of the hull or deck planking and the following are not outriggers: a bowsprit used to secure the tack of a working sail, a bumkin used to sheet the boom of a working sail, or a boom of a boomed headsail that requires no adjustment when tacking.

(b) (1) Any sail may be sheeted to or led above a boom that is regularly used for a working sail and is permanently attached to the mast from which the head of the working sail is set.

(2) A headsail may be sheeted or attached at its clew to a spinnaker pole or whisker pole, provided that a spinnaker is not set.

50.4 Headsails

The difference between a headsail and a spinnaker is that the mid-girth of a headsail, measured from the mid-points of its luff and leech, does not exceed 50% of the length of its foot, and no other intermediate girth exceeds a percentage similarly proportional to its distance from the head of the sail. A sail tacked down behind the foremost mast is not a headsail.

51 MOVABLE BALLAST

All movable ballast shall be properly stowed, and water, dead weight or ballast shall not be moved for the purpose of changing trim or stability. Floorboards, bulkheads, doors, stairs and water tanks shall be left in place and all cabin fixtures kept on board.

52 MANUAL POWER

A boat's standing rigging, running rigging, spars and movable hull appendages shall be adjusted and operated only by manual power.

53   SKIN FRICTION

A boat shall not eject or release a substance, such as a polymer, or have specially textured surfaces that could improve the character of the flow of water inside the boundary layer.

54   FORESTAYS AND HEADSAIL TACKS

Forestays and headsail tacks, except those of spinnaker staysails when the boat is not close-hauled, shall be attached approximately on a boat's centre-line.

55   *FLAGS*

US SAILING prescribes that a boat shall not display flags except for signaling. A boat shall not be penalized for breaking this rule without prior warning and opportunity to make correction.

Part 5 – Protests, Redress, Hearings, Misconduct and Appeals

Section A – Protests and Redress

60   RIGHT TO PROTEST AND REQUEST REDRESS

60.1   A boat may

    (a)   protest another boat, but not for an alleged breach of a rule of Part 2 unless she was involved in or saw the incident; or

    (b)   request redress.

60.2   A race committee may

    (a)   protest a boat, but not as a result of a report by a competitor from another boat or other *interested party* or of information in an invalid *protest*;

    (b)   request redress for a boat; or

    (c)   report to the protest committee requesting action under rule 69.1(a).

60.3   A protest committee may

    (a)   protest a boat, but not as a result of a report by a competitor from another boat or other *interested party* except under rule 61.1(c), or as a result of information in an invalid *protest* except under rule 60.4;

    (b)   call a hearing to consider redress; or

    (c)   act under rule 69.1(a).

60.4   If a protest committee receives a report of an incident that may have resulted in serious damage or serious injury, it may protest any boat involved.

61   PROTEST REQUIREMENTS

61.1   **Informing the Protestee**

    (a)   A boat intending to protest shall always inform the other boat at the first reasonable opportunity. When her *protest* concerns an incident in the racing area that she is involved in or sees, she shall hail 'Protest' and conspicuously display a red flag at the first reasonable opportunity for each. However, boats of hull length less than 6 metres need not display the flag, and if the other boat is beyond hailing distance the protesting boat need not hail but shall inform the other boat at the first reasonable opportunity. A boat required to display a flag shall do so until she is no longer *racing*.

(b) A race committee or protest committee intending to protest a boat under rule 60.2(a) or 60.3(a) shall inform her as soon as reasonably possible, except that if the *protest* arises from an incident it observes in the racing area the committee shall inform the boat after the race within the time limit of rule 61.3.

(c) During the hearing of a valid *protest* or request for redress, if the protest committee decides to protest a boat that was involved in the incident but is not a *party* to that hearing, it shall inform the boat as soon as reasonably possible of its intention, then protest her as required by rule 61.2 and proceed with a hearing as required by rule 63.

61.2 Protest Contents

A *protest* shall be in writing and identify
(a) the protestor and protestee;
(b) the incident, including where and when it occurred;
(c) any *rule* the protestor believes was broken; and
(d) the name of the protestor's representative.

Provided the written *protest* identifies the incident, other details may be corrected before or during the hearing.

61.3 Protest Time Limit

A *protest* by a boat, or by the race committee or protest committee about an incident the committee observes in the racing area, shall be delivered to the race office no later than the time limit stated in the sailing instructions. If none is stated, the time limit is two hours after the last boat in the race *finishes*. Other race committee or protest committee *protests* shall be delivered to the race office within two hours after the committee receives the relevant information. The protest committee shall extend the time if there is good reason to do so.

61.4 *Fees for Protests and Requests for Redress*

US SAILING prescribes that no fees shall be charged for protests *or requests for redress.*

62 REDRESS

62.1 A request for redress or a protest committee's decision to consider redress shall be based on a claim or possibility that a boat's finishing place in a race or series has, through no fault of her own, been made significantly worse by

(a) an improper action or omission of the race committee or protest committee,
(b) physical damage because of the action of a boat that was breaking a rule of Part 2 or of a vessel not *racing* that was required to keep clear,
(c) giving help (except to herself or her crew) in compliance with rule 1.1, or
(d) a boat against which a penalty has been imposed under rule 2 or disciplinary action has been taken under rule 69.1(b).

62.2 The request shall be made in writing within the time limit of rule 61.3 or within two hours of the relevant incident, whichever is later. The protest committee shall extend the time if there is good reason to do so. No red flag is required.

US SAILING prescribes that a request for redress claiming that a boat's finishing place was made significantly worse by an action or omission of a protest committee shall be delivered before 1800 on the day following the protest committee's action or omission or its decision, or later if there is good reason to extend this time limit.

Section B – Hearings and Decisions

63   HEARINGS

63.1   Requirement for a Hearing

A boat or competitor shall not be penalized without a protest hearing, except as provided in rules 30.2, 30.3, 67, 69, A5 and N2. A decision on redress shall not be made without a hearing. The protest committee shall hear all *protests* and requests for redress that have been delivered to the race office unless it allows a boat to withdraw her *protest* or request.

63.2   Time and Place of the Hearing; Time for Parties to Prepare

All *parties* to the hearing shall be notified of the time and place of the hearing, the *protest* or redress information shall be made available to them, and they shall be allowed reasonable time to prepare for the hearing.

63.3   Right to Be Present

(a) The *parties* to the hearing, or a representative of each, have the right to be present throughout the hearing of all the evidence. When a *protest* claims a breach of a rule of Part 2, 3 or 4, the representatives of boats shall have been on board at the time of the incident, unless there is good reason for the protest committee to rule otherwise. Any witness, other than a member of the protest committee, shall be excluded except when giving evidence.

(b) If a *party* to the hearing does not come to the hearing, the protest committee may nevertheless decide the *protest* or request for redress. If the *party* was unavoidably absent, the committee may reopen the hearing.

63.4   Interested Party

A member of a protest committee who is an *interested party* shall not take any further part in the hearing but may appear as a witness. A *party* to the hearing who believes a member of the protest committee is an *interested party* shall object as soon as possible.

63.5   Validity of the Protest or Request for Redress

At the beginning of the hearing the protest committee shall decide whether all requirements for the *protest* or request for redress have been met, after first taking any evidence it considers necessary. If all requirements have been met, the *protest* or request is valid and the hearing shall be continued. If not, it shall be closed. If the *protest* has been made under rule 60.4, the protest committee must also determine whether or not serious damage or serious injury resulted from the incident in question. If not, the hearing shall be closed.

63.6   Taking Evidence and Finding Facts

The protest committee shall take the evidence of the *parties* to the hearing and of their witnesses and other evidence it considers necessary. A member of the protest committee who saw the incident may give evidence. A *party* to the hearing may question any person who gives evidence. The committee shall then find the facts and base its decision on them.

63.7   Protests Between Boats in Different Races

A *protest* between boats sailing in different races conducted by different organizing authorities shall be heard by a protest committee acceptable to those authorities.

64   DECISIONS

64.1   Penalties and Exoneration

(a)   When the protest committee decides that a boat that is a *party* to a protest hearing has broken a *rule,* it shall disqualify her unless some other penalty applies. A penalty shall be imposed whether or not the applicable *rule* was mentioned in the *protest.*

US SAILING prescribes that the penalty for breaking rule 75.2 with reference to Appendix 2, Regulation 21.2.1(h), shall be a warning.

(b)   When as a consequence of breaking a *rule* a boat has compelled another boat to break a *rule,* rule 64.1(a) does not apply to the other boat and she shall be exonerated.

(c)   If a boat has broken a *rule* when not *racing,* her penalty shall apply to the race sailed nearest in time to that of the incident.

64.2   Decisions on Redress

When the protest committee decides that a boat is entitled to redress under rule 62, it shall make as fair an arrangement as possible for all boats affected, whether or not they asked for redress. This may be to adjust the scoring (see rule A10 for some examples) or finishing times of boats, to *abandon* the race, to let the results stand or to make some other arrangement. When in doubt about the facts or probable results of any arrangement for the race or series, especially before *abandoning* the race, the protest committee shall take evidence from appropriate sources.

64.3   Decisions on Measurement Protests

(a)   When the protest committee finds that deviations in excess of tolerances specified in the class rules were caused by damage or normal wear and do not improve the performance of the boat, it shall not penalize her. However, the boat shall not *race* again until the deviations have been corrected, except when the protest committee decides there is or has been no reasonable opportunity to do so.

(b)   When the protest committee is in doubt about the meaning of a measurement rule, it shall refer its questions, together with the relevant facts, to an authority responsible for interpreting the rule. In making its decision, the committee shall be bound by the reply of the authority.

US SAILING prescribes that the authority responsible for interpreting the rules of a measurement or handicapping system is the organization that issued the rating certificate or handicap involved.

(c)   When a boat disqualified under a measurement rule states in writing that she intends to appeal, she may compete in subsequent races without changes to the boat, but will be disqualified if she fails to appeal or the appeal is decided against her.

(d)   Measurement costs arising from a *protest* involving a measurement rule shall be paid by the unsuccessful *party* unless the protest committee decides otherwise.

64.4   Decisions on Protests Involving Appendix P

US SAILING prescribes that when the protest committee is in doubt about the meaning of a rule of Appendix P, it shall refer its questions, together with the relevant facts, to the US SAILING Competitor Classification Committee. In making its decision, the protest committee shall be bound by the Competitor Classification Committee's reply.

65 INFORMING THE PARTIES AND OTHERS

65.1 After making its decision, the protest committee shall promptly inform the *parties* to the hearing of the facts found, the applicable *rules,* the decision, the reasons for it, and any penalties imposed or redress given.

65.2 A *party* to the hearing is entitled to receive the above information in writing, provided she asks for it in writing from the protest committee within seven days of being informed of the decision. The committee shall then promptly provide the information, including, when relevant, a diagram of the incident prepared or endorsed by the committee.

65.3 When the protest committee penalizes a boat under a measurement rule, it shall send the above information to the relevant measurement authorities.

66 REOPENING A HEARING

The protest committee may reopen a hearing when it decides that it may have made a significant error, or when significant new evidence becomes available within a reasonable time. It shall reopen a hearing when required by the national authority under rule F5. A *party* to the hearing may ask for a reopening no later than 24 hours after being informed of the decision. When a hearing is reopened, a majority of the members of the protest committee shall, if possible, be members of the original protest committee.

67 RULE 42 AND HEARING REQUIREMENT

When so stated in the sailing instructions, the protest committee may penalize without a hearing a boat that has broken rule 42, provided that a member of the committee or its designated observer has seen the incident, and a disqualification under this rule shall not be excluded from the boat's series score. A boat so penalized shall be informed by notification in the race results.

68 DAMAGES

The question of damages arising from a breach of any *rule* shall be governed by the prescriptions, if any, of the national authority.

US SAILING prescribes that:

(a) A boat that retires from a race or accepts a penalty does not, by that action alone, admit liability for damages.

(b) A protest committee shall find facts and make decisions only in compliance with the rules. *No protest committee or US SAILING appeal authority shall adjudicate any claim for damages. Such a claim is subject to the jurisdiction of the courts.*

(c) A basic purpose of the rules *is to prevent contact between boats. By participating in an event governed by the* rules, *a boat agrees that responsibility for damages arising from any breach of the* rules *shall be based on fault as determined by application of the* rules, *and that she shall not be governed by the legal doctrine of 'assumption of risk' for monetary damages resulting from contact with other boats.*

Section C – Gross Misconduct

69   ALLEGATIONS OF GROSS MISCONDUCT

69.1   Action by a Protest Committee

(a)   When a protest committee, from its own observation or a report received, believes that a competitor may have committed a gross breach of a *rule* or of good manners or sportsmanship, or may have brought the sport into disrepute, it may call a hearing. The protest committee shall promptly inform the competitor in writing of the alleged misconduct and of the time and place of the hearing.

(b)   A protest committee of at least three members shall conduct the hearing, following rules 63.2, 63.3, 63.4 and 63.6. If it decides that the competitor committed the alleged misconduct it shall either

(1)   warn the competitor or

(2)   impose a penalty by excluding the competitor, and a boat when appropriate, from a race, or the remaining races of a series or the entire series, or by taking other action within its jurisdiction.

(c)   The protest committee shall promptly report a penalty, but not a warning, to the national authorities of the venue, of the competitor and of the boat owner.

(d)   If the competitor has left the venue and cannot be notified or fails to attend the hearing, the protest committee shall collect all available evidence and, when the allegation seems justified, make a report to the relevant national authorities.

(e)   When the protest committee has left the event and a report alleging misconduct is received, the race committee or organizing authority may appoint a new protest committee to proceed under this rule.

69.2   Action by a National Authority

(a)   When a national authority receives a report required by rule 69.1(c) or 69.1(d), or a report alleging a gross breach of a *rule* or of good manners or sportsmanship or conduct that brought the sport into disrepute, it may conduct an investigation and, when appropriate, shall conduct a hearing. It may then take any disciplinary action within its jurisdiction it considers appropriate against the competitor or boat, or other person involved, including suspending eligibility, permanently or for a specified period of time, to compete in any event held within its jurisdiction, and suspending ISAF eligibility under Appendix 2, Regulation 21.3.1(a).

(b)   The national authority of a competitor shall also suspend the ISAF eligibility of the competitor as required in Appendix 2, Regulation 21.3.1(a).

(c)   The national authority shall promptly report a suspension of eligibility under rule 69.2(a) to the ISAF, and to the national authorities of the person or the owner of the boat suspended if they are not members of the suspending national authority.

69.3   Action by the ISAF

Upon receipt of a report required by rules 69.2(c) and Appendix 2, Regulation 21.4.1, the ISAF shall inform all national authorities, which may also suspend eligibility for events held within their jurisdiction. The ISAF Executive Committee shall suspend the competitor's ISAF eligibility as required in Appendix 2, Regulation 21.3.1(a) if the competitor's national authority does not do so.

Section D – Appeals

70 RIGHT OF APPEAL AND REQUESTS FOR INTERPRETATION

70.1 Provided that the right of appeal has not been denied under rule 70.4, a protest committee's interpretation of a *rule* or its procedures, but not the facts in its decision, may be appealed to the national authority of the venue by

(a) a boat or competitor that is a *party* to a hearing, or

(b) a race committee that is a *party* to a hearing, provided the protest committee is a jury.

70.2 A protest committee may request confirmation or correction of its decision.

70.3 A club or other organization affiliated to a national authority may request an interpretation of the *rules,* provided that no *protest* or request for redress that may be appealed is involved.

70.4 There shall be no appeal from the decisions of an international jury constituted in compliance with Appendix M. Furthermore, if the notice of race and the sailing instructions so state, the right of appeal may be denied provided that

(a) it is essential to determine promptly the result of a race that will qualify a boat to compete in a later stage of
an event or a subsequent event (a national authority may prescribe that its approval is required for such a procedure),

(b) a national authority so approves for a particular event open only to entrants under its own jurisdiction, or

(c) a national authority after consultation with the ISAF so approves for a particular event, provided the jury is constituted as required by Appendix M, except that only two members of the jury need be International Judges.

70.5 Appeals and requests shall conform to Appendix F.

71 APPEAL DECISIONS

71.1 No *interested party* or member of the protest committee shall take any part in the discussion or decision on an appeal or a request for confirmation or correction.

71.2 The national authority may uphold, change or reverse the protest committee's decision, declare the *protest* or request for redress invalid, or return the *protest* or request for a new hearing and decision by the same or a different protest committee.

71.3 When from the facts found by the protest committee the national authority decides that a boat that was a *party* to a protest hearing broke a *rule,* it shall penalize her, whether or not that boat or that *rule* was mentioned in the protest committee's decision.

71.4 The decision of the national authority shall be final. The national authority shall send its decision in writing to all *parties* to the hearing and the protest committee, who shall be bound by the decision.

Part 6 – Entry and Qualification

75   ENTERING A RACE

75.1   To enter a race, a boat shall comply with the requirements of the organizing authority of the race. She shall be entered by

(a)   a member of a club or other organization affiliated to a national authority,

(b)   such a club or organization, or

(c)   a member of a national authority.

75.2   Competitors shall comply with Appendix 2.

76   EXCLUSION OF BOATS OR COMPETITORS

76.1   The organizing authority or the race committee may reject or cancel the entry of a boat or exclude a competitor, subject to rule 76.2, provided it does so before the start of the first race and states the reason for doing so. However, the organizing authority or the race committee shall not reject or cancel the entry of a boat or exclude a competitor because of advertising, provided the boat or competitor complies with Appendix 1.

US SAILING prescribes that an organizing authority or race committee shall not reject or cancel the entry of a boat or exclude a competitor eligible under the notice of race and sailing instructions for an arbitrary or capricious reason or for reason of race, color, religion, gender, age or national origin.

76.2   At world and continental championships no entry within stated quotas shall be rejected or cancelled without first obtaining the approval of the relevant international class association (or the Offshore Racing Council) or the ISAF.

76.3   *US SAILING prescribes that a boat whose entry is rejected or cancelled or a competitor who is excluded from a race or series shall be, upon written request, entitled to a hearing conducted by the protest committee under rules 63.2, 63.3, 63.4 and 63.6.*

77   IDENTIFICATION ON SAILS

A boat shall comply with the requirements of Appendix G governing class insignia, national letters and numbers on sails.

78   COMPLIANCE WITH CLASS RULES; CERTIFICATES

78.1   A boat's owner and any other person in charge shall ensure that the boat is maintained to comply with her class rules and that her measurement or rating certificate, if any, remains valid.

78.2   When a *rule* requires a certificate to be produced before a boat *races,* and it is not produced, the boat may *race* provided that the race committee receives a statement signed by the person in charge that a valid certificate exists and that it will be given to the race committee before the end of the event. If the certificate is not received in time, the boat's scores shall be removed from the event results.

78.3   When a measurer for an event concludes that a boat or personal equipment does not comply with the class rules, he shall report the matter in writing to the race committee, which shall protest the boat.

79   ADVERTISING

A boat and her crew shall comply with Appendix 1.

80   RESCHEDULED RACES

When a race has been rescheduled, rule 36 applies and all boats entered in the original race shall be notified and, unless disqualified under rule 30.3, be entitled to sail the rescheduled race. New entries that meet the entry requirements of the original race may be accepted at the discretion of the race committee.

Part 7 – Race Organization

85   GOVERNING RULES

The organizing authority, race committee and protest committee shall be governed by the *rules* in the conduct and judging of races.

86   RULE CHANGES

86.1   A racing rule may not be changed unless permitted in the rule itself or as follows:

(a)   Prescriptions of a national authority may change a racing rule, but not the Definitions; a rule in the Introduction; Sportsmanship and the Rules; Part 1, 2 or 7; rule 43.1, 43.2, 69, 70, 71, 75, 76.2 or 79; a rule of an appendix that changes one of these rules; or Appendix H, M, 1, 2 or 3.

(b)   Sailing instructions may change a racing rule by referring specifically to it and stating the change, but not rule 76.1, Appendix F, or a rule listed in rule 86.1(a).

US SAILING prescribes that sailing instructions shall not change rules 61.4 or 76.3, Appendix P, or its prescriptions to rules 40, 68 or 76.1.

(c)   Class rules may change only racing rules 42, 49, 50, 51, 52, 53 and 54.

86.2   If a national authority so prescribes, these restrictions do not apply if rules are changed to develop or test proposed rules in local races. The national authority may prescribe that its approval is required for such changes.

US SAILING prescribes that proposed rules may be tested in local races.

87   ORGANIZING AUTHORITY; NOTICE OF RACE; APPOINTMENT OF RACE OFFICIALS

87.1   **Organizing Authority**

Races shall be organized by an organizing authority, which shall be

(a)   the ISAF;

(b)   a member national authority of the ISAF;

(c)   a club or other organization affiliated to a national authority;

(d)   a class association, either with the approval of a national authority or in conjunction with an affiliated club; or

(e)   an unaffiliated body in conjunction with an affiliated club, except that in a major event designated by the ISAF, the unaffiliated body shall be owned and controlled by an affiliated club which shall have the approval of the relevant national authority.

87.2   **Notice of Race; Appointment of Race Officials**

The organizing authority shall publish a notice of race that conforms to rule J1, appoint a race committee and, when appropriate, appoint a jury. However, the race committee, an international jury and umpires may be appointed by the ISAF as provided by the ISAF regulations.

88   RACE COMMITTEE; SAILING INSTRUCTIONS; SCORING

88.1   Race Committee

The race committee shall conduct races as directed by the organizing authority and as required by the *rules*.

88.2   Sailing Instructions

(a)   The race committee shall publish written sailing instructions that conform to rule J2.

(b)   The sailing instructions for an international event shall include, in English, the applicable prescriptions of the national authority.

(c)   Changes to the sailing instructions shall be in writing and posted within the required time on the official notice board or, on the water, communicated to each boat before her warning signal. Oral changes may be given only on the water, and only if the procedure is stated in the sailing instructions.

88.3   Scoring

(a)   The race committee shall score a race or series as provided in Appendix A using either the Low Point or Bonus Point system, or as otherwise specified in the sailing instructions.

(b)   When a scoring system provides for excluding one or more race scores from a boat's series score, the score for a breach of rule 2, rule 30.3's next-to-last sentence, or rule 42 if rule 67, N2.2 or N2.3 applies, shall not be excluded. The next-worse score shall be excluded instead.

89   PROTEST COMMITTEE

A protest committee shall be

(a)   a committee appointed by the race committee;

(b)   a jury appointed by the organizing authority, which is separate from and independent of the race committee; or

(c)   an international jury appointed by the organizing authority or as prescribed in the ISAF regulations and meeting the requirements of Appendix M. A national authority may prescribe that its approval is required for the appointment of international juries for races within its jurisdiction, except ISAF events or when international juries are appointed by the ISAF under rule 87.2.

APPENDICES, SECTION I

Appendix A – Scoring

See rule 88.3.

A1 NUMBER OF RACES

The number of races scheduled and the number required to be completed to constitute a series shall be stated in the sailing instructions.

A2 SERIES SCORES

Each boat's series score shall be the total of her race scores excluding her worst score. (The sailing instructions may make a different arrangement by providing, for example, that no score will be excluded, that two or more scores will be excluded, or that a specified number of scores will be excluded if a specified number of races are completed.) If a boat has two or more equal worst scores, the score(s) for the race(s) sailed earliest in the series shall be excluded. The boat with the lowest series score wins and others shall be ranked accordingly.

A3 STARTING TIMES AND FINISHING PLACES

The time of a boat's starting signal shall be her starting time, and the order in which boats *finish* a race shall determine their finishing places. However, when a handicap system is used a boat's elapsed time, corrected to the nearest second, shall determine her finishing place.

A4 LOW POINT AND BONUS POINT SYSTEMS

Most series are scored using either the Low Point System or the Bonus Point System. The Low Point System uses a boat's finishing place as her race score. The Bonus Point System benefits the first six finishers because of the greater difficulty in advancing from fourth place to third, for example, than from fourteenth place to thirteenth. The system chosen may be made to apply by stating in the sailing instructions that, for example, 'The series will be scored as provided in Appendix A of the racing rules using the [Low] [Bonus] Point System.'

A4.1 Each boat *starting* and *finishing* and not thereafter retiring, being penalized or given redress shall be scored points as follows:

Finishing Place	Low Point System	Bonus Point System
First	1	0
Second	2	3
Third	3	5.7
Fourth	4	8
Fifth	5	10
Sixth	6	11.7
Seventh	7	13
Each place thereafter	Add 1 point	Add 1 point

A4.2 A boat that did not *start*, did not *finish*, retired after *finishing* or was disqualified shall be scored points for the finishing place one more than the number of boats entered in the series. A boat penalized under rule 30.2 or 44.3 shall be scored points as provided in rule 44.3(c).

A5 SCORES DETERMINED BY THE RACE COMMITTEE

A boat that did not *start,* comply with rule 30.2 or 30.3, or *finish,* or that takes a penalty under rule 44.3 or retires after *finishing,* shall be scored accordingly by the race committee without a hearing. Only the protest committee may take other scoring actions that worsen a boat's score.

A6 CHANGES IN PLACES AND SCORES OF OTHER BOATS

(a) If a boat is disqualified from a race or retires after *finishing,* each boat that *finished* after her shall be moved up one place.

(b) If the protest committee decides to give redress by adjusting a boat's score, the scores of other boats shall not be changed unless the protest committee decides otherwise.

A7 RACE TIES

If boats are tied at the finishing line or if a handicap system is used and boats have equal corrected times, the points for the place for which the boats have tied and for the place(s) immediately below shall be added together and divided equally. Boats tied for a race prize shall share it or be given equal prizes.

A8 SERIES TIES

A8.1 If there is a series score tie between two or more boats, each boat's race scores shall be listed in order of best to worst, and at the first point(s) where there is a difference the tie shall be broken in favour of the boat(s) with the best score(s). No excluded scores shall be used.

A8.2 If a tie remains between two boats, it shall be broken in favour of the boat that scored better than the other boat in more races. If more than two boats are tied, they shall be ranked in order of the number of times each boat scored better than another of the tied boats. No race for which a tied boat's score has been excluded shall be used.

A8.3 If a tie still remains between two or more boats, they shall be ranked in order of their scores in the last race. Any remaining ties shall be broken by using the tied boats' scores in the next-to-last race and so on until all ties are broken. These scores shall be used even if some of them are excluded scores.

A9 RACE SCORES IN A SERIES LONGER THAN A REGATTA

For a series that is held over a period of time longer than a regatta, a boat that came to the starting area but did not *start,* did not *finish,* retired after *finishing* or was disqualified shall be scored points for the finishing place one more than the number of boats that came to the starting area. A boat that did not come to the starting area shall be scored points for the finishing place one more than the number of boats entered in the series.

A10 GUIDANCE ON REDRESS

If the protest committee decides to give redress by adjusting a boat's score for a race, it is advised to consider scoring her

(a) points equal to the average, to the nearest tenth of a point (0.05 to be rounded upward), of her points in all the races in the series except the race in question;

(b) points equal to the average, to the nearest tenth of a point (0.05 to be rounded upward), of her points in all the races before the race in question; or

(c) points based on the position of the boat in the race at the time of the incident that justified redress.

A11 SCORING ABBREVIATIONS

These abbreviations are recommended for recording the circumstances described:

DNC	Did not *start;* did not come to the starting area
DNS	Did not *start* (other than DNC and OCS)
OCS	Did not *start;* on the course side of the starting line and broke rule 29.1 or 30.1
ZFP	20% penalty under rule 30.2
BFD	Disqualification under rule 30.3
SCP	Took a scoring penalty under rule 44.3
DNF	Did not *finish*
RAF	Retired after *finishing*
DSQ	Disqualification
DNE	Disqualification not excludable under rule 88.3(b)
RDG	Redress given

US SAILING Note: *The scoring systems in Appendix A reward a boat that participates in all the races of a series, even when one or more scores is excluded from her series score. In a long series, such as a season championship spanning several weeks, these systems put a boat that misses some of the races at a disadvantage to a boat that sails more races. The US SAILING website (www.ussailing.org/racemgt) provides texts for alternative scoring systems designed for such long series, including an updated version of Appendix AA that appeared in the 1997-2000 edition of The Racing Rules of Sailing. Those without access to the website may request a copy of these texts by fax on the US SAILING Infofax line, (888) USSAIL-6.*

Appendix B – Sailboard Racing Rules

Sailboard races shall be sailed under The Racing Rules of Sailing *as changed by this appendix.*

B1 DEFINITIONS

Add the following definitions:

Capsized A sailboard is *capsized* when her sail or the competitor's body is in the water.

Recovering A sailboard is *recovering* from the time her sail or, when water-starting, the competitor's body is out of the water until she has steerage way.

B2 PART 2 – WHEN BOATS MEET

B2.1 The last sentence of rule 20 is changed to: 'A sailboard moving astern shall *keep clear* of other sailboards and boats.'

B2.2 Add to Section D:

23   SAIL OUT OF THE WATER WHEN STARTING

When approaching the starting line to *start,* a sailboard shall have her sail out of the water and in a normal position, except when accidentally *capsized.*

24   RECOVERING

A sailboard *recovering* shall avoid a sailboard or boat under way.

B3   PART 3 – CONDUCT OF A RACE

Rule 31 is changed to: 'A competitor shall not hold on to a starting *mark.*'

B4   PART 4 – OTHER REQUIREMENTS WHEN RACING

B4.1   Rule 42 is changed to: 'A sailboard shall be propelled only by the action of the wind on the sail, by the action of the water on the hull and by the unassisted actions of the competitor.'

B4.2   Rule 43.1(a) is modified to permit a competitor to wear a container for holding beverages. The container shall have a capacity of at least one litre and weigh no more than 1.5 kilograms when full.

B4.3   In rule 44.2, delete 'including two tacks and two gybes'.

B5   PART 6 – ENTRY AND QUALIFICATION

Add to rule 78.1: 'When so prescribed by the national authority, a numbered and dated device on a sailboard and her daggerboard and sail shall serve as her measurement certificate.'

B6   PART 7 – RACE ORGANIZATION

In rule 88.2(c), the last sentence is changed to: 'Changes to the sailing instructions may be communicated orally, but only if the procedure is stated in the sailing instructions.'

B7   APPENDIX G – IDENTIFICATION ON SAILS

B7.1   Add to rule G1.1(a): 'The insignia shall not refer to anything other than the manu-facturer or class and shall not consist of more than two letters and three numbers or an abstract design.'

B7.2   Rules G1.3(a), G1.3(c), G1.3(d) and G1.3(e) are changed to: 'The class insignia shall be displayed once on each side of the sail in the area above a line projected at right angles from a point on the luff of the sail one third of the distance from the head to the wishbone. The national letters and sail numbers shall be in the central third of the sail above the wishbone and clearly separated from any advertising and shall be placed at different heights on the two sides of the sail, those on the starboard side being uppermost.'

Appendix C – Match Racing Rules

Match races shall be sailed under The Racing Rules of Sailing as changed by this appendix. Matches shall be umpired unless the notice of race and sailing instructions state otherwise.

C1   TERMINOLOGY

'Competitor' means the skipper, team or boat as appropriate for the event.

'Flight' means two or more matches started in the same starting sequence.

C2 CHANGES TO THE DEFINITIONS AND THE RULES OF PART 2

C2.1 The definition *Finish* is changed to: 'A boat *finishes* when any part of her hull, crew or equipment in normal position, crosses the finishing line in the direction of the course from the last *mark* after completing any penalties. However, when penalties are cancelled under rule C7.2(d) after one or both boats have *finished* each shall be recorded as *finished* when she crossed the line.'

C2.2 Add to the definition *Proper Course*: 'A boat taking a penalty or manoeuvring to take a penalty is not sailing a *proper course.*'

C2.3 Change the last sentence of the definition *Clear Ahead* and *Clear Astern; Overlap* to: 'These terms do not apply to boats on opposite *tacks* unless either rule 18 applies or both boats are subject to rule 13.2.'

C2.4 Rule 13 becomes rule 13.1.

Add new rule 13.2: 'After the foot of the mainsail of a boat sailing downwind crosses the centreline she shall *keep clear* until her mainsail has filled on the other *tack.*'

C2.5 Rules 16.2 and 17.2 are deleted.

C2.6 Rule 18.3 is changed to: 'If two boats were on opposite *tacks* and one of them completes a tack within the *two-length zone* to pass a *mark* or *obstruction,* and if thereafter the other boat cannot by luffing avoid becoming *overlapped* inside her, the boat that tacked shall *keep clear* and rules 15 and 18.2 do not apply. If the other boat can by luffing avoid becoming *overlapped* inside her then rule 18.2(c) shall apply as if the boats were *clear ahead* and *clear astern* at the *two-length zone.*'

C2.7 When rule 19.1 applies, the following arm signals by the helmsman are required in addition to the hails:

(a) for 'Room to tack', repeatedly and clearly pointing to windward; and

(b) for 'You tack', repeatedly and clearly pointing at the other boat and waving the arm to windward.

C2.8 In rule 20 the second sentence is changed to: 'A boat taking a penalty shall *keep clear* of one that is not.'

C2.9 Rule 22.1 is changed to: 'If reasonably possible, a boat not *racing* shall not interfere with a boat that is *racing* or an umpire boat.'

C2.10 Rule 22.2 is changed to: 'Except when sailing a *proper course,* a boat shall not interfere with a boat taking a penalty or sailing on another leg.'

C2.11 Add new rule 22.3: 'When boats in different matches meet, any change of course by either boat shall be consistent with complying with a *rule* or trying to win her own match.'

C3 RACE SIGNALS AND CHANGES TO RELATED RULES

C3.1 Starting Signals

The signals for starting a match shall be as follows. Times shall be taken from the visual signals; the failure of a sound signal shall be disregarded. If more than one match will be sailed, the starting signal for one match shall be the warning signal for the next match.

Time in minutes	Visual signal	Sound signal	Means
10	Flag F displayed	One	Attention
6	Flag F removed	None	
5	Numeral pennant displayed*	One	Warning signal
4	Flag P displayed	One	Preparatory signal
2	Blue or yellow flag or both displayed**	One**	End of pre-start entry time
0	Warning and preparatory signals removed	One	Starting signal

　* Within a flight, numeral pennant 1 means Match 1, pennant 2 means Match 2, etc., unless the sailing instructions state otherwise.

** These signals shall be made only if one or both boats fail to comply with rule C4.2. The flag(s) shall be displayed until the umpires have signalled a penalty or for one minute, whichever is earlier.

C3.2　Changes to Related Rules

(a)　Rule 29.1 is changed to: 'When at a boat's starting signal any part of her hull, crew or equipment is on the course side of the starting line or its extensions, she shall sail completely on the pre-start side of the line before *starting*.'

(b)　Rule 29.2 is changed to: 'When at her starting signal a boat becomes subject to rule C3.2(a), the race committee shall promptly display a blue or yellow flag or both with one sound signal. Each flag shall be displayed until such boats are completely on the pre-start side of the starting line or its extensions or until two minutes after her starting signal, whichever is earlier.'

(c)　When, after her starting signal, a boat sails on the course side of the starting line or its extensions, without having started correctly, the race committee shall promptly display a blue or yellow flag or both. Each flag shall be displayed until such boats are completely on the pre-start side of the starting line or its extensions or until two minutes after her starting signal, whichever is earlier.

(d)　In Race Signal AP the last sentence is changed to: 'The attention signal will be made 1 minute after removal unless at that time the race is *postponed* again or *abandoned*.'

(e)　In Race Signal N the last sentence is changed to: 'The attention signal will be made 1 minute after removal unless at that time the race is *abandoned* again or *postponed*.'

C3.3　Finishing Line Signals

The race signal 'Blue flag or shape' shall not be used.

C4　REQUIREMENTS BEFORE THE START

C4.1

At her preparatory signal, each boat shall be outside the line that is at 90° angle to the starting line through the starting *mark* at her assigned end. In the race schedule pairing list, the boat listed on the left-hand side is assigned the port end and shall display a blue flag at her stern while *racing*. The other boat is assigned the starboard end and shall display a yellow flag at her stern while *racing*.

C4.2   Within the two-minute period following her preparatory signal, a boat shall cross and clear the starting line, the first time from the course side to the pre-start side.

C5   SIGNALS BY UMPIRES

(a)   A green and white flag with one long sound signal means: 'No penalty.'

(b)   A coloured flag identifying a boat with one long sound signal means: 'The identified boat shall take a penalty by complying with rule C7.'

(c)   A red flag with or soon after a coloured flag with one long sound signal means: 'The identified boat shall take a penalty by complying with rule C7.3(d).'

(d)   A black flag with a coloured flag and one long sound signal means: 'The identified boat is disqualified, and the match is terminated and awarded to the other boat.'

(e)   One short sound signal means: 'A penalty is now completed.'

(f)   Repetitive short sound signals mean: 'A boat is no longer taking a penalty and the penalty remains.'

(g)   A coloured shape displayed from an umpire boat means: 'The identified boat has an outstanding penalty.'

C6   PROTESTS AND REQUESTS FOR REDRESS BY BOATS

C6.1   A boat may protest another boat

(a)   under a rule of Part 2, except rule 14, by clearly displaying flag Y immediately after an incident in which she was involved.

(b)   under any rule not listed in rule C6.1(a) or C6.2 by clearly displaying a red flag as soon as possible after the incident.

C6.2   A boat may not protest another boat under

(a)   rule 14, unless damage results;

(b)   a rule of Part 2, unless she was involved in the incident;

(c)   rule 31 or 42; or

(d)   rule C4 or C7.

C6.3   A boat intending to request redress because of circumstances that arise before she *finishes* or retires shall clearly display a red flag as soon as possible after she becomes aware of those circumstances, but not later than two minutes after *finishing* or retiring.

C6.4   (a)   A boat protesting under rule C6.1(a) shall remove flag Y before or as soon as possible after the umpires' signal.

(b)   A boat protesting under rule C6.1(b) or requesting redress under rule C6.3 shall, for her *protest* to be valid, keep her red flag displayed until she has so informed the umpires after *finishing* or retiring.

C6.5   Umpire Decisions

After flag Y is displayed, the umpires shall decide whether to penalize any boat. They shall signal their decision in compliance with rule C5(a), (b) or (c).

C6.6   Protest Committee Decisions

(a)   The protest committee may take evidence in any way it considers appropriate and may communicate its decision orally.

(b)   If the protest committee decides that a breach of a *rule* has had no significant effect on the outcome of the match, it may

  (1) impose a penalty of one point or part of one point,

  (2) order a resail, or

  (3) make another arrangement it decides is equitable, which may be to impose no penalty.

 (c) The penalty for breaking rule 14 when damage results will be at the discretion of the protest committee, and may include exclusion from further races in the event.

C7 PENALTY SYSTEM

C7.1 Rule Changes

Rules 31.2 and 44 are deleted.

C7.2 All Penalties

 (a) A penalized boat may delay taking a penalty within the limitations of rule C7.3 and shall take it as follows:

  (1) When on a leg of the course to a windward *mark,* she shall gybe and, as soon as reasonably possible, luff to a close-hauled course.

  (2) When on a leg of the course to a leeward *mark* or the finishing line, she shall tack and, as soon as reasonably possible, bear away to a downwind course.

 (b) Add to rule 2: 'When *racing,* a boat may wait for an umpire's decision before taking a penalty.'

 (c) A boat completes a leg of the course when her bow crosses the extension of the line from the previous *mark* through the *mark* she is rounding, or on the last leg when she *finishes.*

 (d) A penalized boat shall not be recorded as having *finished* until she takes her penalty and sails completely to the course side of the line and then *finishes,* unless the penalty is cancelled before or after she crosses the finishing line.

 (e) If a boat has one or two outstanding penalties and the other boat in her match is penalized, one penalty for each boat shall be cancelled except that a 'red flag' penalty shall not cancel an outstanding penalty.

 (f) If a boat has more than two outstanding penalties, the umpires shall signal her disqualification under rule C5(d).

C7.3 Penalty Limitations

 (a) A boat taking a penalty that includes a tack shall have the spinnaker head below the main boom gooseneck from the time she passes head to wind until she is on a close-hauled course.

 (b) No part of a penalty may be taken within two of a boat's hull lengths of a rounding *mark.*

 (c) If a boat has one outstanding penalty, she may take the penalty any time after *starting* and before *finishing.* If a boat has two outstanding penalties, she shall take one of them as soon as reasonably possible, but not before *starting.*

 (d) When the umpires display a red flag with or soon after a penalty flag, the penalized boat shall take a penalty as soon as reasonably possible, but not before *starting.* A 'red flag' penalty shall not cancel an outstanding penalty.

C7.4 Taking and Completing Penalties

(a) When a boat with an outstanding penalty is on a leg to a windward *mark* and gybes, or is on a leg to a leeward *mark* or the finishing line and passes head to wind, she is taking a penalty.

(b) When a boat taking a penalty either does not take the penalty correctly or does not complete the penalty as soon as reasonably possible, she is no longer taking a penalty. The umpires shall signal this as required by rule C5(f).

(c) The umpire boat for each match shall display coloured shapes, each shape indicating one outstanding penalty. When a boat has taken a penalty, or a penalty has been cancelled, one shape shall be removed. Failure of the umpires to display or remove shapes shall not change the number of penalties outstanding.

C8 PENALTIES INITIATED BY UMPIRES

C8.1 Rule Changes

(a) Rules 60.2(a) and 60.3(a) do not apply to *rules* for which penalties may be imposed by umpires.

(b) Rule 64.1(b) is changed so that the provision for exonerating a boat may be applied by the umpires without a hearing, and it takes precedence over any conflicting rule of this appendix.

C8.2 When the umpires decide that a boat has broken rule 31, 42, C4 or C7.3(c) she shall be penalized by signalling her under rule C5(b).

C8.3 When the umpires decide that a boat has

(a) gained an advantage by breaking a *rule* after allowing for a penalty,

(b) deliberately broken a *rule,* or

(c) committed a breach of sportsmanship,

she shall be penalized under rule C5(b) or C5(d).

C8.4 If the umpires or protest committee members decide that a boat may have broken a *rule* other than those listed in rule C6.1(a) or C6.2, they shall so inform the protest committee for its action under rule 60.3 and rule C6.6 when appropriate.

C8.5 When, after one boat has *started,* the umpires are satisfied that the other boat will not *start,* they may signal under rule C5(d) that the boat that did not *start* is disqualified and the match is terminated.

C9 REQUESTS FOR REDRESS OR REOPENINGS, APPEALS, OTHER PROCEEDINGS

C9.1 There shall be no request for redress or an appeal from a decision made under rule C5, C6, C7 or C8. In rule 66 the third sentence is changed to: 'A *party* to the hearing may not ask for a reopening.'

C9.2 A competitor may not base a request for redress on a claim that an action by an official boat was improper. The protest committee may decide to consider giving redress in such circumstances but only if it believes that an official boat, including an umpire boat, may have seriously interfered with a competing boat.

C9.3 No proceedings of any kind may be taken in relation to any action or non-action by the umpires, except as permitted in rule C9.2.

C10   SCORING

C10.1 The winning competitor of each match scores one point (half of one point each for a dead heat); the loser scores no points.

C10.2 When a competitor withdraws from part of an event the scores of all completed races shall stand.

C10.3 When a multiple round robin is terminated with an incomplete round robin, only one point shall be available for all the matches sailed between any two competitors, as follows:

Number of matches completed between any two competitors	Points for each win
1	One point
2	One-half point
3	One-third point
(etc.)	

C10.4 In a round-robin series,

(a)   competitors shall be placed in order of their total scores, highest score first;

(b)   a competitor who has won a match but is disqualified for breaking a *rule* against a competitor in another match shall lose the point for that match (but the losing competitor shall not be awarded the point); and

(c)   the overall position between competitors who have sailed in different groups shall be decided by the highest score.

C10.5 In a knockout series the sailing instructions shall prescribe the minimum number of points required to win a series between two competitors. When a knockout series is terminated it shall be decided in favour of the competitor with the higher score.

C11   TIES

C11.1   Round-Robin Series

A round-robin series means a grouping of competitors who all sail against each other one or more times. Each separate stage identified in the event format shall be a separate round-robin series irrespective of the number of times each competitor sails against each other competitor in that stage.

Ties between two or more competitors in a round-robin series shall be broken by the following methods, in order, until the tie is broken. When the tie is only partially broken, paragraphs (a) to (e) shall be reapplied to the remaining ties. The tie shall be decided in favour of the competitor(s) who

(a)   placed in order, has the highest score in the matches between the tied competitors.

(b)   when the tie is between two competitors in a multiple round robin, has won the last match between the two competitors.

(c)   has the most points against the competitor placed highest in the round-robin series or, if necessary, second highest, and so on until the tie is broken.

When two separate ties have to be resolved but the resolution of each depends upon resolving the other, the following principles shall be used in the C11.1(c) procedure:

(1) the higher place tie shall be resolved before the lower place tie, and

(2) all the competitors in the lower place tie shall be treated as a single competitor for the purposes of rule C11.1(c).

(d) after applying rule C10.4(c), has the highest place in the different groups, irrespective of the number of competitors in each group.

(e) has the highest place in the most recent stage of the event (fleet race, round robin, etc.).

C11.2 Knockout Series

Ties (including 0-0) between two competitors in a knockout series shall be broken by the following methods, in order, until the tie is broken. The tie shall be decided in favour of the competitor who

(a) has the highest place in the most recent round-robin series, applying rule C11.1 if necessary.

(b) has won the most recent match in the event between the tied competitors.

C11.3 When rule C11.1 or C11.2 does not resolve the tie:

(a) If the tie needs to be resolved for a later stage of the event (or another event for which the event is a direct qualifier), the tie shall be broken by a sail-off when practicable. When the race committee decides a sail-off is not practicable the tie shall be broken by a draw.

(b) To decide the winner of an event, or the overall position between competitors eliminated in one round of a knockout series, a sail-off may be used (but not a draw).

(c) When a tie is not broken any monetary prizes or ranking points for tied places shall be added together and divided equally among the tied competitors.

Note: A Standard Notice of Race and Standard Sailing Instructions for match racing are available from the ISAF.

Appendix D – Team Racing Rules

Team races shall be sailed under The Racing Rules of Sailing *as changed by this appendix. If umpires or observers will be used the sailing instructions shall so state.*

D1 CHANGES TO THE RACING RULES

D1.1 The following rules are changed, added or deleted:

(a) Rule 17.2 is changed to: 'Except on a beat to windward, while a boat is less than two of her hull lengths from a *leeward* boat, she shall not sail below her *proper course* unless she gybes.'

(b) Rule 18.4 is deleted.

(c) Add to rule 22.2: 'Except when sailing a *proper course*, a boat shall not interfere with a boat on another leg or lap of the course. For the purpose of this rule, a boat that has *finished* is on a different leg from one that has not.'

(d) Add new rule 22.3: 'When boats in different races meet, any change of course by either boat shall be consistent with complying with a *rule* or trying to win her own race.'

    (e)   Add to rule 41: 'A boat that receives help from a team-mate does not break this rule.'

D1.2 The following additional rules apply:

    (a)   There shall be no penalty for breaking a rule of Part 2 when the incident is between boats in the same team and there is no contact.

    (b)   A boat damaged by a team-mate boat is not eligible for redress based on that damage.

D2   INTENTION TO PROTEST; ACKNOWLEDGEMENT OF BREACHES OF RULES

D2.1 General

    (a)   A boat intending to protest shall hail the other boat immediately and promptly display a red flag.

    (b)   A boat that, while *racing,* may have broken a rule of Part 2, except rule 14 when the boat has caused damage, or rule D1 may take a penalty as provided by rules 44.1 and 44.2, except that only one turn is required. When an incident occurs at the finishing line or when an umpire's penalty is signalled at or beyond the finishing line, a boat shall not be recorded as having *finished* until she has completed her penalty and sailed completely to the course side of the line before *finishing.*

    (c)   When after displaying a red flag a boat is satisfied that the other boat has taken a penalty in compliance with rule D2.1(b) she shall remove her red flag.

    (d)   A boat that has displayed a red flag and then decides reasonably promptly that she, and not the other boat, was at fault shall immediately remove her flag, take a penalty in compliance with rule D2.1(b), and hail the other boat accordingly.

    (e)   The sailing instructions may state that rule D2.2(g) applies to all *protests.*

D2.2 Umpired Races

Races to be umpired shall be identified either in the sailing instructions or by the display of flag U no later than the warning signal.

    (a)   When a boat protests under a rule of Part 2, except rule 14, or under rule D1, 31.1, 42 or 44, she is not entitled to a hearing. Instead, when the protested boat fails either to acknowledge breaking a *rule* or to take a penalty in compliance with rule D2.1(b), the protesting boat may display a yellow flag and request a decision by hailing 'Umpire'.

    (b)   An umpire shall signal a decision as follows:

        (1)   A green flag or a green and white flag means 'No penalty imposed; incident closed'.

        (2)   A red flag means 'One or more boats are penalized.' The umpire shall hail or signal to identify each boat to be penalized.

    The protesting boat shall then remove her flag.

    (c)   A boat penalized by an umpire's decision shall make two 360° turns (720°) in compliance with rule 44.2.

    (d)   When a boat commits a breach of sportsmanship or fails to take a penalty when required by an umpire, or when a boat or her team gains an advantage despite taking a penalty, an umpire may impose one or more 360° turn penalties by displaying a red flag and hailing her accordingly, or report the incident as provided in rule D2.2(e).

(e)   When an incident involves reckless sailing, rule 14 when damage may have been caused, rule 28.1 or failure to comply with an umpire's decision, the umpire may report the incident to a protest committee which may further penalize the boat concerned. The umpire shall signal this intention by displaying a black flag and hailing appropriately.

(f)   Rules 60.2 and 60.3 do not apply. The protest committee may call a hearing only on receipt of a report from an umpire as provided in rule D2.2(e) or under rule 69.

(g)   *Protests* need not be in writing, and the protest committee may take evidence in any way it considers appropriate and may communicate its decision orally.

(h)   There shall be no requests for redress or to reopen a hearing or appeals by a boat arising from decisions or actions or non-actions by the umpires. The protest committee may decide to consider giving redress when it believes that an official boat, including an umpire boat, may have seriously interfered with a competing boat.

D2.3 Races with Observers

Observers may be appointed by the race committee to observe the racing and give opinions on incidents when requested. If so, rule D2.2 applies except that

(a)   a boat need not request an opinion or accept one, in which case any *protest* shall comply with and be decided under the rules of Part 5 as changed by this appendix;

(b)   an observer may display a yellow flag to signal that he has no opinion. If a boat then intends to protest she may do so by complying with the rules of Part 5 as changed by this appendix.

D3 SCORING A RACE

D3.1 (a)   Each boat *finishing* a race, whether or not rules 28.1 and 29.1 have been complied with, shall be scored points equal to her *finishing* place. All other boats shall be scored points equal to the number of boats entitled to *race.*

(b)   In addition, a boat's score shall be increased as follows:

Rule broken	Penalty points
(1) rule 14 when the boat has caused damage, or rule 29.1	10
(2) any other *rule* for which a penalty has not been taken	6

However, a boat that breaks rule 28.1 and does not *finish* shall not have the penalty points in (2) above added to her score for this breach when it gained neither her nor her team any advantage. The protest committee may further increase a boat's score when she has broken a *rule* and as a result her team has gained an advantage.

(c)   The team with the lowest total points wins. If there is a tie on points, the team having the combination of race scores that does not include a first place wins.

D3.2 When all boats of one team have *finished* or retired, the race committee may stop the race. The other team's boats shall be scored the points they would have received had they *finished*.

D3.3 When all the boats of a team fail to *start* in a race, each shall be scored points equal to the number of boats entitled to *race,* and the boats of the other team shall be scored as if they had *finished* in the best positions.

D4 SCORING A SERIES

D4.1 A team racing series shall consist of races or matches. A match shall consist of two races between the same two teams. The team with the lower total points for the race or the match wins.

D4.2 When two or more teams are competing in a series consisting of races or matches, the series winner shall be the team winning the greatest number of races or matches. The other teams shall be ranked in order of number of wins. Tied matches shall count as half a win to each team.

D4.3 When necessary, ties in a completed series shall be broken using, in order of precedence,

(a) the number of races or matches won when the tied teams met;

(b) the points scored when the tied teams met;

(c) if two teams remain tied, the last race between them;

(d) total points scored in all races against common opponents;

(e) a game of chance.

If a multiple tie is only partially resolved by one of these, then the remaining tie shall be broken by starting again at rule D4.3(a).

D4.4 If a series is not completed, teams shall be ranked according to the results from completed rounds, and ties shall be broken initially using the results from races or matches between the tied teams in the incomplete round. If no round has been completed, teams shall be ranked in order of their race (or match) win-loss ratios. Thereafter, rule D4.3(a) to D4.3(e) shall be used to break ties.

D5 BREAKDOWNS WHEN BOATS ARE SUPPLIED BY THE ORGANIZING AUTHORITY

D5.1 A supplied boat suffering a breakdown shall display a red flag as soon as practicable and, if possible, continue *racing*.

D5.2 When the race committee decides that the boat's finishing position was made significantly worse, that the breakdown was not the fault of the crew, and that in the same circumstances a reasonably competent crew would not have been able to avoid the breakdown, it shall make as equitable a decision as possible, which may be to order the race to be resailed or, when the boat's finishing position was predictable, award her points for that position. In case of doubt about her position when she broke down, the doubt shall be resolved against her.

D5.3 A breakdown caused by defective supplied equipment or a breach of a *rule* by an opponent shall not normally be determined to be the fault of the crew, but one caused by careless handling, capsizing or a breach by a boat of the same team shall be. Any doubt about the fault of the crew shall be resolved in the boat's favour.

Appendix E – Radio-Controlled Boat Racing Rules

Races for radio-controlled boats shall be sailed under The Racing Rules of Sailing *as changed by this appendix.*

E1   TERMINOLOGY, RACE SIGNALS, DEFINITIONS AND FUNDAMENTAL RULES

E1.1   Terminology

'Boat' means a boat that is radio-controlled by a competitor who is not on board. For 'race' used as a noun outside this appendix and Appendix A read 'heat'. Within this appendix, a race consists of one or more heats, and is completed when the last heat in the race is finished. An 'event' consists of one or more races. A 'series' consists of a specified number of races or events.

E1.2   Race Signals

Race Signals do not apply. All signals shall be given orally or by other sounds described in this appendix.

E1.3   Definitions

(a)   Add to the definition *Interested Party* 'but not a competitor when acting as an observer'.

(b)   In the definition *Two-Length Zone* change '*Two*' to '*Four*'.

E1.4   Personal Buoyancy

Rule 1.2 is replaced with 'When on board a rescue vessel, each competitor shall be responsible for wearing personal buoyancy adequate for the conditions.'

E1.5   Aerials

Transmitter aerial extremities shall be adequately protected. When a protest committee finds that a competitor has broken this rule it shall either warn him and give him time to comply or penalize him.

E2   PART 2 – WHEN BOATS MEET

Rule 21 is replaced with:

CAPSIZED OR ENTANGLED

If possible, a boat shall avoid a boat that is capsized or entangled, or has not regained control after capsizing or entanglement. A boat is capsized when her masthead is in the water. Two or more boats are entangled when lying together for a period of time so that no boat is capable of manoeuvring to break free of the other(s).

E3   PART 3 – CONDUCT OF A RACE

E3.1   Races With Observers

The race committee may appoint race observers, who may be competitors. They shall remain in the control area, while boats are *racing* and they shall hail and repeat the identity of boats that contact a *mark* or another boat. Such hails shall be made from the control area. Observers shall report all unresolved incidents to the race committee at the end of the heat.

E3.2   Course Board

Rule J2.1(3) does not apply. A course board showing the course and the limits of the control area and launching area(s) shall be located next to or within the control area with information clearly visible to competitors while *racing.*

E3.3   Control and Launching Areas

The control and launching area(s) shall be defined by the sailing instructions. Competitors *racing* shall remain in the control area while a heat is in progress, except that competitors may briefly go to and return from the launching area to perform functions permitted in rule E4.5. Competitors not *racing* shall remain outside the control and launching areas except when offering assistance under rule E4.2 or when acting as race observers.

E3.4   Non-applicable Rules

The second sentence of rule 25 and all of rule 33 do not apply.

E3.5   Starting Races

Rule 26 is replaced with:

'Audible signals for starting a heat shall be at one-minute intervals and shall be a warning signal, a preparatory signal and a starting signal. During the minute before the starting signal, verbal signals shall be made at ten-second intervals, and during the final ten seconds at one-second intervals. The start shall be at the beginning of the starting signal.'

E3.6   Starting Penalties

In rules 29.1 and 30 delete the word 'crew'. Throughout rule 30 oral announcements shall replace the display of flag signals.

E3.7   Starting and Finishing Lines

The starting and finishing lines shall be tangential to, and on the course side of, the starting and finishing *marks*.

E3.8   Individual Recall

Rule 29.2 is changed. Delete all after 'the race committee shall promptly' and replace with 'twice hail "Recall (sail numbers)"'.

E3.9   General Recall

Rule 29.3 is changed. Delete all after 'the race committee may' and replace with 'twice hail "General recall" with two sound signals'. After the recalled start, the warning signal for a new start shall be made.

E3.10   Shortening or Abandoning after the Start

In rule 32.1(b) delete 'foul weather' and replace with 'thunderstorms'. Rules 32.1(c) and 32.2 do not apply.

E4   PART 4 – OTHER REQUIREMENTS WHEN RACING

E4.1   Non-applicable rules

Rules 42.2(b), 42.2(c), 42.3(a), 42.3(c), 43, 47, 48, 49, 50, 52 and 54 do not apply.

E4.2   Outside Help

Rule 41 is replaced with:

(a) A competitor shall not give tactical or strategic advice to a competitor who is *racing*.

(b) A competitor who is *racing* shall not receive outside help except:

   (1) A boat that has gone ashore or aground outside the launching area, or become entangled with another boat or *mark*, may be freed and relaunched only with outside help from a rescue vessel crew.

  (2) Competitors who are not *racing* and others may give outside help in the launching area as permitted by rule E4.5.

E4.3 Propulsion and Prohibited Actions

(a) In rule 42.1 delete all after 'sails and hull'.

(b) In rule 42.2(a) delete all after 'releasing the sail'.

E4.4 Penalties for Breaking a Rule of Part 2

Throughout rule 44 the penalty shall be one 360° turn, including one tack and one gybe.

E4.5 Launching and Relaunching

Rule 45 is replaced with:

(a) Except between the preparatory and starting signals, boats scheduled to *race* in a heat may be launched, taken ashore or relaunched at any time during the heat.

(b) Boats shall be launched or recovered only from within a launching area, except as provided by rule E4.2(b)(1).

(c) While ashore or within a launching area, boats may be adjusted, drained of water, or repaired; have their sails changed or reefed; have entangled objects removed; or have radio equipment repaired or changed.

E4.6 Person in Charge

Rule 46 is changed. Delete 'have on board' and replace with 'be radio controlled by'.

E4.7 Moving Ballast

Rule 51 is replaced with:

During an event and unless class rules specify otherwise,

(a) ballast shall not be shifted, shipped or unshipped;

(b) except for replacements of similar weight and position, no control equipment shall be shifted, shipped or unshipped;

(c) the position of rig counterbalance weights may be adjusted; and

(d) bilge water shall not be used to trim the boat, but may be removed at any time.

E4.8 Radio

(a) A competitor shall not transmit radio signals that cause interference with the radio reception of other boats.

(b) A competitor found to have broken rule E4.8(a) shall not *race* until he has proven compliance with rule E4.8(a).

E4.9 Boat Out of Radio Control

A competitor who loses radio control of his boat shall promptly hail and repeat 'Out of control (the boat's sail number)'. Such a boat shall be deemed to have retired and shall be considered an *obstruction.*

E5 PART 5 – PROTESTS, REDRESS, HEARINGS, MISCONDUCT AND APPEALS

E5.1 Right to Protest and Request Redress

Add to rule 60.1(a): 'A *protest* alleging a breach of a rule of Part 2, 3 or 4 shall be made only by a competitor within the control or launching area and by a boat scheduled to *race* in the heat in which the incident occurred.' After the words 'report by a competitor from another boat' in rules 60.2(a) and 60.3(a) add 'except when acting as an observer'.

E5.2 Informing the Protestee

In rule 61.1(a) delete all after the first sentence and replace with 'When her *protest* concerns an incident in the racing area that she is involved in or sees, she shall twice hail '(Her own sail number) "protest" (the sail number of the other boat)'.'

E5.3 Protest Time Limit

In rule 61.3 delete 'two hours' and replace with '15 minutes'. Add 'A protestor intending to submit a *protest* shall inform the race committee within five minutes of the end of the relevant heat.'

E5.4 Accepting Responsibility

A boat that acknowledges breaking a rule of Part 2, 3 or 4 before the *protest* is found to be valid may retire from the relevant heat without further penalty.

E5.5 Redress

(a) Add to rule 62.1:

    (e) radio interference, or

    (f) an entanglement or grounding because of the action of a boat that was breaking a rule of Part 2 or of a vessel not *racing* that was required to *keep clear.*

(b) The first sentence of rule 62.2 is changed to 'The request shall be made in writing within the time limit of rule E5.3.'

E5.6 Right to Be Present

In rule 63.3(a) delete 'shall have been on board' and replace with 'shall have been radio-controlling them'.

E5.7 Taking Evidence and Finding Facts

Add to rule 63.6: 'Evidence about an alleged breach of a rule of Part 2, 3 or 4 given by competitors shall be accepted only from a competitor who was within the control or launching area and whose boat was scheduled to *race* in the heat in which the incident occurred.'

E5.8 Penalties and Exoneration

Instead of disqualification as provided by rule 64.1(a), the penalty for breaking rule E3.3, E4.2(a) or E4.5 may be determined by the protest committee to be:

(a) exclusion from the next race,

(b) disqualification from the next race, or

(c) one or more penalty turns that must be taken immediately after the boat has started her next race.

In these cases rule 64.1(c) does not apply.

E5.9 Decision on Redress

Add to rule 64.2: 'If a boat given redress was damaged, she shall be given reasonable time, but not more than 30 minutes, to effect repairs before her next heat.'

E5.10 Reopening a Hearing

In rule 66 '24 hours' is changed to 'ten minutes'.

E6   APPENDIX G – IDENTIFICATION ON SAILS

Appendix G is changed as follows:

(a) In rule G1 add 'RSD' after 'ISAF'.

(b) Rule G1.1(c) is replaced by: 'a sail number, which shall be the last two digits of the boat registration number, allotted by the relevant issuing authority.' Where this is a single-digit number, a '0' shall be placed in front. Alternatively an owner may be allotted a personal sail number by the relevant issuing authority, the last two digits of which may be used on all his boats. Where this is a single-digit number, a '0' shall be placed in front.

(c) In rule G1.2(b) delete 'and opposite' and add to the table:

	Minimum height	Minimum space between letters and numerals or edge of sail
numbers on RC boats	100 mm	13 mm
letters on RC boats	60 mm	13 mm

Maximum dimensions shall be the minimum plus 10 mm. The space between marks on opposite sides of the sail shall be 60–100 mm. If a sail is too small to use the specified dimensions, smaller letters and numbers may be used, with 13 mm as the absolute minimum spacing.

(d) Rule G1.3(c) is replaced by: 'Sail numbers shall be placed above the national letters. There shall be space in front of the sail number for the prefix '1', which may be prescribed by the race committee in the event of a conflict between numbers.'

(e) Rule G1.3(e) is replaced by: 'The sail number shall be displayed on both sides of the headsail.'

Appendix F – Appeals Procedures

This appendix is a US SAILING prescription.

See rules 70 and 71. This appendix replaces Appendix F as adopted by the International Sailing Federation. The US SAILING Appeals Committee and, when acting under rule F1.3, the US SAILING Article 14 Review Board act as the national authority within the meaning of rules 70.1 and 71. This appendix shall not be changed by sailing instructions.

F1   WHERE TO FILE AN APPEAL OR REQUEST

F1.1 Appeals of decisions of a protest committee and requests by a protest committee for confirmation or correction of its decisions shall be made to the association appeals committee for the place in which the event was held, except as provided in rules F1.3 and F1.4.

F1.2 Appeals of decisions of an association appeals committee, requests by an association appeals committee for confirmation or correction of its decisions, and all requests for interpretations of *rules* shall be made to the US SAILING Appeals Committee.

F1.3 Appeals of decisions of a protest committee made under rule 69.1 and requests by a protest committee for confirmation or correction of such decisions shall be made to the US SAILING Article 14 Review Board ("Review Board" below).

F1.4   Appeals of decisions of a protest committee for a US SAILING national champion-ship and requests by such a committee for confirmation or correction of its deci-sions shall be made to the US SAILING Appeals Committee.

F2   TO APPEAL OR MAKE A REQUEST

F2.1   To appeal the decision of a protest committee or association appeals committee the appellant shall, within 15 days of receiving the written decision being appeal-ed or a protest committee's decision not to reopen a hearing, send a dated appeal to the appropriate appeals committee (the Review Board if rule F1.3 applies), with a copy of the decision and the appropriate fee. The appeal shall state why the appellant believes the committee's interpretation of a *rule* or its procedures were incorrect. If an appeals fee is required and is not sent with the appeal it must be received before the appeal will be considered. The fee for appeals to US SAILING is $25 for members and $75 for non-members.

F2.2   The appellant shall also send, with the appeal or as soon as possible thereafter, all of the following documents that are available to her:

(a)   the written *protest(s)* or request(s) for redress;

(b)   if the appeal is from a decision of an association appeals committee, the written decision of the protest committee;

(c)   a diagram, prepared or endorsed by the protest committee, showing the positions and tracks of all boats involved, the course to the next *mark* and its required side, the force and direction of the wind, and, if relevant, the depth of the water and the direction and speed of any current;

(d)   the notice of race, sailing instructions, any other conditions governing the event, and any changes to them;

(e)   any additional relevant documents and correspondence; and

(f)   the names and addresses of all *parties* to the hearing and the protest committee chairman.

F2.3   To request confirmation or correction of its decision, a protest committee or association appeals committee shall send to the appropriate appeals committee (the Review Board if rule F1.3 applies) a copy of its decision and all relevant docu-ments and comments. There is no fee for requests for confirmation or correction made to US SAILING.

F2.4   To request an interpretation of the *rules*, a club or other organization affiliated to US SAILING shall send to the US SAILING Appeals Committee its request, which shall include assumed facts. The fee for requests for interpretation of the *rules* is $25.

F3   NOTIFICATION OF THE COMMITTEE WHOSE DECISION
         IS BEING APPEALED

Upon receipt of an appeal, the appeals committee (the Review Board if rule F1.3 applies) shall send a copy of the appeal to the committee whose decision is being appealed, asking it for any documents required by rule F2.2 not supplied by the appellant.

F4   COMMITTEE RESPONSIBILITIES

F4.1 Protest Committee

A protest committee whose decision is being appealed shall supply any of the documents requested under rule F3 and any facts or information requested under rule F5 and, if directed to do so by the appeals committee (the Review Board if rule F1.3 applies), shall conduct a hearing or re-hearing of the *protest* or request for redress.

F4.2 Association Appeals Committee

(a) The association appeals committee shall send to all *parties* to the hearing, and to the committee whose decision is being appealed or reviewed, copies of all relevant documents and comments it has received, except those supplied by that *party* or committee.

(b) An association appeals committee shall consider an appeal it has refused to decide if directed to do so by the US SAILING Appeals Committee.

F4.3 US SAILING Appeals Committee; Article 14 Review Board

The US SAILING Appeals Committee (the Review Board if rule F1.3 applies) shall send to all *parties* to the hearing, to the protest committee and to the association appeals committee whose decision is being appealed or reviewed, copies of all relevant documents and comments it has received, except those supplied by that *party* or committee.

F5   FINDING OF FACTS; ADDITIONAL INFORMATION

An appeals committee (the Review Board if rule F1.3 applies) shall accept the protest committee's finding of facts except when it decides they are inadequate, in which case it may require the protest committee to provide additional facts or other information, or to reopen the hearing and report any new finding of facts.

F6   COMMENTS

An appeals committee (the Review Board if rule F1.3 applies) shall consider written comments on an appeal or request for confirmation or correction of a committee's decision only from *parties* to the hearing, the protest committee, and, if relevant, from the association appeals committee. Such comments shall be sent to the appeals committee (the Review Board if rule F1.3 applies) within 15 days of the *party's* or committee's receipt of the appeal or request and, if possible, to all *parties* to the hearing and all committees involved.

F7   OTHER PROVISIONS

In addition to the provisions of rule 71:

(a) An association appeals committee acting under the rules of this appendix may take any of the actions permitted by the national authority in rules 71.2 and 71.3, subject to further appeal as provided in rule F1.2.

(b) No member of the association appeals committee shall take part in the discussion or decision on an appeal or a request for confirmation or correction to the US SAILING Appeals Committee.

(c) An appeals committee (the Review Board if rule F1.3 applies) may direct a protest committee to conduct a hearing or re-hearing of the *protest* or request for redress.

(d) The US SAILING Appeals Committee may direct an association appeals committee to consider an appeal it has refused to decide.

Appendix G – Identification on Sails

See rule 77.

G1 ISAF INTERNATIONAL CLASS BOATS

G1.1 Identification

Every boat of an ISAF International Class or Recognized Class shall carry on her mainsail and, as provided in rules G1.3(d) and G1.3(e) for letters and numbers only, on her spinnaker and headsail

(a) the insignia denoting her class;

(b) at all international events, except when the boats are provided to all competitors, national letters denoting her national authority from the table below. For the purposes of this rule, international events are ISAF events, world and continental championships, and events described as international events in their notices of race and sailing instructions; and

(c) a sail number of no more than four digits allotted by her national authority or, when so required by the class rules, by the international class association. The four-digit limitation does not apply to classes whose ISAF membership or recognition took effect before 1 April 1997. Alternatively, if permitted in the class rules, an owner may be allotted a personal sail number by the relevant issuing authority, which may be used on all his boats in that class.

Sails measured before 31 March 1999 shall comply with rule G1.1 or with the rules applicable at the time of measurement.

Letters	National Authority	Letters	National Authority
ALG	Algeria	COK	Cook Islands
ASA	American Samoa	CRO	Croatia
AND	Andorra	CUB	Cuba
ANG	Angola	CYP	Cyprus
ANT	Antigua	CZE	Czech Republic
ARG	Argentina	DEN	Denmark
ARM	Armenia	DOM	Dominican Republic
AUS	Australia	ECU	Ecuador
AUT	Austria	EGY	Egypt
BAH	Bahamas	ESA	El Salvador
BRN	Bahrain	EST	Estonia
BAR	Barbados	FIJ	Fiji
BLR	Belarus	FIN	Finland
BEL	Belgium	FRA	France
BER	Bermuda	GAB	Gabon
BRA	Brazil	GEO	Georgia
IVB	British Virgin Islands	GER	Germany
BRU	Brunei Darussalam	CAY	Grand Cayman
BUL	Bulgaria	GBR	Great Britain
BUL	Bulgaria	GRE	Greece
CAN	Canada	GRN	Grenada
CHI	Chile	GUM	Guam
CHN	China	GUA	Guatemala
TPE	Chinese Taipei	HKG	Hong Kong
COL	Columbia		

Letters	*National Authority*	*Letters*	*National Authority*
HUN	Hungary	SVK	Slovak Republic
ISL	Iceland	SLO	Slovenia
IND	India	RSA	South Africa
INA	Indonesia	ESP	Spain
IRL	Ireland	SRI	Sri Lanka
ISR	Israel	LCA	St. Lucia
ITA	Italy	SUD	Sudan
JAM	Jamaica	SWE	Sweden
JPN	Japan	SUI	Switzerland
KAZ	Kazakhstan	TAH	Tahiti
KEN	Kenya	THA	Thailand
KOR	Korea	TRI	Trinidad & Tobago
KUW	Kuwait	TUN	Tunisia
KGZ	Kyrghyzstan	TUR	Turkey
LAT	Latvia	UKR	Ukraine
LIB	Lebanon	UAE	United Arab Emirates
LBA	Libya	USA	United States of America
LIE	Liechtenstein		
LTU	Lithuania	URU	Uruguay
LUX	Luxembourg	ISV	US Virgin Islands
MAS	Malaysia	UZB	Uzbekistan
MLT	Malta	VEN	Venezuela
MRI	Mauritius	YUG	Yugoslavia
MEX	Mexico	ZIM	Zimbabwe
FSM	Micronesia		
MDA	Moldova		
MON	Monaco		
MAR	Morocco		
MYA	Myanmar		
NAM	Namibia		
NED	The Netherlands		
AHO	Netherlands Antilles		
NZL	New Zealand		
NGR	Nigeria		
NOR	Norway		
PAK	Pakistan		
PNG	Papua New Guinea		
PAR	Paraguay		
PER	Peru		
PHI	Philippines		
POL	Poland		
POR	Portugal		
PUR	Puerto Rico		
QAT	Qatar		
ROM	Romania		
RUS	Russia		
SMR	San Marino		
SEY	Seychelles		
SIN	Singapore		

G1.2 Specifications

(a) National letters and sail numbers shall be in capital letters and Arabic numerals, clearly legible and of the same colour. Commercially available typefaces giving the same or better legibility than Helvetica are acceptable.

(b) The sizes of characters and minimum space between adjoining characters on the same and opposite sides of the sail shall be related to the boat's overall length as follows:

Overall length	Minimum height	Minimum space between letters and numerals or edge of sail
under 3.5 m	230 mm	45 mm
3.5 m – 8.5 m	300 mm	60 mm
8.5 m – 11 m	375 mm	75 mm
over 11 m	450 mm	90 mm

G1.3 Positioning

Class insignia, national letters and sail numbers shall be positioned as follows:

(a) Except as provided in (d) and (e) below, class insignia, national letters and sail numbers shall when possible be wholly above an arc whose centre is the head point and whose radius is 60% of the leech length. They shall be placed at different heights on the two sides of the sail, those on the starboard side being uppermost.

(b) The class insignia shall be placed above the national letters. If the class insignia is of such a design that two of them coincide when placed back to back on both sides of the sail, they may be so placed.

(c) National letters shall be placed above the sail number.

(d) The national letters and sail number shall be displayed on the front side of a spinnaker but may be placed on both sides. They shall be displayed wholly below an arc whose centre is the head point and whose radius is 40% of the foot median and, when possible, wholly above an arc whose radius is 60% of the foot median.

(e) The national letters and sail number shall be displayed on both sides of a headsail whose clew can extend behind the mast 30% or more of the mainsail foot length. They shall be displayed wholly below an arc whose centre is the head point and whose radius is half the luff length and, if possible, wholly above an arc whose radius is 75% of the luff length.

G2 OTHER BOATS

Other boats shall comply with the rules of their national authority or class association in regard to the allotment, carrying and size of insignia, letters and numbers. Such rules shall, when practicable, conform to the above requirements.

US SAILING prescribes that unless otherwise stated in her class rules, the sails of a boat that is not in an ISAF International Class or Recognized Class shall comply with rule G1. However, offshore racing boats not in a class that is subject to rule G1 shall carry US SAILING numbers on mainsails, spinnakers and each overlapping headsail having a luff-perpendicular measurement exceeding 130% of the base of the foretriangle. This rule applies only to boats whose owner's national authority is US SAILING.

G3   CHARTERED OR LOANED BOATS

When so stated in the notice of race or sailing instructions, a boat chartered or loaned for an event may carry national letters or a sail number in contravention of her class rules.

G4   WARNINGS AND PENALTIES

When a protest committee finds that a boat has broken a rule of this appendix it shall either warn her and give her time to comply or penalize her.

G5   CHANGES BY CLASS RULES

ISAF classes may change the rules of this appendix provided the changes have first been approved by the ISAF.

Appendix H – Weighing Clothing and Equipment

See Rule 43. This appendix shall not be changed by sailing instructions or prescriptions of national authorities.

H1   Items of clothing and equipment to be weighed shall be arranged on a rack. After being saturated in water the items shall be allowed to drain freely for one minute before being weighed. The rack must allow the items to hang as they would hang from clothes hangers, so as to allow the water to drain freely. Pockets that have drain-holes that cannot be closed shall be empty, but pockets or items that can hold water shall be full.

H2   When the weight recorded exceeds the amount permitted, the competitor may rearrange the items on the rack and the measurer shall again soak and weigh them. This procedure may be repeated a second time if the weight still exceeds the amount permitted.

H3   A competitor wearing a dry-suit may choose an alternative means of weighing the items.

(a)   The dry-suit and items of clothing and equipment that are worn outside the dry-suit shall be weighed as described above.

(b)   Clothing worn underneath the dry-suit shall be weighed as worn while *racing*, without draining.

(c)   The two weights shall be added together.

Appendix J – Notice of Race and Sailing Instructions

See rules 87.2 and 88.2(a). The term 'race' includes a regatta or other series of races.

J1   NOTICE OF RACE CONTENTS

J1.1   The notice of race shall include the following information:

(1)   the title, place and dates of the race and name of the organizing authority;

(2)   that the race will be governed by the *rules* as defined in *The Racing Rules of Sailing*;

(3)   a list of any other documents that will govern the event (for example, the

Equipment Rules of Sailing, to the extent that they apply); |

(4)   the classes to race, conditions of entry and any restrictions on entries;

(5)   the times of registration and warning signals for the practice race or first race, and succeeding races if known.

J1.2   The notice of race shall include any of the following that would help competitors decide whether to attend the event or that conveys other information they will need before the sailing instructions become available:

     (1)   that advertising will be restricted to Category A (see Appendix 1) and other information related to Appendix 1;

     (2)   that the ISAF Competitor Classification System (or some other competitor classification system) will apply;

     (3)   the procedure for advance registration or entry, including fees and any closing dates;

     (4)   an entry form, to be signed by the boat's owner or owner's representative, containing words such as 'I agree to be bound by *The Racing Rules of Sailing* and by all other *rules* that govern this event';

     (5)   measurement procedures or requirements for measurement or rating certificates;

     (6)   the time and place at which the sailing instructions will be available;

     (7)   any changes to the racing rules (see rule 86);

     (8)   any changes to class rules, referring specifically to each rule and stating the change;

     (9)   the courses to be sailed;

     (10)   the penalty for breaking a rule of Part 2, other than the 720° Turns Penalty; |

     (11)   denial of the right of appeal, subject to rule 70.4;

     (12)   the scoring system, including the number of races scheduled and the minimum number that must be completed to constitute a series;

     (13)   prizes.

J2   SAILING INSTRUCTION CONTENTS

J2.1   The sailing instructions shall include the following information:

     (1)   that the race will be governed by the *rules* as defined in *The Racing Rules of Sailing;*

     (2)   a list of any other documents that will govern the event (for example, the *Equipment Rules of Sailing*, to the extent that they apply);

     (3)   the schedule of races, the classes to race and times of warning signals for each class;

     (4)   the course(s) to be sailed, or a list of *marks* from which the course will be selected and, if relevant, how courses will be signalled;

     (5)   descriptions of *marks,* including starting and finishing *marks,* stating the order and side on which each is to be left and identifying all rounding *marks* (see rule 28.1);

     (6)   descriptions of the starting and finishing lines, class flags and any special signals to be used;

(7)   the time limit, if any, for *finishing*;

(8)   the scoring system, included by reference to Appendix A, to class rules or other *rules* governing the event, or stated in full. State the number of races scheduled and the minimum number that must be completed to constitute a series.

J2.2   The sailing instructions shall include those of the following that will apply:

(1)   that advertising will be restricted to Category A (see Appendix 1) and other information related to Appendix 1;

(2)   that the ISAF Competitor Classification System (or some other competitor classification system) will apply;

(3)   replacement of the relevant rules of Part 2 with the *International Regulations for Preventing Collisions at Sea* or other government right-of-way rules, the time(s) or place(s) they will apply, and any night signals to be used by the race committee;

(4)   changes to the racing rules permitted by rule 86, referring specifically to each rule and stating the change;

(5)   that the prescriptions of the national authority will not apply;

(6)   if the prescriptions of the national authority will apply at an international event, a copy in English of the prescriptions;

(7)   changes to class rules, referring specifically to each rule and stating the change;

(8)   restrictions controlling changes to boats when supplied by the organizing authority;

(9)   the registration procedure;

(10)   measurement or inspection procedure;

(11)   location(s) of official notice board(s);

(12)   procedure for changing the sailing instructions;

(13)   safety requirements, such as requirements and signals for personal buoyancy, check-in at the starting area, and check-out and check-in ashore;

(14)   declaration requirements;

(15)   signals to be made ashore and location of signal station(s);

(16)   the racing area (a chart is recommended);

(17)   approximate course length and approximate length of windward legs;

(18)   the time limit, if any, for boats other than the first boat to *finish*;

(19)   time allowances;

(20)   the location of the starting area and any applicable restrictions;

(21)   any special procedures or signals for individual or general recalls;

(22)   boats identifying *mark* locations;

(23)   procedure for changes of course after the start and any special signals;

(24)   any special procedure for shortening the course or for *finishing* a shortened course;

(25)   restrictions on use of support boats, plastic pools, radios, etc.; on hauling out; and on outside assistance provided to a boat that is not *racing*;

(26)   the penalty for breaking a rule of Part 2, other than the 720° Turns Penalty;

(27)   penalization without a hearing under rule 67 for breaking rule 42;

(28)   whether Appendix N will apply;

(29)   protest procedure and times and place of hearings;

(30)   if rule M1.4(b) will apply, the time limit for requesting a hearing under that rule;

(31)   denial of the right of appeal, subject to rule 70.4;

(32)   the national authority's approval of the appointment of an international jury under rule 89(c);

(33)   substitution of competitors;

(34)   the minimum number of boats appearing in the starting area required for a race to be started;

(35)   when and where races *postponed* or *abandoned* for the day will be resailed;

(36)   tides and currents;

(37)   prizes;

(38)   other commitments of the race committee and obligations of boats.

Appendix K – Sailing Instructions Guide

This guide provides a set of tested sailing instructions designed primarily for major championship regattas for one or more classes. It therefore will be particularly useful for world, continental and national championships and other events of similar importance. The guide can also be useful for other events; however, for such events some of these instructions will be unnecessary or undesirable. Race officers should therefore be careful in making their choices.

An expanded version of the guide will be available on the ISAF website (www.sailing.org) and will contain provisions applicable to the largest and most complicated multi-class events, as well as variations on several of the sailing instructions recommended in this appendix. It will be revised from time to time, to reflect advances in race management techniques as they develop, and can be downloaded as a basic text for producing the sailing instructions for any particular event.

The principles on which all sailing instructions should be based are as follows:

1   They should include only two types of statement: the intentions of the race committee and the obligations of competitors.

2   They should be concerned only with racing. Information about social events, assignment of moorings, etc. should be provided separately.

3   They should not change the racing rules except when clearly desirable.

4   They should not repeat or restate any of the racing rules.

5   They should not repeat themselves.

6   They should be in chronological order; that is, the order in which the competitor will use them.

7 They should, when possible, use words or phrases from the racing rules.

*To use this guide, first review rule J2 and decide which instructions will be need-
ed. Instructions that are required by rule J2.1 are marked with an asterisk (*).
Delete all inapplicable or unnecessary instructions. Select the version preferred
where there is a choice. Follow the directions in the left margin to fill in the
spaces where a solid line (_____) appears and select the preferred wording
if a choice or option is shown in brackets ([…]).*

*After deleting unused instructions, renumber all instructions in sequential order.
Be sure that instruction numbers are correct where one instruction refers to
another.*

US SAILING Note: *A guide to simplified sailing instructions suitable for events such
as club or local regattas can be found on the US SAILING website (www.ussailing.org/
racemgt). Those without access to the website may request a copy by fax on the
US SAILING Infofax line, (888) USSAIL-6.*

*On separate lines, insert the full
name of the regatta, the inclusive
dates from measurement or the
practice race until the final race or
closing ceremony, the name of the
organizing authority, and the city
and country.*

_____

_____

_____

_____

SAILING INSTRUCTIONS

1   RULES

*List by name any other documents
that govern the event; for example,
the Equipment Rules of Sailing, to
the extent that they apply.*

1.1* The regatta will be governed by the 'rules' as
defined in *The Racing Rules of Sailing.*

1.2* _____ will apply.

*Include only if the prescriptions will
not apply. Insert the name.*

1.3 The prescriptions of the _____ national authority
will not apply.

*Insert the rule number(s) and class
name. Make a separate statement
for the rules of each class.*

1.4 Rule(s) _____ of the _____ class rules [will not
apply] [is (are) changed as follows: _____].

1.5 If there is a conflict between languages the
English text will prevail.

2   NOTICES TO COMPETITORS

Insert the location(s).

Notices to competitors will be posted on the
official notice board(s) located at _____.

3   CHANGES TO SAILING INSTRUCTIONS

Change the times if different.

Any change to the sailing instructions will be
posted before 0900 on the day it will take effect,
except that any change to the schedule of races
will be posted by 2000 on the day before it will
take effect.

4   SIGNALS MADE ASHORE

Insert the location.

4.1 Signals made ashore will be displayed at _____

Insert the number of minutes.

4.2 When flag AP is displayed ashore, '1 minute' is replaced with 'not less than ___ minutes' in race signal AP.

(OR)

4.2 Flag D with a sound signal means 'The warning signal will be made not less than ___ minutes after flag D is displayed. [Boats are requested not to leave the harbour until this signal is made.]'

Delete if a class rule applies.

4.3 When flag Y is displayed ashore, rule 40 applies at all times while afloat. This changes the Part 4 preamble.

5   SCHEDULE OF RACES

Revise as desired and Insert the dates.

5.1* Racing is scheduled as follows:

Date	Class _____	Class _____
_____	racing	racing
_____	racing	reserve day
_____	reserve day	racing
_____	racing	racing
_____	racing	racing

Insert the classes and numbers.

5.2* The number of races scheduled is as follows:

Class	Number of races	Races per day
_____	_____	_____
_____	_____	_____

(a) Reserve days may be used if races are not completed as scheduled or if the race committee considers it unlikely that races will be completed as scheduled.

(b) One extra race per day may be sailed, provided that no class becomes more than one race ahead of schedule.

Insert the time.

5.3* The scheduled time of the warning signal for the first race each day is _____.

5.4 When more than one race (or sequence of races, for two or more classes) will be held on the same day, the warning signal for each succeeding race will be made as soon as practicable. To alert boats that another race or sequence of races will begin soon, the postponement signal will be displayed for at least four minutes before a warning signal is displayed.

Insert the time.

Insert the classes and names or descriptions of the flags.

5.5 On the last day of the regatta no warning signal will be made after _____.

6   **CLASS FLAGS**

Class flags will be:

Class   Flag

_____   _____

_____   _____

_____   _____

7   **RACING AREAS**

Insert a number or letter.

Attachment _____ shows the location of racing areas.

8   **THE COURSES**

Insert a number or letter. A method of illustrating various courses is shown in Addendum A.

8.1* The diagrams in Attachment _____ show the courses, including the approximate angles between legs, the order in which marks are to be passed, and the side on which each mark is to be left. [The approximate course length will be _____].

Insert either 'Mark ___ ' with the number of the leeward mark or 'the midpoint of the starting line'.

8.2 No later than the warning signal, the race committee signal boat will display the approximate compass bearing from _____ to Mark 1.

8.3 When there is a gate, boats shall sail between the gate marks from the direction of the previous mark and round either gate mark.

8.4 Courses will not be shortened. This changes rule 32.

9   **MARKS**

Change the mark numbers as needed and insert the descriptions of the marks. Use the second alternative when Marks 4S and 4P form a gate, with Mark 4S to be left to starboard and Mark 4P to port.

9.1* Marks 1, 2, 3 and 4 will be _____.

(OR)

9.1* Marks 1, 2, 3, 4S and 4P will be _____.

Insert the descriptions of the marks.

9.2 New marks, as provided in instruction 11.1, will be _____.

Describe the starting and finishing marks: for example, the race committee signal boat at the starboard end and a buoy at the port end. Instruction 10.2 will describe the starting line and instruction 12.1 the finishing line.

9.3* The starting and finishing marks will be _____.

9.4 A race committee boat signalling a change of course is a mark as provided in instruction 11.3.

10   THE START

Include only if the asterisked option in rule 26 will be used. Insert the number of minutes.

10.1 Races will be started by using rule 26 with the warning signal given _____ minutes before the starting signal.

(OR)

Describe any starting system other than that stated in rule 26.

10.1 Races will be started as follows: _____.

10.2* The starting line will be between staffs displaying orange flags on the starting marks.

(OR)

10.2* The starting line will be between a staff displaying an orange flag on the starting mark at the starboard end and the port-end starting mark.

(OR)

Insert the description.

10.2* The starting line will be _____.

Insert the number of minutes.

10.3 Boats whose warning signal has not been made shall avoid the starting area.

0.4 A boat starting later than _____ minutes after her starting signal will be scored Did Not Start. This changes rule A4.1.

11   CHANGE OF THE POSITION OF THE NEXT MARK

11.1 To change the position of the next mark, the race committee will move the original mark (or the finishing line) to a new position. The change will be signalled before the leading boat has begun the leg, although the mark may not yet be in the new position. Any mark to be rounded after rounding the moved mark may be relocated without further signalling to maintain the course configuration.

(OR)

11.1 To change the position of the next mark, the race committee will lay a new mark (or move the finishing line) and remove the original mark as soon as practicable. The change will be signalled before the leading boat has begun the leg, although the new mark may not yet be in position. Any mark to be rounded after rounding the new mark may be relocated without further signalling to maintain the course configuration. When in a subsequent change a new mark is replaced, it will be replaced by an original mark.

Insert the class(es).

11.2 For the _____ class(es), rule 33 is changed so that, instead of displaying a compass bearing, the race committee will display a green [triangular] [board] [flag] if the direction is changed to starboard or a red [rectangular] [board] [flag] if the direction is changed to port.

Reverse 'port' and 'starboard' when the mark is to be left to starboard.

11.3 Except at a gate, boats shall pass between the race committee boat signalling the change of course and the nearby mark, leaving the mark to port and the race committee boat to starboard. This changes rule 28.1.

12 THE FINISH

12.1* The finishing line will be between staffs displaying orange flags on the finishing marks.

(OR)

12.1* The finishing line will be between a staff displaying an orange flag on the finishing mark at the starboard end and the port-end finishing mark.

(OR)

Insert the description.

12.1* The finishing line will be _____.

12.2 When the course is shortened at a gate, a race committee boat near the gate will display flag S and boats shall finish by sailing through the gate from the direction of the previous mark. The finishing line will be between the gate marks. This changes race signal S.

13 PENALTY SYSTEM

Include instruction 13.1 only when the 720° Turns Penalty will not be used. Insert the number of places or describe the penalties.

13.1 The Scoring Penalty, rule 44.3, will apply. The penalty will be _____ places.

(OR)

13.1 The penalties are as follows: _____.

Insert the class(es).

13.2 For the _____ class(es) rule 44.2 is changed so that the 720° turn is replaced by a 360° turn.

13.3 A boat that has taken a penalty or retired under rule 31.2 or 44.1 shall complete an acknowledgement form at the race office within the protest time limit.

13.4 As provided in rule 67, the [protest committee] [jury] may, without a hearing, penalize a boat that has broken rule 42.

(OR)

13.4 Appendix N will apply [as changed by instruction 13.2].

14 TIME LIMITS

14.1* Time limits are as follows:

Insert the classes and times. Omit the Mark 1 time limit if inapplicable.

Class	Time limit	Mark 1 time limit
_____	_____	_____
_____	_____	_____
_____	_____	_____

If no boat has passed Mark 1 within the Mark 1 time limit the race will be abandoned.

Insert the time (or different times for different classes).

14.2 Boats failing to finish within _____ after the first boat sails the course and finishes will be scored Did Not Finish. This changes rules 35 and A4.1.

15   PROTESTS AND REQUESTS FOR REDRESS

15.1 Protest forms are available at the race office. Protests shall be delivered there within the protest time limit.

Change the time if different.

Change the time if different.

15.2 For each class, the protest time limit is 90 minutes after the last boat has finished the last race of the day. [The same protest time limit applies to all protests by the race committee and [protest committee] [jury] and to requests for redress. IThis changes rules 61.3 and 62.2.]

15.3 Notices will be posted within 30 minutes of the protest time limit to inform competitors of hearings in which they are parties or named as witnesses. Hearings will be held in the [jury office] beginning at _____.

Insert the location and time.

15.4 Notices of protests by the race committee or [protest committee] [jury] will be posted to inform boats under rule 61.1(b).

15.5 A list of boats that, under instruction 13.4, have acknowledged breaking rule 42 or have been disqualified by the [protest committee] [jury] will be posted before the protest time limit.

15.6 For the purpose of rule 64.3(b) the 'authority responsible' is the measurer appointed by the organizing authority.

15.7 Breaches of instructions 10.3, 13.3, 17, 18.2, 21, 22 and 23 will not be grounds for a protest by a boat. This changes rule 60.1(a). Penalties for these breaches may be less than disqualification if the [protest committee] [jury] so decides.

15.8 On the last day of the regatta a request for reopening a hearing shall be delivered

(a) within the protest time limit if the party requesting reopening was informed of the decision on the previous day;

Change the time if different.

(b) no later than 30 minutes after the party requesting reopening was informed of the decision on that day.

This changes rule 66.

Include if the protest committee is an international jury or another provision of rule 70.4 applies.

15.9 Decisions of the jury will be final as provided in rule 70.4.

16   SCORING

16.1* The [Low Point] [Bonus Point] scoring system of Appendix A will apply.

(OR)

Describe the system.

16.1* The scoring system is as follows: _____.

Insert the number.

16.2* _____ races are required to be completed to constitute a series.

Insert the numbers throughout.

16.3 (a) When fewer than _____ races have been completed, a boat's series score will be the total of her race scores.

(b) When from _____ to _____ races have been completed, a boat's series score will be the total of her race scores excluding her worst score.

(c) When _____ or more races have been completed, a boat's series score will be the total of her race scores excluding her two worst scores.

17   SAFETY REGULATIONS

Insert the procedure for check-in and check-out.

17.1 Check-in and check-out: _____.

17.2 A boat that retires from a race shall notify the race committee as soon as possible.

18   REPLACEMENT OF CREW OR EQUIPMENT

18.1 Substitution of competitors will not be allowed without prior written approval of the [race committee] [protest committee] [jury].

18.2 Substitution of damaged or lost equipment will not be allowed unless approved by the race committee. Requests for substitution shall be made to the committee at the first reasonable opportunity.

19   EQUIPMENT AND MEASUREMENT CHECKS

A boat or equipment may be inspected at any time for compliance with the class rules and sailing instructions. On the water, a boat can be instructed by a race committee measurer to proceed immediately to a designated area for inspection.

20   OFFICIAL BOATS

Insert the descriptions. If appropriate, use different identification markings for boats performing different duties.

Official boats will be marked as follows: _____.

21   SUPPORT BOATS

21.1 Team leaders, coaches and other support personnel shall stay outside areas where boats are racing from the time of the preparatory signal for the first class to start until all boats have finished or the race committee signals a postponement, general recall or abandonment.

Insert the identification markings. National flags are suitable at international events.

21.2 Support boats shall be marked with _____.

22 HAUL-OUT RESTRICTIONS

Keel boats shall not be hauled out during the regatta except with and according to the terms of prior written permission of the race committee.

23 DIVING EQUIPMENT AND PLASTIC POOLS

Underwater breathing apparatus and plastic pools or their equivalent shall not be used around keel boats between the starting signal of the first race and the end of the regatta.

24 RADIO COMMUNICATION

A boat shall neither make radio transmissions while racing nor receive radio communications not available to all boats. This restriction also applies to mobile telephones.

25 PRIZES

When perpetual trophies will be awarded state their complete names.

Prizes will be given as follows: _____.

26 DISCLAIMER OF LIABILITY

Competitors participate in the regatta entirely at their own risk. See rule 4, Decision to Race. The organizing authority will not accept any liability for material damage or personal injury or death sustained in conjunction with or prior to, during, or after the regatta.

27 INSURANCE

Insert the currency and amount.

Each participating boat shall be insured with valid third-party liability insurance with a minimum cover of _____ per event or the equivalent.

Addendum A – Illustrating the Course

Shown here are examples of course illustrations. Any course can be similarly shown. When there is more than one course, prepare a separate diagram for each course and state how each will be signalled.

A Windward–Leeward Course

Start–1–2–1–2–Finish

Options for use with this course include

(1) *increasing or decreasing the number of laps,*

(2) *deleting the final windward leg,*

(3) *using a gate instead of a leeward **mark**,*

(4) *using an offset **mark** at the windward **mark**, and*

(5) *using the leeward and windward **marks** as starting and finishing **marks**.*

A Windward–Leeward–Triangle Course

Start–1–2–3–1–3–Finish

Options for use with this course include

(1) *varying the interior angles of the triangle (45°–90°–45° and 60°–60°–60° are common),*

(2) *deleting the last windward leg,*

(3) *using a gate instead of a leeward **mark** for downwind legs (but not reaches),*

(4) *using an offset **mark** at the beginning of downwind legs (but not reaches), and*

(5) *using the leeward and windward **marks** as starting and finishing **marks**.*

*Be sure to specify the interior angle at each **mark**.*

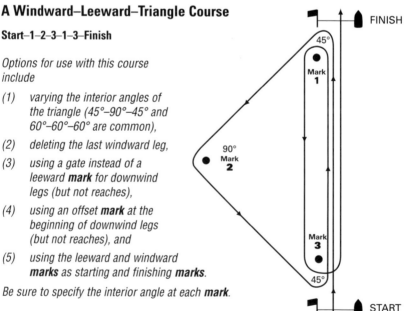

Trapezoid Courses

Start–1–2–3–2–3–Finish   **Start–1–4–1–2–3–Finish**

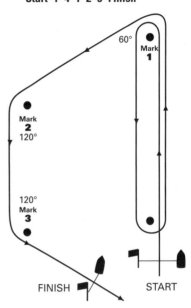

Options for use with this course include

(1)   *adding additional legs,*

(2)   *using gates instead of leeward **marks** for downwind legs (but not reaches),*

(3)   *varying the interior angles of the reaching legs,*

(4)   *using an offset **mark** at the beginning of downwind legs (but not reaches), and*

(5)   *finishing boats upwind rather than on a reach.*

*Be sure to specify the interior angle of each reaching leg. It is recommended that Mark 4 be different from the starting **mark**.*

Addendum B – Boats Provided by the Organizing Authority

The following sailing instruction is recommended when all boats will be provided by the organizing authority. It can be changed to suit the circumstances. When used, it should be inserted after instruction 3.

4   BOATS

4.1   Boats will be provided for all competitors, who shall not modify them or cause them to be modified in any way except that

(a)   a compass may be tied or taped to the hull or spars;

(b)   wind indicators, including yarn or thread, may be tied or taped anywhere on the boat;

(c)   hulls, centreboards and rudders may be cleaned, but only with water;

(d)   adhesive tape may be used anywhere above the water line; and

(e)   all fittings or equipment designed to be adjusted may be adjusted, provided that the class rules are complied with.

4.2   All equipment provided with the boat for sailing purposes shall be in the boat while afloat.

4.3   The penalty for not complying with one of the above instructions will be disqualification from all races sailed in which the instruction was broken.

4.4   Competitors shall report any damage or loss of equipment, however slight, to the organizing authority's representative immediately after securing the boat ashore. The penalty for breaking this instruction, unless the [jury] [protest committee] is satisfied that the competitor made a determined effort to comply, will be disqualification from the race most recently sailed.

4.5   Class rules requiring competitors to be members of the class association will not apply.

Appendix L – Recommendations for Protest Committees

This appendix is advisory only; in some circumstances changing these procedures may be advisable. It is addressed primarily to protest committee chairmen but may also help judges, jury secretaries, race committees and others connected with protest and redress hearings.

In a protest or redress hearing, the protest committee should weigh all testimony with equal care; should recognize that honest testimony can vary, and even be in conflict, as a result of different observations and recollections; should resolve such differences as best it can; should recognize that no boat or competitor is guilty until a breach of a *rule* has been established to the satisfaction of the protest committee; and should keep an open mind until all the evidence has been heard as to whether a boat or competitor has broken a *rule*.

L1   PRELIMINARIES (may be performed by race office staff)

• Receive the *protest* or request for redress.

• Note on the form the time the *protest* or request is delivered and the protest time limit.

• Inform each *party,* and the race committee when necessary, when and where the hearing will be held.

L2 BEFORE THE HEARING

Make sure that

- each *party* has a copy of the *protest* or request for redress. When copies are unavailable let the protestee read the *protest* or request before beginning.
- no member of the protest committee is an *interested party*. Ask the *parties* whether they object to any member. When redress is requested under rule 62.1(a), a member of the race committee should not be a member of the protest committee.
- only one person from each boat (or *party*) is present unless an interpreter is needed.
- all boats and people involved are present. If they are not, however, the committee may proceed under rule 63.3(b).
- boat representatives were on board when required (rule 63.3(a)). When the *parties* were in different races, both organizing authorities must accept the composition of the protest committee (rule 63.7). In a measurement *protest* obtain the current class rules and identify the authority responsible for interpreting them (rule 64.3(b)).

L3 THE HEARING

L3.1 Check the validity of the *protest* or request for redress.

- Were the contents adequate (rule 61.2 or 62.1)?
- Was it delivered in time? If not, is there good reason to extend the time limit (rule 61.3 or 62.2)?
- When required, was the protestor involved in or a witness to the incident (rule 60.1(a))?
- When necessary, was 'Protest' hailed and a red flag flown correctly (rule 61.1(a))?
- When the flag and hail were not necessary was the protestee informed?
- Decide whether the *protest* or request for redress is valid (rule 63.5).
- Once the validity of the *protest* or request has been determined, do not let the subject be introduced again unless truly new evidence is available.

L3.2 Take the evidence (rule 63.6).

- Ask the protestor and then the protestee to tell their stories. Then allow them to question one another. In a redress matter, ask the *party* to state the request.
- Invite questions from protest committee members.
- Make sure you know what facts each *party* is alleging before calling any witnesses. Their stories may be different.
- Allow anyone, including a boat's crew, to give evidence. It is the *party* who must decide which witnesses to call. The question 'Would you like to hear N?' is best answered by 'It is your choice.'
- Call each *party's* witnesses (and the protest committee's if any) one by one. Limit *parties* to questioning the witness(es) (they may wander into general statements).
- Invite the protestee to question the protestor's witness first (and vice versa). This prevents the protestor from leading his witness from the beginning.

- Allow a member of the protest committee who saw the incident to give evidence (rule 63.6) but only in the presence of the *parties.* The member may be questioned and may remain in the room (rule 63.3(a)).

- Try to prevent leading questions or hearsay evidence, but if that is impossible discount the evidence so obtained.

- Accept written evidence from a witness who is not available to be questioned only if all *parties* agree.

- Ask one member of the committee to note down evidence, particularly times, distances, speeds, etc.

- Invite first the protestor and then the protestee to make a final statement of her case, particularly on any application or interpretation of the *rules.*

L3.3   Find the facts (rule 63.6).

- Write down the facts; resolve doubts one way or the other.

- Call back *parties* for more questions if necessary.

- When appropriate, draw a diagram of the incident using the facts you have found.

L3.4   Decide the *protest* or request for redress (rule 64).

- Base the decision on the facts found (if you cannot, find some more facts).

- In redress cases, make sure that no further evidence is needed from boats that will be affected by the decision.

L3.5   Inform the *parties* (rule 65).

- Recall the *parties* and read them the facts found and decision. When time presses it is permissible to read the decision and give the details later.

- Give any *party* a copy of the decision on request. File the *protest* or request for redress with the committee records.

L4   REOPENING A HEARING (rule 66)

When a timely request is made for a hearing to be reopened, hear the *party* making the request, look at any video, etc., and decide whether there is any material new evidence which might lead you to change your decision. Decide whether your interpretation of the *rules* may have been wrong; be open-minded as to whether you have made a mistake. If none of these applies refuse to reopen; otherwise schedule a hearing.

L5   GROSS MISCONDUCT (rule 69)

L5.1   An action under this rule is not a *protest,* but the protest committee gives its allegations in writing to the competitor before the hearing. The hearing is conducted under the same rules as other hearings but the protest committee must have at least three members (rule 69.1(b)). Use the greatest care to protect the competitor's rights.

L5.2   A competitor or a boat cannot protest under rule 69, but the protest form of a competitor who tries to do so may be accepted as a report to the protest committee which can then decide whether or not to call a hearing.

L5.3   When it is desirable to call a hearing under rule 69 as a result of a Part 2 incident, it is important to hear any boat-vs.-boat *protest* in the normal way, deciding which boat, if any, broke which *rule,* before proceeding against the competitor under this rule.

L5.4   Although action under rule 69 is taken against a competitor, not a boat, a boat may also be penalized.

L5.5   The protest committee may warn the competitor when it believes this to be sufficient penalty, in which case no report need be made to the national authority. When the penalty is more severe and a report is made to the national authority, it is helpful to recommend to the national authority whether or not further action should be taken.

L6   **APPEALS (rule 70 and Appendix F)**

When decisions can be appealed,

- leave the papers so that the information can easily be used for an appeal. Is there an adequate diagram? Are the facts found sufficient? (Example: was there an *overlap*? Yes or No. 'Perhaps' is not a fact found.) Are the names of the protest committee members on the form, etc.?

- comments on any appeal should enable the appeals committee to picture the whole incident clearly; the appeals committee knows *nothing* about the situation.

L7   **PHOTOGRAPHIC EVIDENCE**

Photographs and videotapes can sometimes provide useful evidence but protest committees should recognize their limitations and note the following points:

- The *party* producing the photographic evidence is responsible for arranging the viewing.

- View the tape several times to extract all the information from it.

- The depth perception of any single-lens camera is very poor; with a telephoto lens it is non-existent. When the camera views two *overlapped* boats at right angles to their course, it is impossible to assess the distance between them. When the camera views them head on, it is impossible to see whether an *overlap* exists unless it is substantial.

- Ask the following questions:

    Where was the camera in relation to the boats?

    Was the camera's platform moving? If so in what direction and how fast?

    Is the angle changing as the boats approach the critical point?
    Fast panning causes radical change.

    Did the camera have an unrestricted view throughout?

Appendix M – International Juries

See rules 70.4 and 89(c). This appendix shall not be changed by sailing instructions or prescriptions of national authorities.

M1   **COMPOSITION, APPOINTMENT AND ORGANIZATION**

M1.1   An international jury shall be composed of experienced sailors with excellent knowledge of the racing rules and extensive protest committee experience. It shall be independent of and have no members from the race committee, and be appointed by the organizing authority, subject to approval by the national authority if required (see rule 89(c)), or by the ISAF under rule 87.2.

M1.2 The jury shall consist of a chairman, a vice chairman if desired, and other members for a total of at least five. A majority shall be International Judges. The jury may appoint a secretary, who shall not be a member of the jury.

M1.3 No more than two members (three, in Groups M, N and Q) shall be from the same national authority.

M1.4 (a) A jury of ten or more members may divide itself into two or more panels of at least five members each, of which the majority shall be International Judges. If this is done, the requirements for membership of a full jury shall apply to each panel but not to the jury as a whole.

(b) A jury of fewer than ten members may divide itself into two or more panels of at least three members each, of which the majority shall be International Judges. Members of each panel shall be from at least three different national authorities except in Groups M, N and Q, where they shall be from at least two different national authorities. If dissatisfied with a panel's decision, a *party* is entitled to a hearing by a jury composed in compliance with rules M1.1, M1.2 and M1.3, except concerning the facts found, if requested within the time limit specified in the sailing instructions.

M1.5 When a full jury has fewer than five members, because of illness or emergency, and no qualified replacements are available, it remains properly constituted if it consists of at least three members. When there are three or four members they shall be from at least three different national authorities except in Groups M, N and Q, where they shall be from at least two different national authorities.

M1.6 When the national authority's approval is required for the appointment of an international jury (see rule 89(c)), notice of its approval shall be included in the sailing instructions or be posted on the official notice board.

M1.7 If the jury acts while not properly constituted, the jury's decisions may be appealed.

M2 RESPONSIBILITIES

M2.1 An international jury is responsible for hearing and deciding all *protests,* requests for redress and other matters arising under the rules of Part 5. When asked by the organizing authority or the race committee, it shall advise and assist them on any matter directly affecting the fairness of the competition.

M2.2 Unless the organizing authority directs otherwise, the jury shall
(a)   decide questions of eligibility, measurement or boat certificates; and
(b)   authorize the substitution of competitors, boats, sails or equipment.

M2.3 If so directed by the organizing authority, the jury shall
(a)   make or approve changes to the sailing instructions,
(b)   supervise or direct the race committee in the conduct of the races, and
(c)   decide on other matters referred to it by the organizing authority.

M3 PROCEDURES

M3.1 Decisions of the jury shall be made by a simple majority vote of all members. When there is an equal division of votes cast, the chairman of the meeting may cast an additional vote.

M3.2 When it is considered desirable that some members not participate in discussing and deciding a *protest* or request for redress, the jury remains properly constituted if at least three members remain.

M3.3 Members shall not be regarded as *interested parties* (see rule 63.4) by reason of their nationality.

M3.4 If a panel fails to agree on a decision it may adjourn and refer the matter to the full jury.

Appendix N – Immediate Penalties for Breaking Rule 42

This appendix applies only if the sailing instructions so state.

N1 PROTESTS

A member of the protest committee or its designated observer who sees a boat breaking rule 42 may protest her by, as soon as reasonably possible, making a sound signal, pointing a yellow flag at her and hailing her sail number, even if she is no longer *racing.* A boat so protested is not subject to another *protest* under rule 42 for the same incident.

N2 PENALTIES

N2.1 First Protest

When a boat is first protested under rule N1 she may acknowledge her breach by taking a 720° Turns Penalty under rule 44.2. If she fails to do so she shall be disqualified without a hearing.

N2.2 Second Protest

When a boat is protested a second time during the series she may acknowledge her breach by immediately retiring from the race. If she fails to do so she shall be disqualified without a hearing and her score shall not be excluded.

N2.3 Third Protest

When a boat is protested a third time during the series she may acknowledge her breach by immediately retiring from the race and from all other races in the series. If she fails to do so she shall be disqualified without a hearing from all races in the series, with no score excluded, and the protest committee shall consider calling a hearing under rule 69.1(a).

N3 POSTPONEMENT, GENERAL RECALL OR ABANDONMENT

If a boat has been protested under rule N1 and the race committee signals a *postponement,* general recall or *abandonment,* the penalty from her first or second *protest* is cancelled, but the *protest* is counted to determine the number of times she has been protested during the series.

Appendix P – Definitions for Competitor Classification

This appendix is a US SAILING prescription.

This appendix, formerly Appendix R – Definitions for Competitor Eligibility, pro-vides definitions of three groups for competitor classification that can be used singly or in combination by a club, class association or other organizing authority for a race or series. Several variations are possible. For example, a maximum number of competitors of a particular group permitted on each boat may be established; the group requirement for helmsmen may be different from that for crew members; or separate trophies may be awarded for different groups.

An organizing authority that decides to use this appendix shall so state in its notice of race and sailing instructions. When particular group requirements will apply, or when requirements of different groups will apply to different competitors within the event, these requirements shall also be stated.

Although use of this appendix is not required, it shall not be changed by the notice of race or sailing instructions.

P1 DEFINITIONS OF GROUPS FOR COMPETITOR CLASSIFICATION

P1.1 Group US1 Competitor

A Group 1 competitor is one who engages in competitive sailing solely as a pastime, who does not benefit financially from an activity that contributes to the performance of racing boats, and who has not engaged in activity within the past 12 months that would make him a Group 2 competitor or activity within the past 24 months that would make him a Group 3 competitor. As exceptions, the following competitors are included in Group 1

(a) a competitor who otherwise meets Group 1 requirements but occasionally accepts reimbursement for reasonable out-of-pocket expenses of travel, lodging, meals and entry fees necessary for participation in an event;

(b) a competitor who, before he has reached his 24th birthday, is engaged or employed for no more than two periods totaling 100 days or less in a calendar year in an activity that would otherwise make him a Group 2 or Group 3 competitor.

P1.2 Group US2 Competitor

A Group 2 competitor is one who is neither a Group 1 nor a Group 3 competitor and has not been engaged in an activity that would make him a Group 3 competitor within the past 12 months.

P1.3 Group US3 Competitor

A Group 3 competitor is one who directly or indirectly:

(a) is paid to race;

(b) benefits financially from competing;

(c) primarily because of sailing skill or sailing reputation, receives payment or other compensation having a value of more than US $1,000 for allowing his name, likeness, sailing performance or sailing reputation to be used for the advertisement, promotion or sale of any product or service; or

(d) publicly identifies himself as a Group 3 competitor.

P2 FINANCIAL BENEFITS

Financial benefits include, but are not limited to, the following:

(a) income, a gift, loan, or other direct benefit, in excess of reasonable out-of-pocket expenses as permitted in rule P1.1(a), for participating in a race;

(b) a prize of money or its equivalent, a prize readily converted to money, or a non-monetary prize having a value of more than US $1,000, other than a prize of primarily symbolic value such as a trophy or a watch;

(c)   an agreement involving current or future employment based on racing activities or successes.

P3   CHANGES IN GROUP STATUS

P3.1   A Group 3 competitor becomes a Group 2 competitor after 12 months during which he has not been engaged in an activity that would make him a Group 3 competitor.

P3.2   A Group 2 competitor becomes a Group 1 competitor after 12 months during which he has not been engaged in an activity that would make him a Group 2 or Group 3 competitor.

P4   PROTEST DECISIONS

When a protest committee decides that a boat has broken a sailing instruction that applies this appendix, it shall disqualify the boat from any race for which a valid *protest* was made. A protest committee acting under Appendix P shall report its decision to US SAILING.

P5   US SAILING CLASSIFICATION DETERMINATION AND REVIEW

P5.1   A competitor may request the US SAILING Competitor Classification Committee to determine his status under Appendix P, or US SAILING may initiate such a determination. In making the determination, the committee may require the competitor to provide information and evidence. The competitor will be charged an administrative fee ($25 for US SAILING members; $75 for others) except when US SAILING initiates the determination. A competitor may request a new determination at any time, and should do so whenever a change in circumstances might place him in a numerically higher group.

P5.2   A competitor who believes that his classification determination is incorrect may request a review, in which case members of the committee who did not make the original determination will conduct the review. Payment of the administrative fee will again be required.

P5.3   Classification determinations made under rule P5.1 or rule P5.2, or the earlier Appendix R, shall expire on the last day of the second full calendar year after the date of the determination, or earlier when a change in circumstances places the competitor in a numerically higher group.

Appendix Q – Sound-Signal Starting System

This Appendix is a US SAILING prescription.

US SAILING prescribes that, when the sailing instructions so indicate, the Sound-Signal Starting System described below shall be used. This system is recommended primarily for small-boat racing and makes it unnecessary for competitors to use stopwatches. Supplemental visual course and recall signals are also recommended when practicable.

Q1   Course and postponement signals may be made orally.

Q2   Audible signals shall govern, even when supplemental visual signals are also used.

Q3 The starting sequence shall consist of the following sound signals made at the indicated times:

Signal	Sound	Time before start
Warning	3 long	3 minutes
Preparatory	2 long	2 minutes
	1 long, 3 short	1 minute, 30 seconds
	1 long	1 minutes
	3 short	30 seconds
	2 short	20 seconds
	1 short	10 seconds
	1 short	5 seconds
	1 short	4 seconds
	1 short	3 seconds
	1 short	2 seconds
	1 short	1 second
Starting	1 long	0

Q4 Signals shall be timed from their commencement.

Q5 A series of short signals may be made before the sequence begins in order to attract attention.

Q6 Individual recalls shall be signalled by the hail of the sail number (or some other clearly distinguishing feature) of each recalled boat. Flag X need not be displayed.

Q7 Failure of a competitor to hear an adequate course, postponement, starting sequence or recall signal shall not be grounds for redress.

APPENDICES, SECTION II

The appendices of this Section, which are both ISAF regulations and racing rules, may be amended or changed at any meeting of the ISAF Council. Any amendment or change will be posted on the ISAF website (www.sailing.org) as soon as practicable and may be obtained directly from the ISAF.

Appendix 1 – ISAF Advertising Code

See rule 79. This appendix shall not be changed by sailing instructions or prescriptions of national authorities. When governmental requirements conflict with parts of it, those requirements apply to the extent that they are more restrictive.

REGULATION 20

20. ADVERTISING CODE

20.1 *Definition of Advertising*

For the purposes of this code, advertising is the name, logo, slogan, description, depiction, a variation or distortion thereof, or any other form of communication that promotes an organization, person, product, service, brand or idea so as to call attention to it or to persuade persons or organizations to buy, approve or otherwise support it.

20.2. *General*

20.2.1 Advertising shall not be displayed on a boat, except as required or permitted by the ISAF Advertising Code.

20.2.2 Advertisements and anything advertised shall meet generally accepted moral and ethical standards.

20.2.3 Advertisements on sails shall be clearly separated from national letters and sail numbers.

20.3. *Advertising*

20.3.1 The following types of advertising are permitted or required as stated and apply at all times:

(a) Boats and Sailboards

The class insignia shall be displayed on her sails as required by RRS Appendix G.

(b) (i) Boats

One sailmaker's mark, which may include the name or mark of the sail-cloth manufacturer and the pattern or model of the sail, may be displayed on both sides of any sail and shall fit within a 150mm x 150mm square. On sails, other than spinnakers, no part of such mark shall be placed farther from the tack point than the greater of 300mm or 15% of the length of the foot.

(ii) Sailboards

One sailmaker's mark, which may include the name or mark of the sail-cloth manufacturer and the pattern or model of the sail, may be displayed on both sides of the sail and shall fit within a 150mm x 150mm square.

No part of such mark shall be placed farther from the tack point than 20% of the length of the foot of the sail, including the mast sleeve. The mark may also be displayed on the lower half of the part of the sail above the wishbone (boom) but no part of it shall be farther than 500mm from the clew point.

(c) (i) Boats

One builder's mark, which may include the name or mark of the designer, may be placed on the hull, and one maker's mark may be displayed on each side on spars and on each side of other equipment. Such marks shall fit within a 150mm x 150mm square.

(ii) Sailboards

Any number of manufacturers' names or logos may be placed on the board (hull) and in two places on the upper third of the part of the sail above the wishbone (boom). One maker's mark may be displayed each side on spars, and on each side of any other equipment.

(d) (i) Boats

The forward part of the hull on each side of all participating boats in an event shall only display advertising chosen and required to be displayed by that event organizer as follows:

- for boats under 6.5 metres, 25% of the **hull length**, and
- for boats over 6.5 metres, 20% of the **hull length**

excluding **bow numbers**. If such advertising is required, it shall be so stated in the Notice of Race. If advertising is for alcohol or tobacco, the word "may" instead of "shall" applies.

(ii) Sailboards

There shall be no reserved hull space on sailboards for event organizers.

The **organizing authority** of a sponsored event may permit or require the display of an advertisement of the event on both sides of the sail between the sail numbers and the wishbone (boom), on both sides of the sail aft of the foot median and on a bib worn by the competitors.

(e) competitors may display advertising on clothing and personal equipment without restriction.

20.3.2 In addition to 20.3.1, additional advertising chosen by the individual boat may be displayed in the following categories:

(a) Category A

No additional advertising.

(b) Category C

Advertising is permitted as per Category A, and in addition on hulls, spars and sails without restriction except the space reserved for identification by Appendix G and under section 20.3.1(b), (c) and (d).

20.3.3 When equipment is supplied by the event's **organizing authority**, Category C advertising on the supplied equipment is available to the **organizing authority**.

20.4 All Classes (except when participating in events listed in Regulation 20.6) - ISAF and Non-ISAF Status, National Classes

20.4.1 The right to choose Category A or C applies to all ISAF **Classes**, except Olympic

Classes which shall be unrestricted Category C.

20.4.2 (a) The Class Associations of ISAF *Classes* may decide the advertising category to be applied to their class to be either A or C. If the Class Association makes no ruling, Category A shall apply.

(b) The Class Associations of Non-ISAF *Classes* (excluding *National Classes* referred to in Regulation 20.4.2(c) below) may decide the advertising category to be applied to their Class to be either A or C. If the Class Association makes no ruling, Category A shall apply.

(c) For *National Classes* the National Authority of the *Class* decides Category A or C. If the National Authority makes no ruling, Category A shall apply.

20.4.3 If Category C status is chosen, only the National Authority may introduce an Individual Advertising License System to permit its *competitors* to display advertising on their boats/sailboards. (A breach of a National Authority's license system is not protestable under this Code).

20.4.4 For *club or invitational events* the *organizing authority* may restrict advertising to Category A, with the approval of the National Authority of the organizing club.

20.4.5 If Category C is decided, the ISAF Classes (except for Olympic Classes) and non-ISAF Classes (including *National Classes*) may decide the maximum level of advertising. Any restrictions within Category C shall be included in the Class Rules and subject to ISAF Council's approval. Olympic Classes cannot restrict Category C in anyway.

20.4.6 Except as provided by Regulations 20.3.1 and 20.3.3 the right to have any or all advertising on the hulls, sails and spars shall be solely the right of and at the direction of the *competitor* provided that such right may be contracted or assigned to others at the competitor's discretion.

20.5 *Handicapping Systems and Rating Rules*

20.5.1 The National Authority of a *competitor* in respect of the boat in which the *competitor* is competing, may decide the advertising category to be applied to boats racing under a handicap/measurement system to be either A or C. If Category C is decided, the said *competitor's* National Authority may decide the maximum level of advertising. If the National Authority makes no ruling, Category A shall apply. Any "*Class*" (see definition of Class) or individual boat racing under a handicap/measurement system shall have its advertising category determined in accordance with the provisions of this clause.

20.5.2 For the purposes of Regulation 20.5.1, the provisions of Regulations 20.4.3, 20.4.4 and 20.4.6 shall apply.

20.6 *Special Events/Events of Classes/ISAF Events*

20.6.1 Category C applies.

20.6.2 ISAF will administer an Event Advertising System and/or Individual Advertising System for boats participating in the following events:

(i) Special Events
America's Cup Match and Challenger/Defender Series
Volvo Ocean Race

        Global Ocean Races
        Trans-Oceanic Races
        ORC World Championships
        Professional Windsurfers Association Events (PWA)

(ii) Events of Classes
        International America's Cup Class
        Volvo 60'
        Maxi One Design
        Open 60 Monohull Class (incorporates Open 50 Class)
        Open 60 Multihull Class
        PWA Classes
        49'er Grand Prix series

(iii) Proposals for other Special Events and/or Events of Classes of equal or similar status may, on the initiative of the Executive Committee or on application by an event *organizing authority* (with the approval of the relevant National Authority) to the Executive Committee and with its consent, be made to the Council for its approval.

(iv) ISAF Events
        ISAF World Youth Sailing Championship
        ISAF Combined Olympic Classes World Championship
        ISAF World Sailing Championship
        ISAF Match Racing World Championship
        ISAF Women's World Match Racing Championship
        ISAF Team Racing World Championship
        ISAF Women's Keelboat World Championship
        And any other ISAF Events which may be introduced.

20.7 *Fees*

20.7.1 All boats carrying Category C advertising in line with Regulations 20.4 and 20.5 may be required to pay a fee only to their National Authority (no share to ISAF or any other National Authorities).

20.7.2 All Events under Regulation 20.6 carrying Category C advertising shall pay a fee to ISAF (no share to any National Authority).

[Note: Sections 20.7.1 and 20.7.2 to be reviewed after 2 years (November 2003), before a final decision on the distribution of fees is decided].

20.8 *Entry Fees*

There should be no variation of entry fees based on the *competitor's* category of advertising for the boat in which he is competing.

20.9 *Protests under this Code*

20.9.1 When, after finding the facts, a protest committee decides that a boat or her crew has broken a section of this Code, it shall:

(a) give a warning; or

(b) disqualify the boat in accordance with RRS 64.1; or

(c) disqualify the boat from more than one race or from the series when it decides that the breach warrants a stronger penalty; or

(d) act under RRS 69.1 when it decides that there may have been a gross breach.

20.10 *Definitions*

The following definitions shall apply to this Code only:

Note: There are some definitions which are not needed in the present text of the Code.

(a) "All Classes"

Shall include all Classes as defined below and shall include Classes which are designated as ISAF Classes as well as Classes which are not designated as ISAF Classes.

(b) "Class"

A Class of boat/sailboard includes boats/sailboards which conform to a physical specification intended to allow competitive racing among the Class, and without limiting the generality of the foregoing, includes Classes with one-design, restricted, and developmental specifications as these terms are applied generally and for which there is an existing organization to administer the Class which has:

(i) an Executive or similar body which administers the Class,

(ii) a membership which is open to all owners of boats/sailboards which meet the specification of the Class, and

(iii) which holds a meeting of members at least once a year, and which gives notice of such meetings to all members.

(c) "National Class"

A National Class for the purposes of this Regulation is a class where the National Authority has substantial authority in the direction or management of the Class.

(d) "Club or Invitational Event"

A Club event is an event that is sponsored, organized or held by a Club which has sailing as one of its activities. An Invitational event is one in which the participants are invited and is not open to members of a participating class except by invitation.

A yacht club hosting an event which is a qualifier in any way for an International Class event cannot declare an Event Category "A" by making the event an "invitational".

(e) "Hull Length"

For the purposes of this Regulation, Hull Length is as defined in the applicable Class rules for Hull Length or any comparable measurement less Hull Appendages and if no means of measurement exists in the Class rules, Hull Length and Hull Appendage shall have the meaning set out in the Equipment Rules of Sailing, D.3.1 and E.1.1.

(f) "Organizing Authority"

Shall have the definition contained in RRS 87.1.

(g) "Competitor"

In addition to its natural meaning, a competitor in respect of any boat shall include any person who has the right to use the boat as owner or by charter, loan or otherwise.

(h) "Competitor Advertising"

In respect of any boat is advertising which is applied to a boat, its equipment or the person or the equipment of a competitor or competitors as the condition of or as the result of a payment made to or made as a result of the direction of one or more of the competitors in respect of such boat.

(i) "Other Advertising"

Advertising which is not competitor advertising.

(j) "Bow Number"

An identifier assigned to a boat, usually for the duration of an event, by the organizer which is required to be displayed on the bow of a boat which may be a combination of numbers and letters.

Note: Regulation 20 is subject to change by the ISAF Council. The current text of the regulation is available from the ISAF by mail, fax or e-mail (sail@isaf.co.uk).

Appendix 2 – ISAF Eligibility Code

See rule 75.2. This appendix shall not be changed by sailing instructions or prescriptions of national authorities.

REGULATION 21

21.   ISAF ELIGIBILITY CODE

21.1   *ISAF Eligibility Rules*

To be eligible to compete in an event listed in rule 21.2.1, a competitor shall:

(a) be governed by the regulations and rules of the ISAF;

(b) be a member of a Member National Authority or one of its affiliated organizations. Such membership shall be established by the competitor

(i) being entered by the national authority of the country of which the competitor is a national or ordinarily a resident; or

(ii) presenting a valid membership card or certificate, or other satisfactory evidence of identity and membership;

(c) not be under suspension of ISAF eligibility.

21.2   *Events Requiring ISAF Eligibility*

21.2.1 ISAF eligibility is required for the following events:

(a) the sailing regatta of the Olympic Games;

(b) the sailing regattas of regional games recognised by the International Olympic Committee;

(c) events including 'ISAF' in their titles;

(d) world and continental championships of ISAF international classes and of the Offshore Racing Council;

(e) any other event approved by the ISAF as a world championship and so stated in the notice of race and the sailing instructions;

(f) any event approved by a national authority or the ISAF as an Olympic qualifying event;

(g) all other international events involving an ISAF International Judge, Umpire, Race Officer or Measurer. For the purposes of this rule, international events are ISAF events, world and continental championships, and events described as international events in their notices of race and sailing instructions; and

(h) all events using the Racing Rules of Sailing.

21.2.2 ISAF eligibility may be required for any other event when so stated in the notice of race and the sailing instructions with specific reference to this regulation.

21.3 Suspension of ISAF Eligibility

21.3.1 After proper inquiry by either the national authority of the competitor or the ISAF Executive Committee, a competitor's ISAF eligibility shall be promptly suspended with immediate effect, permanently or for a specified period of time

(a) for any suspension of eligibility in accordance with RRS 69.2; or

(b) for breaking RRS 5; or

(c) for competing, within the two years preceding the inquiry, in an event that the competitor knew or should have known was a prohibited event.

21.3.2 A prohibited event is an event:

(a) permitting or requiring advertising beyond that permitted by the ISAF Advertising Code;

(b) with prizes or other benefits referred to in Regulation 8.2 that is a national event not approved by the national authority of the venue or an international event not approved by the ISAF;

(c) that is described as a world championship or uses the word "world", either in the title of the event or otherwise, and that is not approved by the ISAF; or

(d) *that does not conform to the requirements of RRS 87, and is not otherwise approved by the ISAF.*

21.3.3 When an event described in rule 21.3.2 has been approved as required, that fact shall be stated in the notice of race and the sailing instructions.

21.4 Reports; Reviews; Notification; Appeals

21.4.1 When a national authority suspends a competitor's ISAF eligibility under rule 21.3.1, it shall promptly report the suspension and reasons therefor to the ISAF. The ISAF Executive Committee may revise or annul the suspension with immediate effect. The ISAF shall promptly report any suspension of a competitor's eligibility, or of its revision or annulment by the ISAF Executive Committee, to all national authorities, international class associations, the Offshore Racing Council and other ISAF affiliated organizations, which may also suspend eligibility for events held within their jurisdiction.

21.4.2 A competitor whose suspension of ISAF eligibility has been either imposed by a national authority, or imposed or revised by the ISAF Executive Committee, shall be advised of the right to appeal to the ISAF Review Board and be provided with a copy of the Review Board Rules of Procedure.

21.4.3 A national authority or the ISAF Executive Committee may ask for a review of its decision by the ISAF Review Board by complying with the Review Board

Rules of Procedure.

21.4.4 The Review Board Rules of Procedure shall govern all appeals and requests for review.

21.4.5 Upon an appeal or request for review, the ISAF Review Board may confirm, revise or annul a suspension of eligibility, or require a hearing or rehearing by the suspending authority.

21.4.6 Decisions of the Review Board are not subject to appeal.

21.4.7 The ISAF shall promptly notify all national authorities, international class associations and the Offshore Racing Council of all Review Board decisions.

21.5 *Reinstatement of ISAF Eligibility*

The ISAF Review Board may reinstate the ISAF eligibility of a competitor who:

(a) applies for reinstatement;

(b) establishes substantial, changed circumstances justifying reinstatement; and

(c) has completed a minimum of three years of suspension.

Note: Regulation 21 is subject to change by the ISAF Council. The current text of the regulation is available from the ISAF by mail, fax or e-mail (sail@isaf.co.uk).

Appendix 3 – ISAF Anti-Doping Code

See rule 5. This appendix shall not be changed by sailing instructions or prescriptions of national authorities.

REGULATION 19

19. **ISAF ANTI-DOPING CODE**

The doping definition of the ISAF Medical Commission, like that of the International Olympic Committee (IOC), is based on the banning of pharmacological classes of agents.

The definition has the advantage that also new drugs, some of which may be especially designed for doping purposes, are prohibited.

The list published in Appendix "A" of Olympic Movement Anti-Doping Code (OMADC) – and detailed at the end of Regulation 19 - represents examples of the different dope classes to illustrate the doping definition. Unless indicated, all substances belonging to the banned classes may not be used for medical treatment, even if they are not listed as examples. If substances of the banned classes are detected in the IOC accredited laboratory, the ISAF Medical Commission will report to the ISAF Executive Committee who will act upon the advice of the ISAF Anti-Doping Panel.

The presence of the drug in a sample of urine or blood constitutes an offence, irrespective of the route of administration.

Doping Controls shall be undertaken in the sport of sailing.

When governmental requirements conflict with parts of this ISAF Anti-Doping Code those requirements apply.

The following are basic ISAF requirements:

Procedures

19.1 *Selection of Competitors*

19.1.1 A reasonable number of doping control tests, both in-competition (ICT) and out-of-competition (OOCT), shall be undertaken.

19.1.2 In-competition is defined as that period of time between the scheduled time of the warning signal of the first race of the event, up to the closure of protest time following the final race of the event

19.1.3 Out-of-competition testing is defined as testing which takes place at other times outside the ICT period. When a doping control is conducted on the day of a competition in which the affected competitor has competed or is entered or expected to compete, the test shall be considered as in-competition. All other unannounced doping control shall be deemed to be OOCT. OOCT may be conducted by ISAF, by an ISAF authorized organisation or on behalf and in collaboration with the World Anti-Doping Agency (WADA) or by WADA authorized organisation at any time, or a recognised governmental agency, including at the time or location of any competition in every member country. Preferably it shall be carried out without any advance notice to the competitor or his/her Member National Authority (MNA).

19.1.4 ISAF and/or WADA may keep a register of competitors who are being subject to OOCT. Member National Authorities have the obligation to submit names, current places of living, addresses, telephone numbers, training times and training and competition locations for individuals and teams requested by ISAF and WADA, to enable ISAF and WADA to conduct OOCT.

19.1.5 ISAF and/or WADA can select competitors being subject to OOCT among all Member National Authority competitors. The selection can be done by ballot or any other principle that is decided by ISAF and/or WADA.

19.1.6 A competitor selected for sample taking shall not refuse to have a sample taken either in or out-of-competition, when required to do so by an accredited sampling officer acting on behalf of a Member National Authority, ISAF, WADA, IOC or a recognised governmental agency.

19.1.7 Doping Control is administered in order to uphold the requirements of RRS Fundamental Rule 5.

19.1.8 At an authorized event where doping control is undertaken, the protest committee chairman shall select competitors to be sampled on a specific day. Selection may be by means of a draw and specific competitors may be selected, as decided by the protest committee chairman. If on that day a race is postponed to a following day or abandoned, or if a competitor does not start in a race that is taking place, the protest committee chairman may still require the sampling of the specific competitor(s) already selected and may select any other competitors to be tested on that day. When there is more than one competitor in each boat, any or all of them may be selected. The race committee shall give to the sampling officer the names of the competitors selected for sampling. A competitor may be sampled more than once during an event.

19.2 *Sample Taking*

19.2.1 (a) The accredited sampling officer or his/her representative shall inform a competitor by written notice, which shall be given to the competitor, in confidence, that he or she has been selected for sample taking and is required to provide a urine or a blood sample at the time and place specified in the notice. The notice shall specify the name of the sampling officer appointed for the event (or OOCT) and of the designated laboratory (IOC accredited) to which the specimens will be sent.

(b) The competitor shall, during in-competition testing, sign an undertaking to be present at the Doping Control Station by a specific time, which will usually be not later than one hour after the time of notification. In back to back racing a competitor shall be notified at the conclusion of the race from which he/she has been selected, and extra time shall be allowed for the competitor to take part in any subsequent races that day, before returning to shore for Doping Control.

After notifying the competitor the organizing committee representative for doping control should remain with the competitor at all times (unless racing) until they together arrive at the Doping Control Station.

(c) The competitor may be accompanied by one person of his or her choice.

(d) A competitor who fails to appear at the appointed time and place, or who refuses to provide a sample shall be disqualified and sanctioned, together with the boat in which he or she was sailing, from the event and all the results to date shall be expunged. The protest committee shall call a hearing in accordance with RRS Part 5 Section B, to investigate the circumstances, to consider reasons offered to explain the failure to provide a sample in proper time, and report its findings to the initiating national authority, and to the national authority of the competitor.

19.2.2 The protocol for sample taking procedures at Doping Controls is detailed in Appendix "C" of the OMADC.

19.2.3 The competitor and the accompanying person shall be attended in the waiting room of the Doping Control Centre by a member of the doping control team.

19.2.4 The member of the doping control team shall check the identity of the competitor and his/her sail number.

19.2.5 The time of arrival and personal data of the competitor shall be recorded.

19.2.6 Wherever possible only one competitor plus attendant/team official at a time should be called into the Doping Control Office. Where several tests are taking place this may not be possible.

19.2.7 In addition to the competitor and accompanying person only the following may be present in the Doping Control Office:

- A representative from ISAF;
- A member of the ISAF Medical Commission or their nominee;
- The officials in charge of taking samples and keeping records;
- An interpreter if required.

Photographs may not be taken in the Doping Control Station during the doping control procedure, unless required by the Doping Control Official in charge of the Doping Control Station. Representatives of the press are not allowed to be present during testing.

19.2.8 (a) When a competitor has been selected for OOCT the Sampling Officer (SO) appointed by ISAF or International Doping Control Officer (IDCO) appointed by WADA may either make an appointment to meet the competitor or, at preference, he/she may arrive unannounced to the competitor's training camp, accommodation or any other place where the competitor is likely to be found. In either case, the SO/IDCO shall provide proof of identity and provide a letter of appointment from ISAF or WADA. The SO/IDCO shall also require proof of identity of the competitor. The actual collection of the sample shall be in as much accordance with OMADC and Regulation 19 as is reasonable.

(b) Arrangements for collection of the sample shall be made as soon as possible after the appointment with the competitor has been made. It is the competitor's responsibility to check the arranged date, time and the precise location of the meeting.

(c) Where the SO/IDCO arrives unannounced he/she must give the competitor reasonable time to complete activity in which he/she is engaged, but testing should commence as soon as possible.

(d) In case a Team Doctor is not available or present at the OOCT, the competitor is responsible for declaring all medication taken by him/her in the 72 hours prior to the sample collection time. The Team Doctor does not need to be present to give written details or declare medication that the competitor is subject to. It is understood that the OOCT sample procedure is fully valid without the presence and without the declaration on the report form from the Team Doctor.

(e) Each competitor selected for OOCT shall, as part of the collection procedure, in conjunction with the SO/IDCO complete such laboratory forms as are required by the initiating authority or laboratory to whom the sample is to be dispatched.

(f) If the competitor refuses to provide a urine sample, the SO/IDCO shall note this on the doping control form used, enter his name on the form and ask the competitor to sign the form. The SO/IDCO shall also note any other irregularities in the doping control process.

(g) The nature of unannounced OOCT makes it desirable that little or no prior warning is given to the competitor. Every effort will be made by the SO/IDCO to collect the sample speedily and efficiently with the minimum of interruption to the competitor's training, social or work arrangements. If there is interruption, however, no competitor may take any action to gain compensation for any inconvenience incurred.

(h) If OOCT are conducted by WADA or by a WADA authorized organisation, the original copy of the doping control form will be sent to ISAF and a copy will be kept in the possession of WADA.

(i) ISAF shall nominate a contact person responsible for the OOCT Testing liaison with WADA

(j) There has been signed an agreement between WADA and ISAF, the articles, terms and conditions of which are on record at ISAF. Under this agreement WADA will conduct OOCT services on behalf of ISAF in accordance with the OMADC and Regulation 19.

19.2.9 In ICT and OOCT the sampling procedure shall be carefully explained to the competitor in his/her own language or with the aid of an interpreter. It shall be made clear to the competitor that the sampling officer who directly supervises the passing of the urine sample shall be of the same sex as the competitor.

19.2.10 If the competitor refuses to provide a sample the possible consequences shall be explained to the competitor. If the competitor still refuses, this fact shall be noted in the records. These shall be signed by the official in charge of the station, the technician, representatives of the national authority which organized the sampling, and of any representative of ISAF who may be present and may be signed by the competitor and accompanying person. Following investigation the Member National Authority shall report findings and decisions relating to sanctions applied, to ISAF.

19.2.11 (a) The appropriately provided urine sample will be divided by the competitor into two samples "A" and "B" and placed in individual bottles which are sealed into individual containers. Codes shall identify the bottles and containers such that the laboratory does not know the name of any competitor.

(b) Samples collected during testing shall be forwarded in the appropriate sealed containers to the designated, IOC accredited, laboratory concerned. The sample taking, transportation and analysis shall be as detailed in Appendix "C" of the OMADC. During transportation to the laboratory a record of the chain of custody shall be made from the time of production of the sample by the competitor to the time of opening of a container in the laboratory. At all times following its collection the sample shall be stored in the conditions required by the laboratory.

19.2.12 The analysis of sample "A" shall be conducted by the accredited laboratory, and the result made available to the initiating authority, within 30 days of the taking of the sample at the Doping Control Centre.

19.2.13 The competitor shall provide a postal, fax or e-mail address at which during the 60 days following the taking of the sample required, he or she may be informed of the laboratory analysis results of sample "A". Should sample "A" provide a positive result the address given will be used to inform the competitor, and to invite the competitor to attend or to be represented at the laboratory during the subsequent analysis of the "B" sample. Sample "B" shall be analysed within 10 days of the date of notification of the "A" sample result.

Failure by a competitor to acknowledge receipt of the notice requiring his/her presence for the provision of a sample, or to sign the doping control form, or to provide a contact address will not be grounds for cancelling any penalty imposed for breaking RRS Fundamental Rule 5.

19.3 *Sample Analysis*

19.3.1 The Laboratory Analysis Procedures shall follow the protocol detailed in Appendix "D" of the OMADC.

19.3.2   Analysis shall only be carried out in laboratories accredited by the IOC. Such laboratories are listed as Appendix "C" to the OMADC and shall be regularly inspected to maintain accreditation standards.

19.3.3   Sample "A" is analysed first. If sample "A" is negative, i.e. no proscribed medication or its metabolites are present, or no abnormal ratios or quantities for the presence of certain substances by the OMADC are noted, no further action is taken.

19.3.4   When "A" sample is positive, i.e. proscribed medication, metabolites or abnormal substance levels are noted:

(a) the initiating authority shall so inform the competitor and his/her national authority immediately. No race results shall be changed at this stage; and

(b) the laboratory will proceed to test sample "B", the competitor or his/her representative may be present at the testing, and shall be informed of its time and place.

(c) when sample "B" is negative, the initiating authority shall so inform the competitor and his/her national authority, no further action shall be taken.

(d) when no result has been obtained from sample "B" after 60 days from the date of the sample taking, the procedure shall be considered void and no further action shall be taken.

(e) when sample "B" is positive the initiating national authority, or ISAF in testing initiated by ISAF, will inform the competitor in writing at the address provided (see Regulation 19.2.13) and his/her national authority.

(f) any penalties imposed by the national authority against a competitor/participant who is found in breach of RRS Fundamental Rule 5, or of Regulation 19 shall be reported promptly to ISAF.

19.3.5   Sanctions shall be applied in the first instance by the Member National Authority, which shall inform ISAF of its decisions. If the Member National Authority imposes no penalty, or an inadequate penalty, the possibility of imposing sanctions may be reviewed by ISAF.

19.4   Penalties

19.4.1   The penalties for doping are stated in the OMADC.

19.4.2   In addition to any penalty imposed under Regulation 21.3 a competitor who has found in breach of RRS Fundamental Rule 5 shall have his/her ISAF Eligibility suspended as provided in Regulation 21 - Eligibility Code.

19.4.3   The competitor may appeal as provided in Regulation 21 and as Regulation 19.5.5 below.

19.5   Hearings and Appeals Procedure

19.5.1   The competitor has 20 days from the date of the communication required by Regulation 19.3.4(e) to request a hearing or appeal to his/her Member National Authority, or to ISAF if the testing was initiated by ISAF.

19.5.2   If no appeal has been lodged after the last day for any such appeal has passed, one or more of the penalties provided for in Regulation 19.4 will be applied with effect from the event during which the relevant testing took place and any subsequent event prior to the testing of the "B" sample and during 20 days thereafter.

19.5.3 The findings of positive results shall be reported to ISAF, together with details of sanctions applied by the Member National Authority.

19.5.4 Competitors who have positive doping control results and who appeal against the finding of a breach of any of the anti-doping codes to which the competitor is subject or against the sanctions applied may be referred to the ISAF Anti-Doping Panel. The Anti-Doping Panel will consider evidence and report to the ISAF Executive Committee. The participant appealing is entitled to a copy of such procedures at the time he/she is notified of a positive result pursuant to Regulation 19.3.4(e).

19.5.5 Since ISAF recognises the Court of Arbitration for Sport a participant may appeal the decision of the ISAF Executive Committee to the Court of Arbitration for Sport in accordance with the provisions for appeal of the Court. A copy of those provisions shall be provided to the participant at the time he/she is notified of the Panel's decision.

19.6 Exemptions

19.6.1 A competitor may request, only in writing, prior approval from the ISAF Medical Commission for the use of a banned substance, or a banned method, for special medical reasons. The reasons to be supported by written evidence from a specialist doctor. For the Olympic Games, dispensation can only be granted by the IOC Medical Commission, via an appeal made by the ISAF Medical Commission, the request to be made on behalf of the competitor, to ISAF, by his/her Member National Authority.

19.6.2 In Offshore races of more than 50 nautical miles, the use during a race of any banned substance or banned procedure for emergency medical treatment shall be reported promptly to the protest committee, which shall inform the appropriate national authority and the ISAF. The ISAF Medical Commission may retroactively approve such use.

19.7 Expenses

19.7.1 Any expenses in travel to observe analysis of a "B" sample, or to give evidence on his/her own behalf, incurred in connection with this ISAF Anti-Doping Code by a competitor shall be his or her responsibility and neither the participant's National Authority or ISAF shall have any obligation for any such expenses.

19.8 Team Doctors

19.8.1 With the approval of ISAF or a Member National Authority or National Olympic Committee (NOC), a Team Doctor or a Doctor who is responsible for sailing competitors, officials and others in the care of that Doctor, may carry and employ such medications as the circumstances may require, and as might be expected to be properly used in the undertaking of the Hippocratic oath.

19.9 Team Disqualification

19.9.1 In the event that a competitor who is a member of a team is found guilty of doping, the boat upon which the offending sailor was a crew member shall be disqualified from the event. In sailing events in which more than one boat represents an individual national or other team, the boat upon which the offending sailor was a crew member shall be disqualified, but not other boats within a group of boats sailing as a team in either one or a number of classes.

19.10 *Declaration of Medications*

19.10.1 The use of the proscribed beta-2 agonists, which are classified as stimulants, is permitted, by inhalation only, in cases of proven asthma. They are permitted following written request, prior to an event, by the competitor to the relevant medical authority. The relevant doctor shall issue a certificate granting permission for the inhaler(s) to be used, and shall maintain a record of the issue of the certificate.

The relevant medical officer shall preferably be the Member National Authority doctor. In the event of the Member National Authority having no doctor appointed the request should be made to the ISAF Medical Commission.

Diabetics requiring insulin are also required to notify the relevant medical authority to obtain a certificate.

Notification Procedure

1. *Competitors requiring treatment involving permitted beta-2 agonists by inhalation, or insulin, should note details of the treatment in writing, including diagnosis and the name and address of the prescribing physician.*

2. *A copy of this information is sent in confidence to the Member National Authority Medical Officer, or in his absence to the ISAF Medical Commission.*

3. *The Member National Authority Medical Officer may wish to seek further information from the competitor or physician.*

4. *If diagnosis and treatment are accepted, the Member National Authority Medical Officer will send a certificate agreeing to the medication to the competitor, and maintain a record at the Member National Authority.*

5. *Further notification may be required, at intervals, for long term treatment.*

19.11 *Dispensation for taking Proscribed Medication*

19.11.1 If dispensation is requested for medication other than that listed in Regulation 19.10 above the Member National Authority Medical Officer will be required to request full medical details from the competitor, including diagnosis, names of specialists consulted, their address, hospital letters etc. These should be sent in confidence to the Chairman ISAF Medical Commission, with a request, backed by the Member National Authority, that dispensation for the taking of the listed medications be granted.

Following investigation such a dispensation may be granted by the ISAF Executive Committee for a fixed period subject to review. This will enable the sailor to compete in events held under ISAF rules.

19.11.2 For the Olympic Regatta dispensation can only be granted by the IOC, acting upon the advice of the IOC Medical Commission. To obtain this dispensation the Member National Authority should apply to the ISAF Medical Commission. The Member National Authority will be requested to provide full details as outlined above. The ISAF Medical Commission will then, if they agree to the request, submit a documented application to the IOC Medical Commission.

19.11.3 An ISAF Dispensation alone does not permit the sailor to compete in the Olympic Regatta.

19.12 *Classes of Prohibited Substances in Certain Circumstances*

19.12.1 Where in the OMADC in Appendix "A" under III provides an option in the adoption of any substance on the proscribed list of medication, this choice of adoption will be made by the ISAF Executive Committee upon the advice of the Medical Commission.

19.12.2 Pursuant to Regulation 19.12.1:

- Beta Blockers are permitted in sailing <u>except for Match Race Helms</u>

19.13 *ISAF Anti-Doping Panel*

19.13.1 The ISAF Anti-Doping Panel will consist of:

- Executive Committee member - Chair
- Chairman, or alternative appointed by Chairman, of Medical Commission,
- Chairman, or alternative appointed by Chairman, of Racing Rules Committee,
- Chairman, or alternative appointed by Chairman, of Constitution Committee.

and may be called upon to consider breaches of the OMADC and Regulation 19 and then report to the ISAF Executive Committee.

NOTE: Regulation 19 is subject to change by the ISAF Council. The current text of the regulation is available from the ISAF by mail, fax or e-mail (sail@isaf.co.uk).

The Olympic Movement Anti-Doping Code, Appendix A (IOC Prohibited Classes of Substances and Prohibited Methods), List of Examples of Prohibited Substances and Prohibited Methods, and other current information about the Code are also available on the ISAF website.

PROTEST FORM
also for requests for redress and reopening

Date & time received _____

Received by _____ Number _____

1. EVENT_____ Organizing authority_____ Date _____ Race no. _____

2. TYPE OF HEARING
   - ☐ Protest by boat against boat
   - ☐ Protest by race committee against boat
   - ☐ Protest by protest committee against boat
   - ☐ Request for redress by boat or race committee
   - ☐ Consideration of redress by protest committee
   - ☐ Request by boat or race committee to reopen hearing
   - ☐ Consideration of reopening by protest committee

3. BOAT PROTESTING, OR REQUESTING REDRESS OR REOPENING

   Class _____ Sail no. _____ Boat's name _____Tel. _____

   Represented by _____ Address _____

4. BOAT(S) PROTESTED OR BEING CONSIDERED FOR REDRESS

   Class _____ Sail no. _____ Boat's name _____

5. INCIDENT

   Time and place of incident _____ Rule(s) alleged to have been broken _____

   Witness(es) _____

6. INFORMING PROTESTEE How did you inform the protestee of your intention to protest?

   - ☐ By hailing When? _____ Word(s) used _____
   - ☐ By displaying a red flag When? _____
   - ☐ By informing her in some other way Give details _____

7. DESCRIPTION OF INCIDENT
   (use another sheet if necessary)

Diagram: one square = one hull length
Show position of boats, wind and
current direction, marks

Protest Form

Number _____
Heard together with numbers _____

☐ Withdrawal requested; signed _____ ☐ Withdrawal permitted.

Protest time limit _____

Protest, or request for redress or reopening ☐ is within time limit.   ☐ Time limit extended.

Protestor, or party requesting redress or reopening, represented by _____

Other party, or boat being considered for redress, represented by _____

Names of witnesses _____

Interpreters _____   **Remarks**

Objection about interested party.................................☐ _____

Written protest or request identifies incident.......................☐ _____

'Protest' hailed at first reasonable opportunity ....☐ _____

No hail needed, protestee informed at first reasonable opportunity.. ☐ _____

Red flag conspicuously displayed at first reasonable opportunity ... ☐ _____

Red flag seen by race committee at finish ....☐ _____

Protest or request valid, hearing will continue ☐   **Protest or request invalid, hearing is closed** ☐

FACTS FOUND

☐ Diagram of boat _____ is endorsed by committee.   ☐ Committee's diagram is attached.

CONCLUSIONS AND RULES THAT APPLY

DECISION
Protest   ☐ is dismissed.

    Boat(s) _____ ☐ is (are) disqualified.

                ☐ is (are) penalized as follows

Redress ☐ is not given.   ☐ is given as follows _____

Request to reopen a hearing ☐ is denied.   ☐ is granted.

PROTEST COMMITTEE

Members _____

Chairman's signature _____ Date and time _____

Index

Definitions

A term used as stated below is shown in italic type or, in preambles, in bold italic type.

Abandon A race that a race committee or protest committee *abandons* is void but may be resailed.

Clear Astern and **Clear Ahead; Overlap** One boat is *clear astern* of another when her hull and equipment in normal position are behind a line abeam from the aftermost point of the other boat's hull and equipment in normal position. The other boat is *clear ahead.* They *overlap* when neither is *clear astern* or when a boat between them *overlaps* both. These terms do not apply to boats on opposite *tacks* unless rule 18 applies.

Finish A boat *finishes* when any part of her hull, or crew or equipment in normal position, crosses the finishing line in the direction of the course from the last *mark,* either for the first time or after taking a penalty under rule 31.2 or 44.2 or, under rule 28.1, after correcting an error made at the finishing line.

Interested Party A person who may gain or lose as a result of a protest committee's decision, or who has a close personal interest in the decision.

Keep Clear One boat *keeps clear* of another if the other can sail her course with no need to take avoiding action and, when the boats are *overlapped* on the same *tack,* if the *leeward* boat can change course in both directions without immediately making contact with the *windward* boat.

Leeward and **Windward** A boat's *leeward* side is the side that is or, when she is head to wind, was away from the wind. However, when sailing by the lee or directly downwind, her *leeward* side is the side on which her mainsail lies. The other side is her *windward* side. When two boats on the same *tack overlap,* the one on the *leeward* side of the other is the *leeward* boat. The other is the *windward* boat.

Mark An object the sailing instructions require a boat to leave on a specified side, and a race committee vessel surrounded by navigable water from which the starting or finishing line extends. An anchor line and objects attached temporarily or accidentally to a *mark* are not part of it.

Obstruction An object that a boat could not pass without changing course substantially, if she were sailing directly towards it and one of her hull lengths from it. An object that can be safely passed on only one side and an area so designated by the sailing instructions are also *obstructions.* However, a boat *racing* is not an *obstruction* to other boats unless they are required to *keep clear* of her, give her *room* or, if rule 21 applies, avoid her.

Overlap See **Clear Astern** and **Clear Ahead; Overlap**.

Party A *party* to a hearing: a protestor; a protestee; a boat requesting redress; a boat or a competitor that may be penalized under rule 69.1; a race committee in a hearing under rule 62.1(a).

Postpone A *postponed* race is delayed before its scheduled start but may be started or *abandoned* later.

Proper Course A course a boat would sail to *finish* as soon as possible in the absence of the other boats referred to in the rule using the term. A boat has no *proper course* before her starting signal.

Protest An allegation made under rule 61.2 by a boat, a race committee or a protest committee that a boat has broken a *rule*. |

Racing A boat is *racing* from her preparatory signal until she *finishes* and clears the finishing line and *marks* or retires, or until the race committee signals a general recall, *postponement* or *abandonment*.

Room The space a boat needs in the existing conditions while manoeuvring promptly in a seamanlike way.

Rule (a) The rules in this book, including the Definitions, Race Signals, Introduction, preambles and the rules of relevant appendices, but not titles;

(b) the prescriptions of the national authority, unless the sailing instructions state that they do not apply;

(c) the class rules, or the rules of the handicapping or rating system, except any that conflict with the rules in this book;

(d) the notice of race;

(e) the sailing instructions; and

(f) any other documents that govern the event.

Start A boat *starts* when after her starting signal any part of her hull, crew or equipment first crosses the starting line and she has complied with rule 29.1 and rule 30.1 if it applies.

Tack, Starboard or Port A boat is on the *tack, starboard* or *port,* corresponding to her *windward* side.

Two-Length Zone The area around a *mark* or *obstruction* within a distance of two hull lengths of the boat nearer to it.

Windward See **Leeward** and **Windward**.

About the Author

DAVE PERRY grew up sailing on Long Island Sound. Learning to sail in Sunfish, Blue Jays and Lightnings from his parents and in the junior program at the Pequot Yacht Club in Southport, Connecticut, he won the Clinton M. Bell Trophy for the best junior record on L.I.S. in 1971. While at Yale (1973-77) he was captain of the National Championship Team in 1975, and was voted All-American in 1975 and 1977. Other racing accomplishments include: 1st, 1978 Tasar North Americans; 5th, 1979 Laser Worlds; 1st, 1979 Soling Olympic Pre-Trials (crew); 10th overall, 1981 SORC (crew); 3rd, 1982 Soling Worlds; 1st, 1982 Prince of Wales Match Racing Championship; 1st, 1983 Star South American Championship (crew); 1st, 1983 and 1984 Congressional Cup; 2nd, 1984 Soling Olympic Trials; 6th, 1985 Transpac Race (crew); 1st, 1988 and 1992 Knickerbocker Match Race Cup; and 1st, 1994 and 1999 Ideal 18 North American Championship.

Dave has been actively working for the sport since 1977. He has led hundreds of US SAILING instructional seminars in over 50 one-design classes; directed U.S. Olympic Yachting Committee Talent Development Clinics; coached the 1981 World Champion U.S. Youth Team; and given seminars in Japan, Australia, Sweden, Argentina, Brazil and Canada. He has been the Youth Representative on the US SAILING Board of Directors and the Chairman of the U.S. Youth Championship Committee, and has served on the following other US SAILING committees: Olympic, Training, Class Racing and O'Day Championship. He is currently a member of the US SAILING Appeals Committee and a US SAILING Senior Certified Judge. In 1992 he was voted into the *Sailing World* Hall of Fame; in 1994 he received an honorary Doctorate of Education from Piedmont College; in 1995 he became the first recipient of US SAILING's Captain Joe Prosser Award for exceptional contribution to sailing education; and in March 2001 Dave received the W. Van Alan Clarke, Jr. Trophy, US SAILING's national award for sportsmanship. He is currently the Director of Athletics at Greens Farms Academy, a K-12 coed independent day school in Westport, Connecticut.

About the Illustrator

BRAD DELLENBAUGH grew up in Fairfield, Connecticut where he learned to sail at the Pequot Yacht Club. He has been coaching and teaching sailing for over 20 years. Presently the Director of Offshore Sailing at the U.S. Naval Academy in Annapolis, Brad also coached the intercollegiate team at Brown University from 1980-1990, as well as the U.S. Women's team from 1984-1987. From 1977-1980 he coached the sailing team at the Hotchkiss School in addition to teaching in the art department, and taught junior sailing from 1973 through 1982 on Long Island Sound. He continues to be actively involved in teaching junior and adult racing clinics across the U.S. both on the water and in the classroom, and lectures frequently on racing tactics and the rules.

An avid racer, Brad has been involved in three Olympic campaigns in the Soling class (including one with Dave in 1981-1984), as well as serving as tactician or helmsman in numerous national, continental and world championships in a wide variety of one-designs and offshore boats. He has won the 1987 and 1988 US SAILING Team Racing Championship, the 1989 J/24 World Championship, the 1990 and 1991 J/22 World Championships and the 1997 US SAILING Prince of Wales Match Racing Championship. He is an International Judge and Umpire, a member of several US SAILING committees including Appeals, Judges and Championships, and served as the rules advisor to *Young America* and the 2000 U.S. Olympic Sailing Team.

Brad graduated from Brown University with a major in fine arts and has pursued this interest as a freelance artist, illustrating for a number of sailing magazines and books.

US SAILING

PO Box 1260, 15 Maritime Drive

Portsmouth, RI 02871

401 683-0800

Fax 401 683-0840

Infofax 888 US SAIL-6

info@ussailing.org

www.ussailing.org